Lesbian Detective Fiction

Lesbian Detective Fiction

Woman as Author, Subject and Reader

PHYLLIS M. BETZ

McFarland & Company, Inc., Publishers
Jefferson, North Carolina, and London

LIBRARY OF CONGRESS CATALOGUING-IN-PUBLICATION DATA

Betz, Phyllis M. (Phyllis Marie), 1953–
　　Lesbian detective fiction : woman as author, subject and reader / Phyllis M. Betz.
　　　　p.　　cm.
　　Includes bibliographical references and index.

　　ISBN-13: 978-0-7864-2548-8
　　softcover : 50# alkaline paper ∞

　　1. Lesbians' writings, American — History and criticism.
　　2. Detective and mystery stories, American — History and criticism.
　　3. American fiction — Women authors — History and criticism.
　　4. Lesbians in literature.　5. Lesbians — Books and reading.
　　I. Title.
　　PS153.L46B48　2006
　　813'.0872093526643 — dc22　　　　　　　　　　　2006013448

British Library cataloguing data are available

©2006 Phyllis M. Betz. All rights reserved

No part of this book may be reproduced or transmitted in any form or by any means, electronic or mechanical, including photocopying or recording, or by any information storage and retrieval system, without permission in writing from the publisher.

Cover photograph ©2006 Dex Stock Images.

Manufactured in the United States of America

McFarland & Company, Inc., Publishers
　Box 611, Jefferson, North Carolina 28640
　　www.mcfarlandpub.com

To Joan,
For her constant support,

and

in memory of
Paul R. Betz

Acknowledgments

Such efforts as this are built on the support of a wide range of people — colleagues, friends, and family. I know that I will have omitted some of their names by mistake, but I have not forgotten them overall.

On the academic side, I must thank Adrienne Gosselin for considering my ideas on lesbian police fiction worth including in her anthology, *Multicultural Detective Fiction: Murder from the "Other" Side*, and Garland Press for permission to use that material; Richard Schneider, Jr., for accepting my first work on lesbian detective fiction for *The Harvard Gay & Lesbian Review*, as it was known in 1994, and also for permission to use the article for this book; to the several chairs of panels at the Modern Language Association and the Northeast Modern Language Association for including my work and giving me the opportunity to offer my analyses to a critical audience.

My colleagues at La Salle University, Philadelphia, Pennsylvania, let me use them as sounding boards and offered constant encouragement. I particularly wish to thank my chair, Dr. Kevin Harty, for his knowledge about getting things published, and Genevieve Carlton, for reading the whole draft.

There is no way to thank my friends and family sufficiently for their support, so putting their names in print is the least I can do: my mother, Mildred Betz; Judith and her husband Mike and my niece Kathleen; Raymond and his wife Katherine and my nieces Madeline and Caitlin; Virginia and my nephew Todd; Frederick, David, and Rebecca.

Table of Contents

Acknowledgments — vii
Introduction: Reading Lesbians, Reading Mystery — 1
List of Authors and Characters — 15

1. Solving Crime, Resolving Passion — 17
2. Having Sex, Finding Love — 40
3. Playing the Boys' Game — 67
4. Lesbian Tough Guys — 92
5. Marginal Values — 119
6. Real Time, Gay Time — 144

Conclusion: Gathering the Evidence — 171
Chapter Notes — 177
Works Cited — 187
Index — 195

Introduction

Reading Lesbians, Reading Mystery

> Making familiar or making ordinary is the radical "work" done by popular forms.—Philip Fisher, 1987, 19

> It is a good and self-affirming thing to read these books because they have a positive attitude toward being queer that counteracts all the negative flak coming at you from everywhere.—Helen Hodgman, 1996, 29

What and why we read always comes down to the question of value. What is it in a book that connects with our interests, experiences, or desires, and how does the work achieve this? Why is it necessary for us to find ourselves and our lives reflected in the literature we read? These questions suggest that searching for value reflects two distinct approaches: the first built on objective critical theories and analyses of the text, the second on the subjective reactions of readers to what they discover in the words. While we search for value throughout our lives in numerous ways, literature seems to be the place that allows us to discover a personal sense of meaning and at the same time enables us to connect with a larger circle. Anyone else reading the same work becomes part of a community that has also determined that some value exists in the shared reading experience. This ability of literature to be unique and communal at the same time becomes the locus of critical and social debate about the meaning and use of the literary work. After all, one person's valuable text is another's trash.

The idea of value is itself, a loaded term, of course, carrying with it a wide range of political, cultural, moral, and critical contexts. Any attempt to establish a definition of value must deal with the often contradictory meanings implied in the word and its applications, which include the commercial and material as well as the intangible. However, certain levels of consensus and compromise can be reached within a limited group or larger community. The criticism of the text provides us with a vocabulary to express the meanings and values we believe reside within its pages; criticism will also reflect our personal value systems—whether ideological, political, or ethical. Theory encourages us to expand our reading and enjoyment of the text, but theory can only offer a frame of reference against which our personal response interacts. Ultimately, the determination of value rests with the individual reader.

This fluid nature of defining and assigning value in texts becomes the crux of how we respond to any written work. We will agree, to a point, that some works—Shakespeare's plays or Toni Morrison's novels—have an intrinsic value, and that it is worthwhile for us to read them. Other literature is subject to the shifts of critical and popular fashion, which sometimes makes selecting a book to read a confusing experience. Many of us have found ourselves defending some of our reading choices in the face of these fashions, especially those of us who enjoy popular fiction. To say that we enjoy mysteries or romances or science fiction for their own value is often met with surprise or nonchalance. The now classic comment that such works are not serious, that they have no deeper meaning than the provision of a few hours of relaxation, still carries weight with its speakers. In some instances, of course, the statement is valid; our decisions to read reflect several rationales, and escape is one. However, the dismissal of popular fiction is continually challenged by the expanding production and consumption of such work and the growing attention paid by the critics.

Commentators on popular culture and literature describe a complex relationship between the production and consumption of genre fiction. Tied from its beginnings to technological advances in publication and distribution systems, situated in the urban environment, and directed to a diverse, often segregated readership, popular fiction has the task of bridging such differences, at least temporarily. As Scott McCracken (1998) states, "[p]opular fiction ... mediates social conflict. In other words, it acts as a medium between reader and world through which the social contradictions of modernity can be played out"(6). The ability of genre fiction to accomplish this mediation comes from its ability to respond more quickly to the shifts in social belief and behavior. During the Cold War period, for instance, the enemy in thrillers was a Communist country; now the enemies of America are terrorists. Hard-boiled detectives more and more give way to forensic investigators. Popular fiction, too, often integrates major questions about or fears of changing social mores: in the 1990s, for instance, the narratives of many mystery novels were centered on child abuse or abduction. Once a theme or topic is introduced in popular fiction, subsequent versions of it will appear and reappear, frequently diluting the original impact of the subject's representation. However, this repetition is the essential source of genre literature's power and value.

The major complaint directed toward the popular genres is the fact that, despite adaptations to their conventions, they tell the same story of the same characters in the same way. Plots become stale, characters are stereotyped, the impact is diminished. The lack of innovation and dependence on formula relegates this literature to the category of the second rate. Familiarity may breed contempt for some, but for readers of genre fiction familiarity provides points of reference that enable us to maintain a sense of stability while at the same time allowing us to consider change. As McCracken (1998) notes:

> In an information age more than ever before the reader is constantly drawing a line between what makes sense in terms of her or his life and what does not. Reading the texts available involves a search for forms and structures that will give those texts meaning. The quest for meaning in narratives gives the reader the opportunity to confront the opportunity of new and exciting selves and the threat that they may dissolve as quickly as they appear [11].

Readers of popular fiction do not sleepwalk through the story; we rely on the conventional components to give us the freedom to examine the new. Philip Fisher's quotation that heads this Introduction calls attention to this blending of the revolutionary and the ordinary. By embodying the unfamiliar for a particular cultural place and time, "popular forms colonize entirely new terrains. They enter what are only temporarily exotic configurations of experience as a necessary practice for a transformation of moral life that is approaching" (Fisher 1987, 20). The innovations do not appear in technique; rather they are articulated through how characters are positioned within the narrative, the interactions among those characters, and the new delineation of social and physical environments. What is transformed is not the genre but how we incorporate what the story tells us.

Theorists of reading have long identified the interplay between what appears in the text and how the reader interprets that text. Wolfgang Iser (1978) describes the reading of a text as a continuous process of synthesis; the reader pieces together multiple points of information to create an individual meaning of what has been read. What this facilitates is the opening of a text to many interpretations: "[a]s there is no definite frame of reference to regulate this process, successful communication must ultimately depend on the reader's creative activity" (112). At first, this would seem to contradict the preceding assertion of the importance of genre conventions because popular formulas can be seen as clear-cut frames of reference that restrict interpretation. However, the paradox of literary formulas is the simultaneous expression of restriction and freedom that encourages "the audience to explore in fantasy the boundary between the permitted and the forbidden and to experience in a carefully controlled way the possibility of stepping across this boundary" (Cawelti 1976, 35). Only in popular fiction, after all, can an African American maid not only solve the crime, but also expose the basic injustices faced by people of color when confronted by police structures. Only in popular fiction can a member of a race switch and blend gender roles, forcing a reorientation of the concept of personal interaction. Only in popular fiction can the romantic hero and heroine both be women.

The security of genre conventions frees the reader to identify with what goes on in the text and with the main characters; it is easier for us to become the detective who solves the crime than it is to be Lady Macbeth. Serious literature, according to Fisher, "build[s] nuances of texture, structure, detail, and psychology into nearly exhausted terrains. The popular forms colonize entirely new terrains. They enter what are only temporarily exotic configurations of experience as a necessary practice for a transformation of moral life that is approaching" (20). Within the pages of a mystery or romance novel, we discover the extraordinary becoming routine. For example, the hard-boiled detective was once considered strictly male because of the typical plot situations he found himself in and the violent actions that were required to bring about the solution. However, when Marcia Muller introduced Sharon McCone in the 1977 mystery *Edwin of the Iron Shoes*, the paradigm shifted. From Sarah Paretsky's V.I. Warshawski to Sue Grafton's Kinsey Millhone, from Lauren Wright Douglas' Caitlin Reece to J. M. Redmann's Micky Knight, contemporary women detectives have appropriated the tactics and behavior of the hard-boiled detective. Once a woman takes on the role of hard-bitten loner private eye, though, she reconceptualizes and reapplies it. This is the transformation suggested by Fisher. Linking women and violence instigates a complex set of responses that must be accommodated by the writer and reader. How do we accept a woman who uses violence to achieve her objective? Can she keep her public role as detective separate from her private life so that the violence does not seep into intimate relationships? Will a woman who uses, indeed relies on, violence remain feminine? Since the introduction of the hard-boiled female detective, the answers to these questions have presented a diversity of characters who have realigned the relationship between women and violence. The gradual acceptance of hard-boiled female investigators is supported by the bestseller status of the works of Grafton, Muller, and others. Each of the characters mentioned in this paragraph is the star of a multivolume mystery series, and each new volume increases her popularity. Yet of the four women listed only two have attained consistent mass appeal; every mystery fan knows Kinsey and V. I., even the critics. The critics of detective fiction reinforce the prominence of McCone and Millhone's reputation and status. It is hard not to find critical commentary on and analysis of the characters and their impact on the mystery genre or the cultural view of women's changing roles or the changing meaning of gender.

Caitlin Reece and Micky Knight, however, have not enjoyed wide popular audiences for reasons of availability; both series are published by small independent presses that lack the economic power of the corporate publishers in terms of distribution and advertising. These novels are sold by independent bookstores more often than by the large chain retailers.[1] Difficulty of access and limited runs represent only part of the explanation, however. That authors J. M. Redmann and Lauren Wright Douglas found publishers willing to publish their work initially and continue that relationship points to the underlying factor for their limited audience. Both characters are lesbians, operating within a specifically lesbian defined and focused environment. Both characters acknowledge their sexuality and live full lives as lesbians. Both characters develop and maintain intimate relationships, including sexual relationships, as lesbians. While their plots adhere to the standard hard-boiled formulas and their characters reflect many of the private eye's traditional qualities, Reece, Knight, and many others have failed to find mainstream popular readers because of this foregrounding of lesbian being and sensibility. The familiarity of the detective story is seen as threatened by a figure constructed as marginal by the dominant culture, which is surprising, given that the majority of private eyes themselves are marginalized figures within the society of their narratives. What is in contention centers on the fact that lesbian experience is normalized within the pages of lesbian detective fiction. In other words, the mystery genre is performing the transformative function of all popular literature: making the unknown knowable, and turning the dangerous into the ordinary.

The mystery novel is especially open to Fisher's concept of popular fiction's process of familiarization because of its strong reliance on its conventions and our willingness, as readers, to accept and engage them Dove (1997) notes: "The reader's expectations are shaped by the traditions and conventions of the genre, to the degree that the reader, relieved of anxiety, is free to enjoy the playing out of the game" (24).[2] Like the detective, the reader confronts a break in the stability of the world (the crime) and follows a consistent procedure to secure a resolution of some kind. In earlier detective fiction the solution of the crime restored the characters' world to an assured order; in more recent works the outcome is less guaranteed but at least temporarily possible. The appeal of the mystery resides not in the crime, but in its resolution; depending on the type of mystery, the process of detection determines the level of our response. We know that Micky Knight or Detective Inspector Carol Ashton will always catch the criminal. What we are continually attentive to is the manner in which this is accomplished. Within the rigidity of the mystery narrative we are paradoxically exposed to a number of variations and adaptations in the working out of the solution. Most critics of detective fiction stress, however, that these stories are inherently conservative, dependent on the maintenance of plot, characters, and resolution that block the writer from attempting to make any radical innovations. Yet, in spite of our familiarity with the traditions of the detective story, we anticipate a degree of experimentation with them. These texts are able to contain innovations within their pages because the security of the format enables readers to accept their presence; in other words, we trust that the writer will not overstep the boundaries of the genre. George Dove describes this as

> a reciprocal relationship, whereby the horizon of the genre sets the terms of reception of the book, which upon acceptance becomes part of the "henceforth familiar expectation." ... Over a period of time, the new approach disappears, and the innovation itself has become part of the reader's own expectations. In a rigid genre like detective fiction, however, an additional step enters the process: before it can be absorbed into the reader's horizon, it must demonstrate its compatibility with the formula [98].

The nature of detective fiction's technical innovations can be characterized as a progressive widening of its narrative situations—both in terms of physical settings and the circumstances of the crime. Crimes are still committed in recognizable environments, although the configurations have shifted to accommodate modern experience. Technological advances, like cell phones, the Global Positioning System, and computers, have replaced older forms of surveillance: the methods of detection have evolved to require new expertise on the part of the investigator. This replacement of old techniques with new is essential for the detective story, especially if the story is set in the modern world. Unless the story is placed within a clearly established historical setting, we expect to find a familiar and knowable situation and discover credible motives and outcomes. Without this, our pleasure in the text is diminished. However, only part of our pleasure comes from the working out of the genre's formulas; as Scott McCracken suggests, there is a deeper value inherent in solving the mystery: "through the narrative the reader is offered the apparatus for negotiating the boundaries that define identity. Whether the crime is regarded as a banal, normal event or as a shocking incident, it supplies a narrative event through which questions about the self and society can be worked" (66). These negotiations take place inside the detective novel, as the investigator pieces together the threads of suspects and motives to solve the crime, and between the reader and the text itself. We consider how this particular story reflects or amplifies our earlier experiences of reading detective novels not only on its technical merits, but also on how *this* particular work reflects our sense of relationship to and with the narrative. Readers continually judge a work against past experience, whether it is the work of a favorite author or a new entry in the genre; we decide if the story, the characters, and the resolution match our expectations. If something has been added or modified, we consider how it succeeds or fails.

McCracken's idea of the way popular texts, including mysteries, confront and define identity moves beyond the limits of the specific text, however. Just as the detective takes on new social identities— African American, Latina/o, gay or lesbian — due to the shifting configurations of the modern world, the reader is also "offered an apparatus for negotiating the boundaries that define identity" (50). In other words, because readers connect so strongly with what happens in the detective novel, we become involved in the same process of transforming our expectations of what is possible. Like the detective — who, after all, is our surrogate for finding a resolution that may offer justice for the victim and punishment for the perpetrator — we also become both interrogators of the crime and the suspects. We are confronted in the text by new means by which people can become victims of crime; we are presented with new ways that justice can be manipulated to benefit the criminal; we are shown how the detective is able to overcome such threats by devising new methods of investigation and forming new types of relationships. Increasingly we see in the detective genre the integration of previously neglected portions of society, the environments and the circumstances of populations not typically portrayed. It is not only that marginalized communities and individuals are included, but that they are made the dominant focus of the story; witness, for example, the increasing number and popularity of African American writers and detectives.[3] The expansion of who can be included within the detective genre's conventions opens the way for new readers of detective fiction and requires the realignment of those conventions to accommodate those readers. When women became detectives and members of police forces in the real world, the mechanisms of their fictional representations had to change; issues such as the use of physical force, the woman's position within an institution and her ability to rise in the ranks, questions of authority and its manifestations, the conflation of a woman's cultural roles—as nurturer, for instance—and her professional role had to be reconciled with the requirements of the detective novel.

These adaptations are not only cosmetic; as new social experiences become ordinary components of the fiction, a gradual shifting of perspective occurs. Female characters challenge and are challenged by prejudices about their abilities and often in the text, or throughout a series, surmount them. This gradual assimilation in the fiction reflects the social reality; at the same time, the fiction establishes a basis for future possibility. McCracken (1998) notes:

> Popular narratives play a vital role in mediating social change, informing their audience of new currents and allowing the reader to insert him- or herself into new scenarios in a way that can be related to her or his own experience.... We use fiction to help us refine our conception of the world [185].

This ability of popular genres to address and accept change brings us full circle to the purpose and value of such literature. The normalizing function of the reliance on formula and repetition gives popular fiction the ability to contain the potentially dangerous shifts in the modern world. By relying on the reader's familiarity with form while simultaneously allowing for adaptation, popular fiction facilitates a balancing of old and new. The safety of genre conventions permits the introduction of difference because, as readers, we trust that the author will still meet our reading expectations. For a reader of detective stories this means there will still be a crime and a process of detection; depending on the type of detective story, the investigator will adhere to the standard methods of identifying, pursuing, and capturing the criminal; and some form of justice, sanctioned or not, will be achieved. Assured of the framework, readers of detective fiction can anticipate how authors will manipulate these techniques to keep us attentive and challenged, not only to the plot but to the inclusion of the unfamiliar as well, showing us how the unfamiliar fits into the framework, how difference is only temporary.

This examination represents another contribution to the conversation about the values of popular fiction, specifically of lesbian mystery/detective fiction. My selection of such texts rests not only on my critical interests but also on personal interest. As a lesbian reader, I desire to find myself represented in books, and often the best — indeed, often the only — place to find such images lies within the pages of popular fiction. It is still difficult to find a complete representation of lesbian life in mainstream literature, despite the increase in the number of lesbian authors being published by major presses. And ghost hunting, to appropriate Terri Castle's (1993) concept of the "apparitional lesbian," demands attentiveness to a text, determining what's not there, and understanding the cultural dynamics at work that keep the lesbian figure and content subordinated within the text's narrative. Traditional heterosexual narratives, according to Castle, play a balancing game of acknowledging the lesbian through language or plot situation, but refusing to grant her full status within the text's pages. If present in the text, the lesbian is often characterized in some negative manner. She is either desexed as the maiden aunt chastely living a solitary life, or she is demonized as a predatory seducer of innocence, who will eventually face just punishment, or she is dehumanized as a male impersonator tragically doomed to madness or death because she can never become what she desires. However, the very fact that the lesbian character intrudes into heterosexual literature indicates her essential power: Castle writes: "One might think of lesbianism as the 'repressed idea' at the heart of patriarchal culture. By its very nature ... lesbianism poses an ineluctable challenge to the political, economic, and sexual authority of men over women. It implies a whole new social order, characterized — at the very least — by a profound feminine indifference to masculine charisma" (61–62). The lesbian haunts the text and requires the constant attention and effort of the dominant heterosexual writer and culture to exorcise her. Instead of being banished, however, the lesbian has maintained her hold on literature, and in the hands of modern lesbian writers has become "an affirming presence" (65).

Castle's concept of the apparitional lesbian, the character simultaneously there and not there in a text, has instigated a debate among lesbian critics on the issue of how lesbians read a text: what is the nature of the lesbian reader's engagement with the text? Is there a difference in the way the lesbian reads a heterosexual text and a specifically lesbian text? What constitutes a lesbian text and the particular representation of the lesbian? Much of the theoretical opinions are directed more to what must be identified as the lesbian canon of writers and texts — Virginia Woolf, Radclyffe Hall, Adrienne Rich, Jeanette Winterson, Audre Lorde, and others. However, more recently, attention has been given to popular texts and authors. The basic issues of this critical position rest on the idea that

> Lesbians are always aware that the dominant heterosexual narrative of most fiction is a myth that fails to reveal the context of lesbian lives. Thus lesbian readers search for the lesbian subtext that speaks to them and their experiences ... they are constantly involved in altering the entire text [Inness, 1997, 82].

The way the text will be altered relates to the type of text being read.

Traditional narrative strategies are decoded to reveal new possibilities in the relationships presented in the text, what Bonnie Zimmerman calls "perverse reading." Heterosexual texts, whether canonical or popular, involve the lesbian reader in a process of taking "an active role in shaping the text she reads in accordance with her perspective on the world" (Zimmerman, 1993, 139). In other words, the lesbian, because she is adept at simultaneous double-reading, will reconstruct the story to fit her own sense of expectation and outcome. Often, of course, a tension exists between the lesbian's desired conclusion and the actual narrative development. In a traditional heterosexual romance, after all, the girl always gets the guy. However, as Sherrie Inness demonstrates, the lesbian reader of straight literature forces the text to open up to new interpretations, making it possible for the inclusion of previously rejected meanings (84).

With a specifically lesbian text, one dealing with explicitly lesbian situations and characters, the work of reading is less problematic. Obviously, the difficulty of finding the lesbian in the text is removed; she dominates the action and controls the story's resolution. The act of reading, then, becomes focused on the relationship constructed by the reader with the text; the lesbian reader brings a set of clearly articulated expectations, not only about the type of book being read, but also about the way lesbian life and experience will be represented. In nongeneric literature by and about lesbians this engagement may be expressed in a highly complex manner through the creation of characters, situations, and relationships that explore the intricacies of their lives. In popular fiction, the transaction between reader and text is more overt because of the stable foundation provided by this literature's literary conventions. Because the lesbian reader of lesbian romance or mystery already knows the narrative structure and movement, as well as the range of characters, she is able to focus on the adaptations of those technical requirements. For example, she looks not only at how the private detective will sidestep the interference of the police; she will understand more intimately and identify with the implications of those maneuvers when the detective is a lesbian. The standard tenuous allegiances of private eye and police officer are intensified because of the supraoutsider status of the lesbian. Unlike the traditional male private eye, who, at the least, shares the viewpoints and behavior of the dominant heterosexual culture, the lesbian private eye is doubly marginalized. Like all private investigators, she is looked on as suspect by the police hierarchy; however, because she is lesbian, this investigator cannot rely on the basic camaraderie that the straight detective enjoys. Although the novel may not accentuate this as the story develops, the lesbian will understand more completely the double-bind in which the investigator operates.

However, since lesbian authored popular texts perform the same task of making the unfamiliar familiar, the initial conflicts presented in the text, whether explicitly part of the plot or implicit in the particular social background delineated in the work, become reconciled. Not only will the detective solve her case, but she will also achieve some kind of accommodation with the dominant heterosexual environment. In lesbian detective/mystery novels this process is most readily seen in the increasing movement of the investigator — private and police — from the margin to the center. Often this process involves the detective coming out to friends or colleagues during the course of the novel, and in serial mysteries, the lesbian detective's sexuality becomes secondary to the major narrative's development. Claire McNab's Inspector Carol Ashton, Penny Micklebury's Lt. Gianna Maglione, and Barbara Johnson's insurance investigator Colleen Fitzgerald are only three of many lesbian detectives who successfully maneuver this integrative process. Of course, not all lesbian investigators confront such a choice, and their sexuality will be included in the text in a number of ways. The important issue for the lesbian reader, though, is her continued exposure to lesbians who overcome the internal and external pressures these characters experience. Marilyn Farwell (1996) describes this basic connection between the lesbian reader and text as follows:

> [T]he lesbian character in popular lesbian fiction offers a sense of power and possibility to hungry lesbian readers who have encountered little either inside or outside of school which portrays them with anything but disdain. As could be expected, these stories are satisfying because writers assign the active narrative role to a self-conscious lesbian who makes her own decisions and decides her own fate [137].

The mystery/detective novel is particularly open to the normalizing function of popular fiction because it combines a clearly articulated set of technical expectations regarding plot, character, and resolution while at the same time remaining open to the admission of variations. The ability and readiness of detective fiction to incorporate difference can be seen in its history; from a genre dominated by white male characters in key roles, mystery novels have expanded to included African Americans, Asian Americans, Hispanic Americans, and gays and lesbians at the center of the narrative. These changes are not only cosmetic, however. In addition to addressing the race and sexuality of its main characters, the mystery novel has moved beyond its traditional settings and storylines. Issues not typically found in such works appear frequently: the assimilation of marginalized people into the dominant culture, the manipulation by various institutions or legal systems to control others, and the addressing of societal issues (spousal and child abuse, hate crimes, violence against women, political injustices, gender identity). Crimes occur in Rehoboth Beach, gay bars, abortion clinics, at drag shows, in women's collectives, the Castro as well as conventional places.

Most importantly, the detective story, because of its reliance on standardized techniques, gives lesbian writers the ability "to tell the familiar story of the solving of a crime from a different perspective" (Wilson 1994, 219). A new sensibility and awareness is detailed as the lesbian writer follows her detective as she negotiates the solution to a crime as well as the confrontations with a society that views her very existence as flawed. Faced not only with the problem of identifying the criminal, the lesbian investigator must also respond to challenges—and threats—to her abilities and her very right to act. The requirements of the genre, of course, call for the successful resolution of the crime, but for lesbian readers, often the more vital resolution is the success of the lesbian in engaging with and triumphing over people and institutions that would deny her existence. These are the outcomes that underscore the appeal of this literature for its particular audience. But solving the crime is only part of the attraction; situated within the dominant narrative of detection a second story is being told. This is the everyday life of its lesbian characters. The lesbian reader observes the detective living as complete a life as possible within genre limits. If she is a private investigator, she faces the typical problems of finding clients and paying bills; if she is a police officer, she deals with keeping up with the paperwork and department politics. Issues of family, intimate relationships, and all the mundane components of experience are detailed. More and more lesbian mystery and detective novels give narrative space to this detailing of the personal life of the investigator. In other words, the very ordinariness of these situations and the character's responses indicates to the lesbian reader that both she and the detective are no different from anyone else. Like all lesbian readers, I want to see the community I am familiar with represented in the stories I read. I want to see the working out of private and public relationships that do not diminish my value. I want to see images that recognize the variety in my community. Lesbian detective and mystery novels provide that recognition.

In the analysis that follows I will be examining lesbian detective/mystery fiction regarding its representation of lesbian characters and experience within the confines of the genre. My discussion will also offer a reading of these texts that highlights the various ways in which they reveal the increasing inclusion of the lesbian into the wider society. The first two chapters discuss the intersection of the main character's private and public lives, which often centers on the coming out process or the movement from the character's isolation to connection with a wider support community. The movement from separation to connection is a hallmark of the lesbian detective story. Many of the first novels in detective series frequently combine the detective's search for the criminal with her own search for and understanding of her sexuality. Barbara Wilson, the author of the Pam Nilsen and Cassandra Reilly novels, has said that all mysteries are at heart stories about identity — the identification of the crime and the perpetrator as well as the investigator.[4] These chapters will also examine the role of intimacy in the lesbian detective's life, particularly the influence it exerts on the performance of her investigation. Many lesbian detective novels interrupt the narrative of investigation to describe the private relationship of their main characters, including, sometimes, vivid sexual scenes. These incidents provide more than titillation; they illustrate the detective's need for release from the pressures of the outside world, since such scenes usually occur between the detective and her lover. In fact, rarely in these texts does sex become a means to an end for the investigation itself. Sex is not used to coerce or blackmail suspects. When sex or a character's sexuality is used in these ways, it is often the impetus for the crime or a tactic of the criminal.

Chapters 3 and 4 focus on how the lesbian detective confronts two crucial qualities of any investigator: the role and use of violence and the acquisition and expression of authority within police systems. Like all women detectives, the lesbian must first deal with questions of the suitability of using violent methods for solving the problem under investigation. Unlike her straight counterpart, however, the lesbian faces a paradoxical situation; using violence makes a woman unwomanly, yet, lesbians are often not regarded as real women by the straight world. This outsider status, then, offers the lesbian detective permission to be aggressive and to utilize violence to accomplish her goal. Lesbians operating within the structures of police systems face greater difficulties of assimilation and accommodation than their straight female colleagues. Where the private detective enjoys the freedom to pursue lines of inquiry and use methods not available to the police officer, she must adhere to the rule of law and follow departmental procedures. The lesbian police officer must also deal with institutionalized misogyny and homophobia in her efforts to bring about a successful resolution to her investigations. Embedded within the surface investigation of lesbian police procedurals lies the question of whether the officer will be able to negotiate her transgressive status as a lesbian with her socially sanctioned position a as member of a public institution.

The focus of my analysis shifts in chapters 5 and 6 to examine the wider cultural environments in which many lesbian mystery/detective stories are situated. Many novels involve the lesbian detective in confronting or dealing with social issues that were dominant at the time of their publication; for example, Vicki McConnell's mysteries, published in the early 1980s, deal with the basic questions of gay and lesbian visibility. *Mrs. Porter's Letter* contains no immediate crime; McConnell's Nyla Wade is involved in an investigation, a personal one, to find out the circumstances behind a letter discovered in an old desk she has purchased. During her pursuit Nyla will come out, find a community, and discover the letter's author and recipient. Later lesbian novels treat such topics as questions of gender roles and behavior within the lesbian community, the nature of families, including whether to have children, loyalty to one's personal relationships and politics when there is a clash with the demands of the investigation, as well as others. In addition, lesbian writers of detective fiction incorporate stories that examine society's treatment of children, hate crimes, especially directed toward gays and lesbians, sex crimes, and other topics receiving public attention. Chapter 6 investigates the motive behind the use of history in numerous lesbian detective novels. Some authors create characters and settings that are typical of the historical mystery, but with important changes: the history represented is a specifically gay/lesbian history or specifically lesbian and gay characters are placed within the historical situation and force a reexamination of the assumptions of heterosexual norms. More common is the use of a character's personal history and how her relationship to those events impacts her sexuality. Interestingly, some authors, Katherine Forrest, Joan Albarella, and Joan Drury most notably, have their investigators deal with the consequences of the Vietnam War.

My intention with the following examination is to add to the ongoing discussion of why we read popular fiction, particularly what lesbians find in the detective/mystery narrative that continues to draw them into the story. As suggested in the preceding pages, lesbian readers come to these texts with a range of expectations— about the genre and about how they will see themselves in the work. In the world of the novel, we find representations of our experience normalized and validated; after all, a successful mystery is one that brings about a resolution of the crime. The world, which has been thrown out of order, is made right, and since a lesbian detective is the agent of restoration in these works, we enjoy and applaud her efforts. As more and more lesbian detective/mystery novels are published, not only by small feminist or lesbian presses but by major corporations, we find our fictional representatives recognized and accepted and valued.

List of Authors and Characters

This list identifies the authors discussed in the following pages and their detective characters. Amateur detectives are indicated by (A) and professional private detectives by (P). Members of police forces are identified by their rank. The titles of the specific works are listed in the Works Cited at the back of the book.

Kate Allen	Officer Alison Kane
N. H. Avenue	Det. Amanda Ross
Kim Baldwin	Kat Demetrious (P)
M. F. Beal	Kat Alcazar (A)
Elaine Beale	Lou Spenser (A)
Becky Bohan	Britt Evans (A)
ReBecca Beguin	Hazel Preston (A)
Baxter Clare	Lt. L. A. Franco
R. S Corliss	Agents Alexia Reis and Teren Mylos
Diane Davidson	Lt. Toni Underwood
Lisa Davis	Blackie Cole (A)
Lauren Wright Douglas	Caitlin Reece (P)
Sarah Dreher	Stoner McTavish (A)
Marian Foster	Harriet Fordham Croft (A)
Katherine V. Forrest	Det. Kate Delafield
Sharon Gilligan	Alix Nicholson (A)
Gabrielle Goldsby	Det. Foster Everett
Ellen Hart	Jane Lawless (A)
Molly Hite	Det. Scilla Carmody
Lynne Jamneck	Agent Samantha Skellar
Laurie King	Det. Kate Martinelli

Dolores Klaich	Tyler Divine (P)
Lori Lake	Officers Dez Reilly and Jaylynn Savage
Catherine Lewis	Officer Abigail Fitzpatrick
Julia Lieber	Loy Lombard (P)
Randye Lordon	Sydney Sloane (P)
Jean Macy	Meg Darcy (P)/Det. Sarah Lindstrom
Jaye Maiman	Robin Miller (P)
Melanie McAllister	Det. Elizabeth Mendoza
Vicki McConnell	Nyla Wade (A)
Claire McNab	Det. Inspector Carol Ashton
Penny Mickelbury	Lt. Gianna Maglione
Carlene Miller	Capt. Tory Gordon
Mary Morell	Det. Lucia Ramos
C. Paradee	Agent Kristine Bartley
Cath Phillips	Det. Jayne Stewart
Deborah Powell	Hollis Carpenter (A)
Radclyffe	Det. Rebecca Frye/J. T. Sloan (P)
J. M. Redmann	Micky Knight (P)
Tracy Richardson	Det. Stevie Houston
Margie Schweitzer	J. Z. Mackenzie (P)
Linda Kay Silva	Officer Delta Stevens
Talaran	Det. Nicole Stone
Jean Taylor	Maggie Garrett (P)
Pat Welch	Helen Black (P)
Barbara Wilson	Pam Nilsen (A)
Mary Wings	Emma Victor (P)
C. N. Winters	Lt. Denise van Cook

Chapter 1

Solving Crime, Resolving Passion*

> American society was characterized in large part by rigid gender-role differentiation within the family and within society as a whole, leading to the emotional segregation of women and men.... It was within just such a social framework, I would argue, that a specifically female world did indeed develop, a world built around a generic and unself-conscious pattern of single-sex or homosocial networks.... Within such a world of emotional richness and complexity, devotion to and love of other women became a plausible and socially accepted form of human interaction. — Carroll Smith-Rosenberg, 1986, 60
>
> Come out of the closet — is that what you're asking me to do? — Claire McNab, 1990, 192

A crime discovered, a body found, the mystery revealed, the scene and actors in place, and the detective story begins. The skillful mystery writer takes the conventional requirements and sets into motion a series of expected actions and outcomes. The author brings carefully developed suspects and clues together to produce the required and satisfying resolution. Mystery readers approach such a book anticipating this pleasurable working out of these conventions. Reader satisfaction, as the critics of genre fiction have noted, comes from several sources. A puzzle has been presented, and, if the story is constructed fairly, the reader enjoys the challenge of bringing the story to a clear-cut finish. Or, the threat of chaos is represented by the subversion of social codes. Only the detective hero is able to restore order, often only temporarily, by successfully resolving the mystery. As the detective finds and deciphers clues, the reader cheers those efforts. Or, the world is pictured as a hostile, inhuman place, representing an archetypal clash of good and evil, and again, only the detective manages

---

*An earlier version of this chapter appeared in *The Harvard Gay & Lesbian Review*, 1, no. 3 (Summer 1994). Used with permission.

to return it to some semblance of balance. Or, the crime illustrates the breakdown of social and personal interactions, and by finding the solution, the detective salvages some sense of personal honor and integrity. The reader admires the detective's individual moral stance and, perhaps, sees in those efforts a model of behavior. Whatever the motive, a devoted mystery reader finds in this fiction compelling reasons to read the same story over and over.[1]

These are the clichés of the mystery genre, and like all clichés, they reside within a framework of credibility. The stories, the characters, even the outcomes are predictable and familiar. It is that very predictability that makes such books so enjoyable for the mystery reader: "A writer writes (and a reader reads) with an understanding of what is acceptable within the limits of the literary form, of what inventions and experiments are permissible, and what traditions must be observed" (Dove 1997, 4). As Dove indicates, the mystery, while adhering to certain narrative standards, also contains the flexibility to encompass alterations in them, and the mystery/detective text has succeeded in incorporating changes in the identity of the detective, the nature of the crime, the disposition of the villain, and the implications of the resolution. The essential concern, of course, is the impact such alterations have on the specific work and on the genre as a whole. The writer who takes innovation too far runs the risk of alienating the readers. However, since the mystery's beginnings, adaptations in the formulas have dramatically refashioned reader expectations about the type of crime and the manner of its resolution and opened the door to further expansions of the conventions. Such a reconfiguration lies at the heart of this current study: What happens to the genre when its framework is shifted, when the outlines of the detective story are redefined and reapplied, specifically, what changes when the detective story and hero become lesbian?[2]

Something more than just the typical working out of the solution to the crime appears in lesbian detective fiction. Besides fulfilling the genre's requirements, lesbian mysteries also present another story, one that, because the situations and characters have been specifically recast as lesbian and lesbian centered, may have a greater impact for its particular readers. It is the discovery of this other story that intrigues me. Is the detective story radically different when the detective is a lesbian? How does the development and resolution of the story change when it involves a lesbian focus and sensibility? What may be the purpose for the inclusion of this other story inside the primary narrative of a crime and its outcome?

As basic detective stories, many lesbian crime novels offer little innovation in technique, characterization, or storyline. Like their mainstream counterparts, these books adhere to the particular specifications of the genre and, when appropriate, their subgenres. Lesbian detective fiction fits easily into the standard classifications of the mystery: police procedurals (Forrest's Kate Delafield, McNab's Claire Ashton and Clare's Lt. Franco series); the hard-boiled loner, whether an amateur or professional (Douglas's Caitlin Reece, Wing's Emma Victor, Kat Alcazar, Redmann's Micky Knight, or Madison McGuire); the genteel amateur (Jane Lawless, Harriet Croft, Stoner McTavish, and Nyla Wade). Like most crime stories, lesbian writers and their detectives cross and blend these categories. With the similarities so strong, the main question must be how lesbian mysteries differ from the typical crime novel, especially from the typical crime novel with a female protagonist. Superficial alterations—making the hero a lesbian, incorporating a clear-cut political issue that impacts gays and lesbians, situating the plot within a specifically gay environment—are the starting point for the lesbian crime novel's reshaping of the genre. Merely altering the setting or the hero's sexual orientation, however, does not distinguish lesbian detective fiction from mainstream works. What differentiates them is how the lesbian story uses these redesigned surface features to direct the reader to the deeper mystery.

Solving the crime remains, of course, the detective's main function; however, the lesbian mystery novel interrupts the hero's pursuit of that resolution with another pursuit. This second narrative strand develops simultaneously with the primary story although the detective does not always recognize it or its connection to her main goal. For the lesbian reader, this second story offers another layer of interest because of an intrinsic tension between the overt detective plot and this sublimated one. Katherine Forrest's *The Beverly Malibu* (1989) typifies this dual focus tension. During the investigation of the murder at the Beverly Malibu apartments, Kate Delafield, the detective in charge, finds herself attracted to Aimee Grant, one of the residents and a possible suspect. While such a scenario appears frequently in heterosexual, mainstream mysteries, in this novel any action by Delafield compromises not only the investigation itself, but more importantly, her position with the police hierarchy. The straight detective, whether male or female, may face censure for complicating the investigation with romance, but the attraction itself is never suspect. Delafield's attraction has the potential to jeopardize her public identity and function, a potentially dangerous threat. Her personal feeling can seriously impact the necessary objectivity required to complete her task, and unlike a straight detective in this situation, who could act on these impulses and not have her or his identity as an officer *and as a person* challenged, Kate Delafield cannot. For Delafield, in this novel, the separation of her personal life and public duty is essential:

> [I]t's clear and precise what my duty is. To do what I can to guard the last elements of that person's dignity, to protect, even in death that person's right. To search for Owen Sinclair's killer no matter how much it takes, no matter how long it takes [183–84].

Kate Delafield's clear idealism and moral stance regarding her role in solving murder is a consistent trait that, as the series progresses, will be challenged. The source of that challenge is her increasing desire and need to integrate her sexual identity with her public identity.

In *The Beverly Malibu*, then, two mysteries must be solved: who killed Owen Sinclair and what happens to this demand for objectivity when Kate's sexuality — not only her personal interest in Aimee Grant, but in her own public acknowledgment that she is a lesbian — surfaces. Delafield achieves the resolution to the murder through solid police work, bringing the case to a firm conclusion; the second resolution, however, remains tentative. Aimee has acknowledged a reciprocal attraction to Kate, and Kate has taken a bold step in giving Aimee a key to her apartment. The story ends with the two women clearly establishing an intimate partnership, and while there is the suggestion that this relationship will be happy, Kate's position in the police force can work against its success. At this point in the series of novels about Kate Delafield, she has not publicly acknowledged her sexual orientation to her colleagues, nor does she intend to, given the overt homophobia of her partner as well as the implicit support of such behavior by the Los Angeles police institution itself. The dependence on the solidarity of other officers could disappear for Kate because she understands that coming out would set her apart, isolating her from the necessary professional relationships that will help her pursue an investigation. Rather than lose such access, Kate relegates her lesbian identity to an extremely confined portion of her life. A major concern for Delafield in the early novels of the series centers on her fear of being recognized as a lesbian. Before Delafield can fully engage in a satisfying relationship with Aimee Grant, she will have to take the risk of coming out; she must publicly acknowledge what she has previously kept private.

The importance of coming out cannot be understated: "The coming out story is one of the fundamental lesbian myths of origin, the first basic tale of all lesbian communities. Coming out is an expression of activity, implying movement from one state of being to another" (Zimmerman 1993, 34). Bonnie Zimmerman's (1993) *The Safe Sea of Women: Lesbian Fiction, 1969–1989* emphasizes the necessity for the lesbian character to achieve a new state of awareness through the coming out process, which involves desire for another woman, understanding the negative response of the dominant culture, and acceptance of her new identity (35). At the heart of this process lies the question of how the individual determines her identity. Answering this question involves looking at a complex pattern of historical, cultural, and psychological components that move far beyond the scope of my topic. However, a brief description of some of the essential influences on the development of sexual identity establishes a set of reference points against which these narratives can be placed. After all, to discover who one is must be the first mystery to be solved.

Most historical studies of homosexuality situate its recognition as a distinct form of sexual expression in the last quarter of the nineteenth century.[3] Lesbianism was frequently seen by the then new science of psychology as a perversion of typical feminine behavior, a woman who wanted to be a man, an "invert," a "deviant." This negative view dominated professional and popular images for many years; lesbians were viewed either as morally bankrupt figures, aggressive and assertive, who were usually lying in wait to seduce unsuspecting young girls, or as sexually immature women waiting for the right man to initiate them into their proper submissive roles. If she did not reject her desires for another woman, the lesbian faced diagnoses of madness and could face forced hospitalization and treatment, legal penalties, and physical violence. Popular culture's representations echoed such views, and often added the lesbian's suicide as the only choice when she realized her failure to abide by society's standards. Even though homosexuality was removed in 1973 from the American Psychiatric Association's list of mental disorders, such popular versions of lesbians can still be presented. The movie *Basic Instinct*, although loudly protested, managed to incorporate both stereotypic views of lesbians in the Sharon Stone character. However, in spite of the open hostility to their very lives, from the earliest periods lesbians found ways to recognize one another and to build communities that provided the safety from which they would create their art, politics, and lives.[4] Particularly as the twentieth century progressed, lesbians became more visible and vocal in their assertions of their place in the dominant society.

Identity is a private as well as a public construct. Even before a woman can connect with a community of others like herself, she must come to terms with the pull of attraction for another woman. This process involves the positioning of desire — physical and emotional — within the mechanisms of constructing one's identity. Summarized by Joseph Bristow (1997), the descriptions of this intersection of defining a self and determining the actions of that self range from economic theory (the individual is the product of a capitalistic system that requires constant consumption of desired objects), to feminist critiques and analyses of the tension between gender expectations and sexual behavior, to psychoanalytic theories ranging from

Freud's discussion of the Oedipal/Electra complexes to Foucault's concept of sexuality as a discourse between power and social control of sexual expression. A central position held by modern theorists asserts that one's identity is a fluid construction, influenced by shifting cultural, political, and economic forces. Particularly vulnerable to these shifts is one's gender(ed) expression; whether personal or private, the individual's behavior is subject to a range of stereotyped or traditional expectations.

Lesbians often confront this dilemma of how to establish an identity that balances the notions of proper sex/gender behavior as delineated by mainstream, heterosexual culture and their own interpretations of that range of possible models. These constraints are obviously tied to a specific historical time and place. For example, Carroll Smith-Rosenberg (1985) in "The Female World of Love and Ritual" examines the existence, and often support, of intense same-sex female relationships during much of the nineteenth century; her research reveals intense expressions of love between women, often lasting throughout the individuals' lives. By the end of the nineteenth century, however, a reconfiguration of social categories and expectations positioned these relationships outside the mainstream. Using the new psychosexual descriptions of appropriate gender identity and behavior, intimacy between women, whether sexual or emotional, became highly charged and suspect.

As the twentieth century progressed, the lesbian's public position shifted, depending on the willingness of the dominant culture to tolerate her presence, and her personal identity often reflected those shifts. The lesbian could be viewed as exotic and fascinating as she defied traditional gender boundaries during the post–World War I years when other segments of society were rebelling against traditional views, or she was seen as a threat to masculine power as she moved into the public arenas of education, career, and self-determination and, therefore, needed to be contained. In whatever way her position was seen by the rest of society, the lesbian relied on a set of standardized traits from which to fashion an identity, one that was recognizable not only to other lesbians, but to the rest of society as well. For most of the twentieth century a lesbian's options were limited to the butch-femme dichotomy: if you were a woman, then you acted like a woman; if you didn't want to act like a woman, then you could only behave as a man. Of course, behaving like a man meant that you were contradicting the natural order and were, therefore, outside the normal social boundaries. As the century progressed, the butch-femme model was no longer "viewed simply as an imitation of heterosexual, sexist society. Although they derived in great part from heterosexual models, the roles also transformed those models and created an authentic lesbian lifestyle" (Kennedy and Davis

1994, 6). By the last quarter of the century, lesbians were manipulating and reconfiguring these images into lipstick lesbians and drag kings.

Simultaneous to the developing understanding of the historical and psychological reality of the lesbian is the representation of lesbians in literature, although my study cannot do justice to the varied literary expressions of lesbians and lesbian life. Just as the lesbian was not historically acknowledged until the end of the nineteenth century, the lesbian as fully recognized character does not appear in fictional texts until well into the twentieth century.[5] One of the central critical questions has been to discover the mechanisms of representing lesbians, especially in the literature produced before the lesbian became an historical construct. The answers to this question vary according to the theoretical position of the critic, the particular time and place of the literature being examined, the author's gender, and the reputation of the work itself. The first issue to resolve is if lesbians, in fact, can be found in these texts. Can something be said to exist in the fiction if there is no point of reference beyond its pages? Critics like Terry Castle (1996) and Sherrie Inness (1997) offer a compelling response to this question with their similar notions of the "apparitional lesbian" and "disassembl[ing] the dominant heterosexual plot"(83).[6] The recognition of lesbian characters and stories, then, depends on the situation of the reader in relation to what occurs within the text. Obviously, the reader's willingness to search for the ghost or to break down the narrative is tied to her own willingness to read as a lesbian.

Genre narratives contain within them expectations about how the story is framed and the characters who inhabit that story, and those expectations reflect the values of the dominant culture. When the story or its actors are reconstructed to include what was once seen as being outside social norms, those structures are faced with the challenge of adaptation or stagnation. Lesbians in the text, according to Marilyn Farwell (1996),

> must take on the existing structure, function within some of its parameters, yet question its movement and arrangement of subject positions. This interrogation happens first, when female bonding breaks up male bonding, realigning any remaining male characters; second, when the asymmetrical structural patterns of active agent and passive object are revised by the structural interjection of sameness; and finally, when these changes on a structural level affect the movement and thematics of the traditional narrative [62].

When lesbians take prominent positions within the genre text, conventional treatments of the plot and character interaction can no longer be assumed; even the most superficial adaptation — simply making the hero of the story a lesbian — alters its outcome. Even if nothing else changes, a lesbian hero means the story's assumptions of power and authority as characteristics of male action can be challenged; even if nothing else changes, a lesbian hero means the romantic interest and focus of the heroine is opened to new possibilities.

Simply changing the sexual orientation of the hero may seem a sufficiently radical alteration of genre fiction, since the limitations of their literary conventions are assumed to stretch only so far. However, as suggested in the introduction to this study, the paradox of genre fiction appears in the ability of these rigid structures to enable representative fluidity. In other words, because the romance or the western or the detective story demands that the writer adhere to clear-cut narrative guidelines, genre fiction has "the capacity to assimilate new meanings [and] ease the transition between old and new ways of expressing things and thus contribute to cultural continuity" (Cawelti 1976, 36). The ability of genre literature to balance tradition and innovation ultimately accomplishes the transformative function described by Philip Fisher (1987): such works are "examples of culture that invites and then achieves incorporation. Because so much of its reality has leaked out and merged into the common language of perception and moral action, its very success, as mimesis, in altering the categories of reality, hides the extraordinary energy that now seems already ours" (21). So when lesbian authors relate the experience of lesbian characters utilizing genre formats, they are participating in this radical act of reconciling the margin with the center.

By presenting a more complete picture of lesbian life, one that portrays her as experiencing the same tensions with career, relationships, and society, genre fiction allows its readers to adjust their perceptions. The "otherness" of the lesbian becomes identifiable; her private and public situations become recognizable. This process of identification and integration, at least in the pages of the text, is what pulls the lesbian reader and makes her a participant in the transformation. This is not to imply that the reading of a detective story or romance novel will turn a lesbian audience into activists. What it suggests is that by seeing her life and experience represented in a recognizable fashion in a narrative that asserts the ordinariness of her experience, the lesbian reader can enjoy the luxury of confirmation. Here, in the book's pages, are others like her, dealing with the everyday issues of finding love, balancing career and family, deciding to come out to colleagues, and confronting the daily routines of life. Sherrie Inness (1997) recognizes the importance of this impact of lesbian texts for the lesbian reader:

> representation *does* matter. Representations of lesbians not only have depicted lesbian experiences but have also helped to constitute them. Les-

> bianism and its place in society can only be understood by recognizing how representations have functioned to maintain the status of the lesbian as a hated and feared outsider. Representations, however, have also been used to alter that cultural stereotype and to create new, empowering ways to depict lesbian lives [126; emphasis in text].

Certain genre fiction, of course, weaves this level of representation into the dominant plotline according to its conventional requirements.

In the detective novel this movement from one position of self-awareness to another is complicated by the demands of solving the crime. Whether the detective is part of a police force or a private investigator, an amateur or professional, the criminal investigation must take precedence. In their study of the feminist hard-boiled detective novel, Priscilla Walton and Manina Jones (1999) stress the importance of a writer's maintaining allegiance to the demands of the mystery format; they quote Katherine Forrest's 1995 (a telephone interview) contention that "[t]here just are certain aspects that you know you need to meet. It's not enough to want to make a statement in a book, you still have to fulfill that contract with the reader" (54). In many of the detective novels that will be examined here the authors are faced with the challenge of balancing the main character's coming out, which usually also involves the development of a romantic connection, and the pursuit of the solution to a crime. At least in many heterosexual crime novels, the romance is relegated to the background of the narrative; however, this attraction of the detective for another woman and its implications for her sense of her private and public self often interrupts and delays the resolution of the mystery. Kate Delafield is not the only hero in lesbian detective fiction to confront this tension between public expectations and performance and private desire. Whether she is a professional or an amateur, the lesbian detective faces two distinct problems during the course of her investigation — solving the crime and resolving a developing passionate relationship. Often these investigations run along parallel lines: the pursuit of both the criminal and love are coincidental. More often they intersect as the nature and definition of pursuit and pursuer become intertwined and blurred. Before any successful completion of both pursuits, however, the detective must confront the implications of being lesbian.

Only when the issue of identity is resolved can the detective resume the pursuit of the criminal. Within the pages of the detective novel the lesbian hero/detective faces this moment of identification in a number of ways: in the first and most dramatic, she literally comes to a moment of the declaration of her sexual identity, which is usually faced in the process of solving the mystery. Typically it is an amateur detective who usually confronts the issue of coming to terms with her sexual orientation. Vicki

McConnell's (1982) Nyla Wade typifies this character. The recognition of their sexuality, while not essential the solution of the mystery, establishes for these characters a new point of reference for their engagement with and response to the situations of the mystery. In the subplot to her search for the author and recipient of Mrs. Porter's letter, Nyla becomes involved with a group of prostitutes, organizing to identify the pimp who has gotten away with the murder of one of their own. Sara, the leader of the group, instigates Nyla's interrogation of her shifting emotional experiences:

> Seeing [Sara and Nikki] together, their open concern and affection, released in me a flood of exhilaration that I knew was right. It was not just a crush I felt for Sara, though that was part of it, but a *recognition* of the kind of feeling that two women could share. That was what I wanted, that syncopation of body and mind. I had no past experience to clinch it easily for me, but something clearly felt like square peg finally in square slot [McConnell, 1982, 162; emphasis in text].

Surprisingly, Nyla takes no further action specifically directed to exploring her realization; instead she continues to pursue her goal of locating the writer of the love letters she has previously found in a desk she purchased in a second-hand store.

In spite of this apparently easy acceptance of being lesbian, McConnell hints that Nyla still carries traditional heterosexual expectations about the identities of the couple whose romance has impelled her investigation. Learning that W. Stone is actually Winona momentarily stuns Nyla and brings her to understand "what a victim I was of an ordinary and limited perspective" (198). What the letters and the women whose story Nyla had been assembling offer her (the most important discovery Nyla makes is that both are still alive and still together), is a model of a complete and successful relationship, despite attempts to break up the original couple's commitment as well as prevent Nyla's search than being successful. In fact, this first mystery in the Nyla Wade series stresses the importance of identity, since her goal is to discover the story behind the letters found in the desk. During the course of her investigation Nyla will literally and figuratively be denied access to information that might aid in her search, or she will misinterpret the clues she possesses. This first mystery also emphasizes the essential quality of interpretation that is not only the basic method of detection, but the cornerstone of Nyla's and other characters' recognition. As an investigator, Nyla must examine and reexamine the meaning of the letters as well as the circumstances surrounding their composition and disposition. As a woman coming to identify as lesbian, Nyla must also reexamine and understand her attractions to another woman and the implications of her claiming of that identity: "I can think of it no longer as some abstraction because it is my choice too.... Maybe it won't be simple, and for many who know me, it will seem impossible to understand" (209). In the subsequent novels, McConnell continues to intertwine Nyla Wade's growing understanding of what being a lesbian means with the investigations of more traditional mysteries.

That such a coming out appears in novels describing the accidental investigations of amateur detectives is not surprising. The violence of the crime forces a repositioning of the character's involvement with narrative events, pushing her away from familiar situations and relationships. Whether she is suspected of the crime and must prove her innocence or becomes engaged in solving the crime — either by accident or deliberately — this character discovers that she no longer has a place in the environment in which she moves. Paradoxically, this discovery is not frightening; rather with that recognition comes a feeling of completion and belonging that has been missing from her life. For example, in Foster's *The Monarchs are Flying* (1987), Harriet Croft, after she acknowledges her feelings for Leslie, "closed her eyes and wondered, briefly, at the rightness of this moment and the years it had taken to reach it. She knew that she, ... was at last set free" (217). Many of the characters who follow this narrative pattern are divorced, have had unsatisfactory relationships, whether sexual or emotional, with men, or have established highly structured and solitary lives. Coming out allows these characters to connect physically and emotionally to another individual, often for the first time in their experience. For the lesbian reader, the character's coming out, instead of placing her in a potentially hostile environment, connects her to a supportive one. Rather than being marginalized by coming out, these characters encourage the lesbian reader to participate in a temporary realignment of her status within the dominant heterosexual culture.[7]

However, the euphoria of coming out can only be experienced once. After the initial revelation the character faces the more typical reactions from friends and family to her discovery and must deal with their acceptance or denial. Such developments typically appear in the later novels, if the character and her adventures become a series, but the tensions between the character and others can become part of the immediate narrative. When this occurs within the pages of the novel, in spite of the fiction of the narrative and the characters, the lesbian reader finds a more accurate representation of her own coming out experience. The reason lies in the obvious fact that the source of the newly out lesbian's change is her love of another woman, especially if the relationship moves beyond an emotional one. Physical intimacy challenges social norms, even within the pages of the genre text. In *Murder in the Collective* (B. Wilson 1986), Pam Nilsen's supportive twin sister, Penny, has difficulty dealing with the sexual component of Pam's lesbianism. However, at the same time that the newly out lesbian challenges traditional sexual standards and faces real and potential dangers, her very expression of a sexual self is an essential quality that ultimately proves beneficial for her growth as an individual *and* as a detective. (My discussion of the role of sex in lesbian detective fiction requires a separate chapter that will follow.)

Not all investigations incorporate the detective's first recognition of her sexuality into the process of uncovering the solution to the mystery. Most lesbian detective fiction describes the cases of characters who have already come out as lesbian and have already, at least in their personal lives, dealt with the consequences of that discovery. Of course, these women still confront the prejudice and hostility of the dominant society especially during the progress of an investigation; however, in their work environments and among their immediate circles of friends, they have created supportive communities. In fact, it is these small, selected communities that frequently provide the detective with a wide range of support (examined later in this discussion). So, while coming out as lesbian no longer impinges on the detective's primary investigation, she must still deal with the complexities her sexuality can bring in her pursuit of the crime's resolution. These most often are criminal acts that fulfill the detective genre's foundational narrative premise, that a crime must be committed to set the process of resolution in motion. However, many of these crimes also reflect the bias of the majority culture toward homosexuals, the severity of such crimes ranging from blackmail to murder.

Not only does such tension initiate the investigation, but the detective must also confront fissures within the particular gay environment that often serves as an important setting of the narrative, from internalized homophobia to ideological conflicts. After accepting television personality Val Frazier's case (she is being blackmailed by someone threatening to reveal her lesbian affair and ruin her career) Caitlin Reece ruminates on her client's refusal to reveal her identity and deflate the control of the blackmailer in *The Always Anonymous Beast*:

> I was never ashamed of the fact that I loved women. And I certainly never felt guilty. Now thank heavens, life was infinitely easier. I had to answer to no one.... Val's guilt not only gave the blackmailer a handle on her professional life, but it gave him power over her personal life as well. I sighed. Even if I got the letters back, thereby assuring Val that no one at the television station would ever know The Horrible Truth, the blackmailer would still have an edge. He would still know what she perceived to be a shameful secret [10].

Often then, it is not the detective's but the client's or even a suspect's coming out. This realignment of the discovery of a character's sexual orientation may complicate the smooth process of the investigation, becoming a red herring for the detective as she must pursue the relationship between that character's behavior —feelings of shame and/or guilt, deliberate misdirection of the investigation, or distraction, sometimes comic, sometimes romantic, from the primary investigation — and the successful resolution to the crime, for example in Doris Klaich's *Heavy Guilt* (1988). Typically, in these situations the consequence of the outing adds complexity to the trajectory of the mystery plot without which the reader's enjoyment of the genre can be decreased; George Dove (1997) identifies the second "constitutive convention" of detective fiction as there being "no competitor to the investigation to the strange business" of the essential problem (76). Dove refers to incidental material, often taking the form of explanations of a specified background or esoteric information, which becomes necessary for facilitating the outcome or understanding motive. What seems an interruption to the primary narrative is actually an integral part of the detective story. In a majority of lesbian detective stories these secondary plot or character components often replicate the experience of the lesbian reader. She will also feel guilty or ashamed of her sexuality; she will try to "pass" with straight colleagues; she will go to extremes in an attempt to reconcile her sexuality with the rest of her life. Often, these incidents will come to a positive conclusion for the characters and the readers: the once shamefilled character will begin a movement toward acceptance; the seemingly hostile coworker becomes an ally. Of course, such a "happy ending" is demanded by the genre. Dove's fourth constitutive convention is that the "intentionality of detective fiction [is] that the only acceptable closure is solution of the mystery," and while Dove is describing the dominant narrative, the same demand for finality operates within the secondary components as well (77).

When the detective in a lesbian mystery is a member of a police force, coming out carries with it a more complex set of behaviors and responses. Unlike the amateur or the private investigator who operates from and within a clearly delineated personal environment, the woman member of an institutionalized police system faces the intersection of her public role and private experience. Where the private investigator is able to control the degree and intensity of her interactions with the public, the professional does not have this luxury of choice. While the private detective is able to circulate freely and negotiate her relations with legal, economic, and political systems, the police officer is constrained by the symbiotic linkages among these institutions. Given the tendency of the police system to be conservative, hierarchical, and male-centered, any woman, let alone an out lesbian, faces the reactions of her male colleagues that can range from benign neglect to harassment to overt hostility. Institutions like the police force demand allegiance to the overt systems of organization and power, as well as the implicit codes of conduct practiced by their members, but unwritten codes of support and silence are sometimes more important to the daily routine of police work.[8] In addition to the tensions that accompany the lesbian officer in her daily work interactions, she also confronts the attitudes of the public at large; in a society that finds homosexuality unnatural, the image of the lesbian as the guardian of social norms can be seen as a contradiction. The decision to come out, then, is a dangerous one for the lesbian police officer since it can place her outside the blue wall of the precinct house.

Not surprisingly, the characters who face this decision must weigh the outcome of the revelation with the risk. The moment of the initial revelation, the recipient(s) of that information, and the outcome(s) of the announcement must all be balanced by the detective, especially as these decisions must often be made during the course of the investigation. The lesbian officer does not always have the option of choosing the time or place of coming out: it will be forced on her in order to produce a desired outcome or to prevent interference with the investigation itself or threats to the investigator. Whatever the cause, once the detective's sexuality is revealed, she must come to terms with its impact on her ability to function within the institution. The most important factor that influences these relationships is often tied to the officer's rank. Street officers will confront many of the same tensions as higher ranked officers; however, their expression and their resolution will take different forms. Of course, the officer's sexuality must be interwoven with her attitudes about being in the police force, her expression of those beliefs, and her manner of adjusting to the behavior of her fellow officers. Not surprisingly, these women are portrayed as passionate about the profession and positive representatives of the institution. This is the essential paradox of the lesbian police officer — an outsider who participates in a system that inherently divides the world into insiders and outsiders, the marginalized other whose public role embodies the beliefs of the group that would exclude her.

The characterization of the lesbian officer falls into the standard genre representations: the by-the-book officer (Lucia Ramos/Scilla Carmody/Dez Reilly); the officer willing to bend the rules for results (Tru North/Stevie Houston); the renegade officer who deliberately flouts regulations (Delta Stevens/Foster Everett). The role sexuality plays in the development of the narrative reflects the character's position to the crime and the nature of her involvement with the investigation. Often, because of the nature of the crime, the lesbian officer finds herself having to explain homosexuality to fellow officers; Scilla Carmody and Ashley Johnson are typical of this plot situation, where gays or lesbians are the victims of the crimes committed. In other situations, the lower ranked officer has developed a crush, usually temporary, on the main lesbian character: for instance, Ann Newsome for McNab's Detective Inspector Carol Ashton. What is striking in these situations is that, whatever instigates the revelation, the character's coming out is not the first articulation of or recognition of her sexuality. In each case, the officer has already gone through the process and achieved a clear sense of her lesbian identity. In these instances the coming out produces positive outcomes. The "education" of a straight partner brings about acknowledgment and understanding; the potential sexual tension of the crush is defused for the development of an intimate professional and personal friendship. For the lesbian reader, these secondary plot situations suggest that, when the work environment supports it, one's sexuality does not hamper the shared goal of pursuit and capture. Everyone in the department realizes that whom one sleeps with has no effect on the performance of one's duty. However, not all officers find themselves in supportive situations.

More often, the lesbian police officer faces either overt or subtle hostility from other members of the force. Such responses can take the form of fully expressed loathing, as when Officer Alison Kaine, who has been caught up in an attack at a lesbian bar, is brutally put in her place by the detective in charge in *Tell Me What You Like*:

> "Don't think, Officer Kaine. Don't try to tell me how to do my job. You seem to think you're some kind of expert consultant here. Of course it would be wonderful if we could have homosexual officers on homosexual cases...." He put a broad look of disgust on his face which Jones [his partner] was miming, just in case she was too stupid to get the sarcasm ... [92].

Or they can be expressed as rumor or innuendo about the character's sexuality. How the woman responds to explicit or implicit hostility depends on the level of connection she experiences in the department. She can have a partner who goes out of the way to squelch comments, like Delta Stevens, or who is fully engaged with the woman's life and relationships, like Nicole Stone's partner, Jim, who supports his sister's growing involvement with Nicole. Other novels indicate that because of the quality of her work, she is able to ignore any comments, such as Lori Lake's Dez Reilly. In novels published in the late 1990s and more recently, the lesbian officer's sexuality may be tacitly acknowledged and sometimes even openly supported. There are even situations where the officer's superior may reveal surprising information; in Goldsby's *Wall of Silence*, after the climax that resolves the intertwined crimes, Forster Everett is recuperating after being shot, when she is visited by her captain to recap the motives of those involved. After the debriefing, when Everett has learned of the role her partner played in disrupting the investigation, the captain crosses the barrier from commander to friendship:

> The captain sighed. "Well, I should go." She placed the pad in her briefcase and stood. "It's our niece's birthday, and I promised I would get her a new doll. I'll stop back by in a few days if I have any more questions."
> "You have ... family?" I asked, before I realized it might have sounded rude.
> She grinned. "My partner has two sisters, two brothers, three nieces and one nephew, with one on the way. I guess you wouldn't have known that." She sounded almost regretful [390].

Earlier throughout the novel the relations between Forster and the captain have shown little except strained professionalism since Forster has a reputation for flouting the rules, so the captain's not so subtle revelation of her own lesbianism marks a shift in their working relationship.

The captain's disclosure also highlights an important progression in lesbian detective novels. Although not an accurate reflection of the broader changes in how the wider society regards homosexuality, the increased support by characters who represent the upper echelons of the police institution indicates the acknowledgment of the level of integration into the mainstream that gays and lesbians have achieved.[9] However, not all high-level officers receive this kind of accommodation; more typical responses include outright hostility, indifference, or ignorance. Usually these reactions tend to illustrate the continuity of the old-boy network within a department and the desire to maintain the appearance of unity and harmony. Katherine Forrest's *Apparition Alley* (1997) illustrates that even in 1997 gay and lesbian officers within any police force faced a blue wall of silence that conspired to diminish their abilities to function as successful members of the organization (chap. 20). Although a number of serial characters in lesbian police detective fiction have attained high rank or status in their particular departments (Carol Ashton is a detective inspector; L. A. Franco is a lieutenant as is Gianna Maglione; Kate Delafield is a homicide detective) even this cannot insulate lesbian detectives from the impact of the conservative environment of the department in which they work. Coming out, therefore, is a decision that requires careful thought and circumspection from the detective; the motivations for the detective to take this step reflect the security felt by the character to reveal her sexuality to the people with whom she works. If she chooses to come out to coworkers, the process is often slow and sporadic.

Often narrative circumstances impact how the revelation will occur, forcing the issue by making the detective's sexuality a part of the investigation. This happens when, during the course of the investigation, the suspect or another character, threatens to out the detective in order to publicly humiliate her or keep her from pursuing the resolution to the investigation; for example, in N. H. Avenue's *Letter Perfect* (2001). Another common plot situation presents the main character coping with the loss of a lover, either by the breakup of the relationship or by her death. The past's impinging on the present sets up the possibility for the detective to face the decision to reveal her sexuality. Surprisingly, in many situations, it is the concern of colleagues that brings the detective to this crossroads; both Kate Delafield and L. A. Franco are seen dealing with this. Unfortunately, neither of these characters formally comes out. They choose instead to remain in the closet at work, and when they do become romantically involved, they attempt, with varying degrees of success, to keep these aspects of their lives separate. A variation of the preceding narrative situation appears when the main character's romantic involvement becomes a strong, and positive, motivation for coming out. Over the course of their series Lt. Gianna Maglione and D. I. Carol Ashton deliberately move from the closet to public acknowledgment of their sexuality.

One other motive for coming out can be seen in the following exchange between Lieutenant Toni Underwood and Sergeant Sally Murphy in *Deadly Rendezvous*. Murphy is an officer assigned to assist Underwood find a serial killer, after Murphy has earlier made blunders during the interrogation of a potential witness, the owner of a lesbian bar:

> Looking uncomfortable, Sally blurted out, "Toni, I've got to be honest with you. I don't know much about gay life, or the people in it. I don't know if my input can be of much help."
>
> Toni ... whirled around, facing Sally. "Let's get this straightened out here and now, Sally. I'm a lesbian, have been all my life. I've never hidden that fact from anyone, I'm proud of who I am. And if someone has a problem with that, it's their problem, not mine. I do my job, and I do it well. Far as I'm concerned, that's all that counts. If I can try to understand your world, by God, you *will* try to understand mine. Or you're right, you're useless to me..." Toni continued. "Your job here isn't to judge, or decide whether you like my life-style or not. Your job is to help me solve four murders. Their being lesbian or not makes no difference. These women were human beings, and there's a maniac out there who brutally killed them. That's *all* that matters...."
>
> Sally began speaking with a slight tremor in her voice. "You're right, you and I have a job to do here. I admit I don't understand a lot of things, but I think we can make a good team. I'll do the best I can to do that job" [43–44; italics in text].

The obvious preaching tone of this conversation does not undercut the purpose behind Underwood's announcement; it will, in fact, help in finding the solution to the serial murders, since homophobia turns out to be the justification given by the killer for his actions.

Whether determinedly in the closet with her colleagues or proudly out and advocating for the recognition of other lesbians, the lesbian police officer adds another link in the reconfiguration of a shared experience and a reaffirmation of identity for lesbian readers. For this particular audience, the exposure to the variety of coming out stories offers a frame of reference of connectedness as well as mechanisms of fashioning one's identity. These texts illustrate for a lesbian reader a number of strategies by which she can situate her within a specific historical and cultural moment. As Gillian Whitlock (1994) observes, "[t]he 'making' of the lesbian throughout the twentieth century is a fine instance of how provisional, how context dependent, are ideas of identity, authenticity, the 'natural.' These categories are constantly in the process of being made, of being discursively constructed, in an ongoing social process of contest, struggle and change" (108–19). Whitlock continues by stressing the value of popular genres in this process of articulating a definition of lesbian that remains open to political and cultural shifts. What the lesbian reader discovers, and here I must interject a personal note, is a charged moment of recognition, the discovery of another like oneself and the replication of one's own experience. At the same time, however, as a consumer of the genre, one understands this identification operates within the closed system of its conventions. Solving the mystery must take precedence; the contract between the reader and the author cannot be radically broken at the expense of a reader's search for models.

The preceding discussion of the lesbian detective's coming out would suggest that the risks outweigh any strong benefit for the character. However, running parallel to the resolution of the detective's sense of identity is that character's connecting with a distinct community of other lesbians, which offers her the security of acceptance and the opportunity to explore that identity. The configurations of these communities is not monolithic in these fictions: they encompass a wide group of politically active members, as in the several groups that Emma Victor connects with over her series; they represent a particular lesbian/gay neighborhood, seen in McConnell's Nyla Wade or Stoner McTavish or the Cassidy James books; they center on a circle of friends who offer all levels of support, for example, the Caitlin Reece, Meg Darcy, and Nell Fury series; they may reflect a sometimes unspoken recognition within the workplace as illustrated in the Dez Reilly, Delta Stevens, and Rebecca Frye series, as well as portrayed in many single police procedurals. Whatever the community's makeup it establishes a concrete expression of what being lesbian means for the main character. Within the particular group she will discover various representations of lesbian presentation—from the superficialities of dress and residence to the intrinsic ways of response and being. Most importantly for the main lesbian character is the ability the community offers for exploring the multiple meanings of intimacy. Whether she is newly or gradually out, the lesbian detective's second investigation centers on the discovering the solution to her isolation. The boundaries of communities, after all, are extraordinarily flexible; they can expand to include the entire West Coast lesbian and gay community in an effort to save a house rich in gay history, as detailed in McConnell's *The Burnton Widows* or contract to embrace two people.

What happens to the second mystery, then, is a stretching of the detective's understanding of what it means to claim her lesbian identity and what effect that will have on her actions in the public and private sphere. In addition to a sense of personal burdens lifted, she is often able to establish a new moral base from which she will attempt, and sometimes succeed, to bring about needed change. These outcomes may be incredible outside the pages of the genre text; in *The Burnton Widows* that house is saved and becomes a museum dedicated to the preservation of and education about the gay past. More realistically, the main character, by solving the crime in which a lesbian or gay individual was the victim, asserts the value of a life seen as diminished by the perpetrator as well as marginalized by the society at large. The novels indicate this shift in the detective's moral position by having her become an advocate; this advocacy may take the more active form of Kat Alcazar's political engagement (*Angel Dance*), or Maggie Garrett's help in organizing a demonstration (*We Know Where You Live*). The character's professional circumstances may require a more limited form, such as Kate Delafield's buying books for a local lesbian bar (*Murder at the Nightwood Bar*) or Carol Ashton's insistence that a victim's HIV status not be kept secret (*Dead Certain*). Whatever form this commitment takes, these acts tie her more securely to a group and, perhaps, a cause that brings her out of the conventional isolation ascribed to the detective.[10] In *Murder at the Nightwood Bar* (Forrest 1989a), Maggie Schaeffer, the owner, tells Kate Delafield that "we have the power in us to make our own families" (212). And becoming part of a new family means taking on the responsibilities of the group, however they may be defined. Even the most independent detectives realize the importance of maintaining and strengthening such relationships.

Perhaps more important than the detective's understanding of the necessity for such connection is her acceptance not only of the link itself, but of her own need to take that step to community. The community with which the detective will align herself offers a safe space for that exploration. Beyond an ideological or practical linkage, the detective discovers that once open to the influence of others she becomes open to the possibility of deeper, more personal connections. Many of these characters are presented as isolated from affection, from emotional intimacy of any kind with another person. Throughout much of the story, the detective works to keep herself detached from events. Of course, such disengagement is a prerequisite for a successful outcome to the investigation, but as the primary story — finding the solution to the crime — intersects with the secondary one — finding the resolution to identity — the detective finds herself more and more engaged in the process of uncovering her need to belong to this new community. This is especially important for those characters who have previously been unconnected to any wider group, since, as indicated above, some have already well-established relations. Those who come to realize the importance of widening their relationships do so because not only do they provide assistance in solving the original crime, but they offer her the ability to become more comfortable with herself.

This progression appears more often in the narratives of serial characters. Carol Ashton, for example, in the first novel, *Lessons in Murder* (McNab 1988), stays firmly in the closet throughout the investigation. Becoming romantically attracted to a major suspect forces her to confront being open about her sexuality. With each subsequent novel, Ashton moves slowly but resolutely to coming out to an increasing number of friends and associates. The fifth book in the series, *Dead Certain*, has the father of the victim threatening to expose Ashton's sexual orientation as a way to prevent his own son's homosexuality from being announced. Although the threat is real, Carol Ashton defuses it by taking control of the revelation; having taped the conversation where the threat is made, Carol plays it for her superiors and colleagues. Instead of being publicly humiliated or privately ostracized, Carol discovers that neither occurs. As Mark Bourke, her partner, tells her, "You know, we cops close ranks over some things — no one's going to be talking to the media about you." Carol's response is "inspecting this new shift in the center of her universe. She was out now, to her own family and to her police family. She was no fool — there would be problems, serious ones. But it felt right. And good. Very good indeed..." (200–201; ellipsis in text). As the Aston series continues, she does confront the implications of her coming out, but the impact moves from her public position to her personal relationships.

Being open about one's sexuality does make one vulnerable to potentially harmful responses, and the harm can have immediate and long-term effects. Yet not all consequences to coming out are negative; the acceptance of her lesbian identity allows the detective to bridge an important gap in her personal life — becoming attracted to another woman during the course of the investigation. The obvious question to be asked is what is the purpose or value of including the romantic plot with the crime plot. Many detective novels work successfully without this complication, and in the major critical works devoted to explorations of the genre the romantic situation is given little, if any, attention. The introduction of a love interest into the criminal investigation is a conventional narrative strategy. Depending on the particular subgenre, the romance will provide a distraction for the detective: the love interest is a suspect using the attraction to shift suspicion. The romance occurs, deliberately or accidentally, between partners and may disrupt their working relationship. The romance develops with the growing attraction between the detective and a witness or peripheral character and offers the detective interludes of rest from the pursuit. Lesbian detective fiction takes these standard plotlines and transforms them, first by making both participants women. This is the most startling shift, perhaps, for straight readers, but for the lesbian reader, no other pairing is possible. The detective's struggle to claim her lesbian identity must be rewarded in some way; the attraction for another woman signals the completion of that effort. Finding an emotional connection marks the initial stage; pursuing the relationship, even with the potential for it disrupting the primary investigation, becomes the hallmark of many lesbian detective narratives. The relationship may be a long-term one carried out over the course of a series, like Carol Ashton's, Kate Delafield's, or Robin Miller's, or a brief connection experienced during a single novel, as with Emma Victor, Mickey Knight, or Denis Cheever. Whatever the duration of the romance, the experience of intimacy dramatically impacts the detective, and even though the relationship may be temporary, the outcomes are generally positive.

The second way that lesbian detective fiction transforms the conventional romance plot occurs in the way the development of that plot is slightly altered. If the subject of the detective's romantic attraction is a suspect, rarely does she become the perpetrator of the crime. Within the hard-boiled category, for example, the femme fatale character's negative qualities are greatly diminished; instead of sexual attraction diverting the detective's pursuit of the investigation, it becomes the means for the detective's reconciliation of her private identity with her public reputation. If the attraction develops between partners, rather than acting as an obstacle, it becomes the impetus to improving their professional performance.[11] However, at the same time that lesbian detective fiction manipulates the criteria of the genre, it must not distort them beyond the willingness of the reader to accept them. Lesbian readers, like all avid consumers of popular fictions, actively participate in the construction and reconstruction of the genre and its representations. Gillian Whitlock (1994) describes these readers "not as addict[s], lacking in preferences, but as historical subjects with some understanding and control of their own behaviours..." (110). So the innovations in plotting of the crime and investigation and characterization of the lead detective presented by lesbian authors addresses the expectations of lesbian readers.

Lesbian detective stories fulfill their genre requirements: murders are solved and villains are punished. These same imbedded assurances appear within the second resolution as well. The lesbian reader discovers that she must claim her sexual identity to become a complete person, that acceptance encourages one's movement into a community that preserves and protects all its members, that becoming a participant in the community opens the way to passion, and that passion leads to greater possibilities of self-awareness. This may seem an easily dismissed and idealized description of the purpose for lesbian detective fiction's combing the search for identity with the search for a criminal. What appear as conflicting narrative topics, however, become an integrated pursuit by the detective and one where the resolution of one leads to the resolution of the other. In *Adventure, Mystery and Romance*, John Cawelti (1976) states that detective fiction "offer[s] a temporary release from doubt." It enables the reader to distance and control potentially threatening situations (105). When the conventions work to their inevitable conclusion, the reader reasserts moral and social values, at least during the experience of the text. Good does triumph; people can be led to change their beliefs and behavior. Lesbians can move from the margin to the center.

Any genre fiction is constrained and yet, at the same time freed by its conventional requirements. As George Dove states (1997):

> The bounds of a genre naturally offer a challenge, to which creative authors respond by probing those limits and seeking points of breakthrough. What takes place then is a continual founding and altering of horizons. If the reading public accepts these alterations, the rules of the game will be revised and new horizons of expectations established [96].

Specifically lesbian detective fiction carries out this appropriation and reinterpretation of the genre in ways geared to its particular audience. At the same time that the lesbian reader looks for the essential components that make a mystery a mystery, she is anticipating the transformational experience that Philip Fisher calls "making familiar." Making familiar for lesbian readers means seeing our lives clearly represented and our relationships acknowledged. Whether in addition to identifying the perpetrator, the detective discovers her own identity; or while reestablishing a semblance of order, she uncovers a community that helps establish her own emotional relationships, we readers come to recognize ourselves and find pleasure in that recognition.

CHAPTER 2

Having Sex, Finding Love

> To ["the power of action and practical intelligence"] the lesbian detective adds the power of loving women. Her loving becomes an emblem for living with compassion and hope. Like other writers of lesbian detective novels, Forrest gives us strong emotional exchanges between lovers rather than casual, violent, or exploitative sex. She shows the strength of supportive female friendships and provides positive models of validating of various choices for women.—Lois A. Marchino 1995, 77–78

> It occurred to her that things were happening awfully fast all of a sudden. Two days ago she and Jaylynn had been circling one another warily, as if uncertain about the other. Yesterday the barriers had begun to crumble, and last night, *well, so much for barriers*. Today had already started out on a good note, and she wondered how long it could last. ... And yet ... something in her told her to trust.—Lori Lake 2001, 436; emphasis in text.

Whatever else may change about the detective novel, the one consistency is, as Scott McCracken (1998) asserts, "Detectives are loners. It is rare for passionate or romantic love to figure in their lives" (62). The detective's race or ethnicity, social position, ability, even sex may change, but whatever adaptations the writer makes to the physical and psychological identity of this character, love is relegated to the background, if it is considered at all. This is not meant to suggest that detectives are celibate; often they, especially male detectives, are represented as sexual powerhouses, intrinsically attractive to female characters within the novel. The female detective has also been frequently described as sexually attractive and desirable, and, just like her male counterpart, may find herself the object of the sexual interest of several male characters in the text. Sexual appeal and ability may be used as recreation or a means of achieving the desired goal, or the sexual component of the detective's personality is deliberately left ambiguous, particularly in mystery novels that highlight the intellectual aspect of detection. By ambiguity, I mean that the possibility of the detective having a sexual life is never addressed within the story.

However, whatever the circumstances surrounding the detective's sexuality and the uses to which it is put, the sexual orientation of the male or female detective is never assumed to be anything but heterosexual.

Sex, of course, is one thing; romantic love is another. Romance happens quite frequently in the pages of detective fiction, often providing the motive for the crime, or a plot situation that complicates or reinforces the actual investigation. Typically, the main investigator, whether female or male, will discover an attraction for another character; standard variations are the private detective becoming romantically involved with the book's representative of the police or legal system or becoming intimate with, usually against their better judgment, a suspect in the case. If the investigator is a member of the police force, the love interest may be a fellow officer, lawyer, suspect, or other outsider. Sometimes the primary detective is portrayed as married, although this relationship tends to remain in the background of the main plot. But rarely is the development and pursuit of a romantic attachment by the primary detective the centerpiece of the narrative. Some exceptions do appear; for example, Sayers's Lord Peter Wimsey and Harriet Vane, Christie's Tommy and Tuppence Beresford, but the dominant tendency is to downplay the role and impact of romance in the detective genre.

While some lesbian detective novels strictly adhere to the convention that positions romance to the periphery of the narrative, the larger percentage can only be said to deliberately incorporate a second, romantic, narrative impulse into the text: From the earliest lesbian detective novels—M. F. Beal's *Angel Dance* (1977/1990) and the Nyla Wade mysteries of Vicki McConnell—to the most recently published, the main character has confronted two dilemmas: solving the crime and understanding the nature of her attraction for another woman. The romance's progress will follow a variety of paths, including a character's coming out (sometimes the detective herself, sometimes another character), the growing integration of the socially isolated detective into a lesbian community, the breaking down of the detective's emotional barriers to dis(re)cover passion. Whatever trajectory the romance plot takes, its inclusion in the novel provides more for the lesbian reader than simple titillation: "This kind of narrative works to satisfy the need of readers—in this case, lesbians—to see ourselves in representational forms, to see that we do, indeed, exist and that our existence matters. These plots validate the sense of identity that readers have or seek and also show us something about what might constitute that identity" (Juhasz 1998, 68).[1] As I have discussed in the previous chapter, the discovery of the lesbian's sexual orientation opens her to a range of experiences that help her to clarify her sense of self and position in the world.

Feeling a physical, sexual attraction for another woman — or the reawakening of physical desire — is an essential component of that process; it completes the lesbian's integration into a world and community that completes her. What takes place in the romance plot is the transformation of passion, the initial sexual drive is realigned as the two women uncover a deeper sense of purpose and commitment as their relationship develops. The key questions, then, center on the purpose behind the inclusion of a love story, or the introduction of the possibility of a love story into the investigation. Does the romance add to or detract from the criminal investigation? When does sex become romance? What value is attached to the romance for the detective? Answering these questions requires looking at the idea of romance itself as well as looking at how ideas and expectations of romantic relationships change when situated in a story about lesbians.

Any discussion of the romance, however, must confront the long-standing bias of the critics, especially of academics. Of all the major popular genres, the romance faces constant disparagement for its rigid adherence to formula, for its reinforcement of stereotypic concepts of gender, for its subversive influence on women readers to accept the status quo.[2] Despite such negative responses, romance novels consistently appear on bestseller lists and outsell many other types of literature (Regis 2003, xi). Aside from its market dominance, the pervasive influence of the romantic storyline cannot be denied, appearing in a wide range of narratives even when least expected. The very ubiquity of the love story may account for its dismissal. Yet such cultural pervasiveness also suggests that the romance cannot be ignored, since it clearly addresses the needs and pleasures of its audience. What the romantic narrative embodies for its readers, lesbian or straight, is twofold: the representation of a reciprocal desire and a model for establishing a successful relationship.[3]

Any definition of desire must remain flexible because its meaning is determined by the context within which the focus of desire and its attainment operate. To satisfy her desire, the individual must first articulate the thing desired. Naming something or someone as desirable requires that she construct a framework against which to measure the object or person; without some clear understanding of the qualities that will be used to evaluate the suitability of the desired, she may find the pursuit more difficult. For example, if I am seeking a romantic partner, I need to determine the behaviors, appearances, and viewpoints that will satisfy my physical, intellectual, and emotional needs. Should I leave such aspects totally to chance, I may spend all my time and energy in testing numerous possible relationships but ultimately be left unsatisfied. However, if my criteria for a relationship are too rigid, I run the risk of never achieving my desire.

Complicating this is the realization that my ideas about my needs and what will satisfy them change over time. However, to create an awareness of those qualities in another that will fulfill my desires, I must make the effort if I hope to achieve them. Once identified, the individual determines those methods that will bring about a union between the desirer and the desired. As with determining what is desirable, finding the means to attain the desired are as varied. Do I pursue or let myself be pursued? Do I behave in a direct manner or use subterfuge? Such decisions, obviously, assume that the person whom I desire recognizes and accepts my efforts. If she does not, do I continue or bring a halt to my pursuit? Suppose I am the object of someone's desire, how do I structure my response? Quantifying desire and determining its pursuit are subjective, especially when what is desired is a relationship with another person, and most of us look beyond our individual abilities to our particular communities and cultures to assist in our efforts.

The romance narrative is "concern[ed] with desire and the prospect of its satisfaction" (McCracken 1998, 76). By allowing the female reader to participate not only in the construction of the one desired, but the management of her attaining that relationship as well, romantic stories provide reference points for comparing the ideal and the actual. In her analysis of a group of romance novel readers, Janice Radway (1984) identifies the various levels of engagement experienced by these women:

> Dot Evans and the Smithton readers[4] believe very strongly that romance reading changes at least some women. They seem to feel that bad romances especially prompt them to compare their own behavior with that of passive, "namby-pamby" heroines who permit their men to abuse them and push them around. This comparison, they believe, then often leads to greater resolve on the part of the reader who vows never to let her spouse injure her in a similar fashion. Dot and her customers also believe that they learn to assert themselves more effectively as a consequence of their reading because they so often have to defend their choices of material to others and justify their right to pleasure [218].

Radway insists that what may seem like a failure to separate the fantasy of the fictional romance from real life relationships does not occur. Although the Smithton women are voracious readers of romance novels, they retain a clear distinction between what happens in and out of the text. However, Radway also asserts that the reading experience does not produce any deliberate alteration in these readers' belief in or support of traditional gendered notions of intimate relationships.

The tension of the traditional heterosexual romance centers on the conflict between the woman's sense of personal empowerment and the pressure to conform to social expectations. The main female character, through a series of stages, comes to self-awareness and takes deliberate action to control the direction and outcome of her desires.[5] The various kinds of confrontations with the hero and others enable the heroine to realize that she has the ability and the choice to control the direction and outcome of the romance. Despite this awareness, in the typical romance narrative, the heroine cedes this power to the romantic hero. This action is projected in the narrative as a willing resignation, not a rejection of that new knowledge. By consciously giving up her agency, the heroine not only effects the transformation of the hero, from potential threat to perfect mate, but also (re)gains social status. Pamela Regis (2003), a defender of the romance novel, perhaps inadvertently highlights the paradox at the heart of this genre; after describing the basic structure of the novel, she asserts that the reader's enjoyment comes with the heroine's newfound freedom from the various social impediments that have prevented the accomplishment of her desire:

> The heroine's freedom in the form of her life, her liberty, or her property may be in doubt not only in the original society that promotes the barrier, but also in the new society at the end of the work. Nonetheless, the heroine's freedom, however provisional, is a victory. *She is freed from the immediate encumbrances that prevent her union with the hero. When the heroine achieves freedom, she chooses the hero* [16, emphasis added].

In spite of the heroine's growing sense of self-knowledge and control, her ultimate goal is to find a sense of completion with the hero; instead of a further exploration of that self, the heroine accedes to the dominant expectations of a heterosexist culture that continues to define women mainly through their relationship to men.

For many feminist critics, it is this unwieldy combination of the heroine's adherence to conservative expectations, while at the same time holding the radical ideal of self-assertion, that devalues the impact and value of the genre. The likelihood of the heroine breaking free of the pressure of social conformity remains unfulfilled; the romance's dependence on the happy ending — the promised marriage — confines the narrative to that one option. Even the possibility of other choices for the heroine does not exist; alternative male suitors are generally proven to be inadequate to satisfy her physical and emotional desires; retaining her independent life (and the requisite skills to maintain it) is shown to offer little happiness or complete satisfaction. As other avenues of self-development are blocked off, the heroine is left with the only approved outcome, union with a man. Even the smallest hint of the heroine's attraction to another female character must be quashed. Typically, other women in the romance stand as competition for the hero's affection or as emotional support for the heroine in her pursuit. The degree of intimacy in the heroine's relation with other women tends to stay superficial; this watering down suggests an inarticulate maintenance of society's distrust of female friendships.

As Carroll Smith-Rosenberg, Lillian Faderman, Julie Abraham, Terry Castle and others have documented, female friendships throughout the nineteenth century and early twentieth century were viewed as acceptable outlets for women's emotional lives. Overly simplified, these relationships, often begun during childhood, provided a wide range of private and public support: "Within this secure and empathetic world women could share sorrows, anxieties, and joy, confident that other women had experienced similar emotions" (Smith-Rosenberg 1985, 63). Within the friendship, the two women found not only emotional support, but also discovered approval for intellectual pursuits or creative abilities, traded practical information for household management, and provided opportunities for their private experiences to be validated. Most importantly, such relationships were regarded as a normal part of women's experience and often encouraged by parents, husbands, and the wider society. Some relationships even gained public approval: the Ladies of Llangollen, Eleanor Butler and Sarah Ponsonby, or the Boston marriage of Annie Fields and Sarah Orne Jewett. These relationships could also be found in the pages of all ranges of literary production.[6] The intensity of such relationships were as varied as their participants, but the possibility of physical intimacy between the couple cannot be discounted as the letters and diaries quoted by these critics talk of kisses, hugs, shared beds, and other gestures. Social approval did not rest on fear of such physical closeness between women; in fact, these friendships were often seen as a way to acculturate young women about the expectations of the dominant patriarchal culture. Sherrie Inness (1995), in her study of women's college fiction, describes the outcome of an intense college "crush" this way:

> Although crushes help maintain the cohesive structure of the all-woman group, in actuality they also support the patriarchal status quo of that era. The homoaffectionate crush is considered by educators and parents as just one stage a woman undergoes before arriving at "normal" heterosexual adulthood through marriage to a male [46].

Only when the concepts of women's social, emotional, and psychological makeup shift are these intense friendships called into question.

The realignment of social attitudes toward women at the end of the nineteenth century results from a complex intersection of political, medical, economic and other influences. The second wave of feminism instigated a sometimes more vocal and radical attack on male privilege; more women began to enter the workforce, which was viewed as a threat to the sanctity of home and the separation of the sexes; women also began to infiltrate professions — medical, legal, educational — typically seen as the prerogatives of men; women became more visibly engaged in artistic, literary, and other cultural production. Establishment institutions attempted to respond to these transformations using a variety of rationales, from religion to the new study of psychology. Women's actions were now defined as threats to social traditions and systems, and they were labeled an unnatural and deviant in their attempts. Masculinity, itself, was seen as under attack, and during the last quarter of the nineteenth century many popular self-help manuals and guides were published urging men to retake their rightful position both in the public and private sphere. Women's previous behaviors and relationships, like their intense friendships, once viewed as normal became demonized, seen as another indication of social breakdown. The sexologists developed and promulgated the theory of sexual inversion to explain same-sex attraction; later, psychologists, following Freud, theorized the failure of women to achieve maturity in their psychosexual development, which negatively impacted their formation of intimate relationships.[7] By the early decades of the twentieth century all same-sex relationships, whatever the level of physical intimacy, were categorized as diseased, leaving the women open to implicit and explicit social ostracism, legal sanctions including institutionalization, and physical harm. Given the stigma attached to same-sex relationships, it is not surprising that romance novels underplay the connections between the heroine and other female characters.

When attached to detective fiction, the romantic narrative loses its prominence if it appears at all. This is understandable; after all, the primary goal of the detective is to discover the instigator of the crime, bring him or her to justice, and restore some semblance of balance to the world that has been disrupted by the crime. Yet even Sherlock Holmes, the quintessential intellectual detective, had to confront a woman, and the suggestion appears in "A Scandal in Bohemia" that he and Irene Adler share some past. Rarely are women completely omitted from detective novels featuring male protagonists. In the standard male-centered crime novel female characters typically reflect the old dichotomy of woman as virgin or whore. She is the innocent victim of deceit; often due to the machinations of the criminal she becomes suspected of the crime and must be rescued by the detective. Or she is allied with the crime in some way, either as an accomplice or mastermind. She is usually portrayed as alluring, enticing the detective with promises of sexual favors in an attempt to distract him from the investigation. Depending on her treatment in the text, the outcome for this female character is either to become romantically available (although marriage between the detective and this character is not common) or to be punished through incarceration or death. Variations on the portrait of women do appear in these texts—the helpful secretary, the interfering busybody, the sometimes ineffective sidekick. In each case, however, the female character tends to remain sidelined in the narrative's progress; her assistance toward a solution is minimal at best, leaving the male detective as the recipient of the rewards for a successful conclusion to the investigation.

Of all the permutations available to female characters in traditional detective novels, the femme fatale is the most common, setting up the possibility of intimacy within its pages to fail. The femme fatale inhabits the same world as the hard-boiled detective, a territory where the veneer of civilization is easily broken by the uncontrollable corruption that all its citizens exhibit. In this world no one, except the detective can lay claim to any virtue; even women are not immune to the power of greed and corruption. Instead of remaining allied to traditional ideas about their social position, they position themselves as competitors for economic and social status with men. Since the hard-boiled detective's ethical code rests on very conservative notions about appropriate gender roles, when faced with such a reversal of his expectations, "[t]he only possible resolution to the insecurity caused by the conflict between the need for women as sexual and social fulfillment and the threat of feminine independence and domination is the simultaneous possession and destruction of the female" (Cawelti 1978, 159). Even though he may be tempted by the femme fatale, and perhaps even succumb to her enticements, in the end the detective must annihilate the woman and free himself from her illusionary self-representation. It is often surprising how easily swayed the detective is by the femme fatale, and it is plausible to believe that, in the dark world of the novel, the extreme violence of his reaction toward the discovery of her falsehoods rests on his own desire to believe in the possibility of intimacy.

The image of the woman who lives in the pages of the detective story is tinged with qualities of the femme fatale, particularly when she must always be approached with suspicion. None of her statements and actions can be taken at face value by the detective; he is often shown questioning her motives and doubting her assertions: "What she holds out and promises as an erotically cathectable scenario is the possibility of an impossibly thrilling identification with the image of one's own death" (Forter 2000, 33). So, when such a woman declares her desire for a romantic connection with the detective, she confronts an impossible task—to assert her feelings without being seen as posing a threat to his personal codes of behavior or his very sense of self. Unfortunately, the detective cannot overcome his personal allegiance to a greater, abstract morality, and he leaves the scene in the same isolated state in which he entered it.

When women began writing detective novels, they faced the question of how to appropriate and revise the conventions of the genre without betraying their credibility or the new sensibility created by the introduction of a female as the primary investigator. Not unexpectedly, as the majority of the critics of women's mysteries indicate, the female detective took on those standard characteristics and behaviors but utilized them in new ways and for new purposes. This meant "turn[ing] them upside down and inside out, exposing the genre's fundamental conservatism and challenging the reader to rethink his/her assumptions" (Reddy 1998, 2). Instead of working a case out of an idiosyncratic worldview, the female detective often puts personal interests aside and takes the case as much for how it impinges on her sense of solidarity with the victim. Since her clients are generally women, the female detective forges relationships and understanding rather than foregoes them. Often, too, the nature of the crime being investigated highlights issues integrally bound up with women's experience: "[T]he protagonist will expose the reader to some unpleasant social truths: poverty and racism contribute to crime; damaged children can become damaged, transgressing adults, domestic violence can push women to murder; corporate criminals destroy workers' lives" (C. Cole 2004, 140). The women who are victims are vulnerable because they are subjected to a hostile, patriarchal system that devalues their contributions and demeans their very being. Not only are women damaged by the very social institutions that are supposed to support them, but they are also victimized simply because they are women. Crimes of violence against women, especially sexually based ones, appear often in works with female detectives. This creates a new level of identification between the detective and the victim, because the investigator recognizes that she is just as vulnerable to physical attack.

While many of the earliest female detectives, Sharon McCone, Kinsey Millhone, V. I. Warshawski, exhibited strong feminist principles in the cases they undertook, their investigative methods replicate the standard practices of the genre. Just like their male counterparts, the female detectives use illegal means for obtaining information, intimidate witnesses if necessary, and do not hesitate to use violence if no other means produces the desired result. Some of them bring specialized skills or experience to their profession: some are former police officers; others have a legal background. Even the amateur detectives are usually able to bring in their particular area of expertise in solving the crime; among the various abilities are those of herbalists, ministers, caterers, and housecleaners. Female detectives may use these typical investigative practices, but they will adapt them in ways that will not violate their particular moral standards; for example, many do not use weapons of any kind, relying on other skills to accomplish the task.[8] The female detective does, however, appropriate one characteristic of the male investigator and make it her own — tough talk. A signature trait of the hard-boiled detective, the wisecrack becomes a weapon capable of instigating the criminal to reveal his hand, provoking a response (often violent), and revealing the truth. Language, for the male detective, is one way of asserting his resistance to those who assume authority over him. His words are concrete, his sentences clipped, his intentions explicit; most importantly, the detective's talk is readily understood by the other male characters in the text. Women's language, on the other hand, is stereotypically viewed as weak because of its subject matter — emotions, personal issues, domestic concerns — and delivery — softspoken, nonlinear, nonassertive. The female detective uses language like a man, but she is not just parroting the man's tone or merely mouthing his words; rather she is using language as "a means of opposing conventional codes of feminine conduct. ... Talking back has been viewed as inappropriate behavior for women: it is a mode of resistance more plausible and ethical — and potentially subversive — than, say, physical violence" (Walton and Jones 1999, 131). The subversive quality of her speech comes from the fact that the female detective has a greater vocabulary from which to choose; she can and does, as Walton and Jones illustrate, make references to those feminine attributes, menstruation, childbearing, and other bodily functions, that most men find disturbing if not disgusting. She will also play with the delivery of her talk, often couching her words in a seductive or humorous tone. Men's talk is always serious. Rarely heard from either female or male detectives, however, are the words that reflect any romantic feeling or convey the desire for a truly intimate relationship.

The most obvious reason for the female detective (and perhaps for the male as well) is that the language associated with romance makes its speakers open to emotional hurt. Romantic language asks each party in the relationship to be willing to reveal her or his deepest feelings not only about the other, but also about her or himself. The hallmark of all romances, after all, is the expression of desire, and for the detectives, whose raison d'etre is to remain separated from social intercourse, to admit to a longing for connection destabilizes that sense of self. In the romance novel, this breakdown of the hero's defense represents an essential outcome of the narrative; he learns through the development of his relationship with the heroine that he must relinquish his previous habits if their union is to be achieved and succeed.[9] However that desire is articulated in the crime novel, the detective fears being made incapable of fulfilling the obligations of the investigation. These fears are reasonable; after all, the blandishments of the femme fatale aim to undercut the detective's investigation; by promising him sexual or emotional satisfaction, she uses his own needs against him, thus the strong expressions of betrayal made by the detective who discovers the woman's affections are merely a ruse. Even when the detective welcomes the overtures of a female character, he keeps close watch on the progress of the relationship and tries not to let his private feelings intrude into his public life. To acknowledge such a need requires the detective to question the importance of fundamental aspects of both his professional and private behavior, and if the basic premise of his existence is open to challenge, the detective must make a choice that has the potential to reframe his sense of self and purpose. It seems obvious, then, why he prefers to cut off all possibility of intimacy.

Female detectives' confrontations with the issue of desire are complicated by the tendency to stereotype women's expression of and engagement in romantic relationships. Women are still seen as desiring some kind of involvement with another as the dominant drive in their interactions with the opposite sex; those who reject this characterization face being labeled as spinster, frigid, or worse, lesbian. The generalization that a woman does not feel complete unless she is linked with a man has long roots, and still finds expression in the majority of popular forms. Romance novels, especially, reinforce the notion that, even if she is intelligent, strong, and self-aware, the woman will achieve greater satisfaction from her connection to the hero. All of the obstacles she faces and overcomes— with or without the hero's assistance — reveal more that she is the most suitable mate for him than that she is capable of maintaining a self-directed life. Small wonder, then, that many female detectives, amateurs as well as professionals, are given an explicit or implicit romance. Usually, the romantic figure becomes the female detective's source of practical or moral support; many become interested in the chief investigator of the crime or are outsiders to the investigation who are able to assist her with information and other help; and they will act on that interest later in the novel or the series. Yet, as Patricia Johnson (1994) observes, the placement of the female detective in a romantic situation also has the potential to harm her. Because the detective, in spite of positioning herself against the attempts of patriarchy to define and limit her, must still behave in ways that are "feminine and not only feminine but (hetero)sexually desirable and active" (99). Like her male counterpart, then, the female detective often becomes sexually/romantically involved with a male suspect who, at the novel's conclusion, is revealed as the murderer. This situation may seem an exact duplicate of the male detective and the femme fatale, but as Johnson notes, ultimately, his loss of power is temporary:

> [T]he *femme fatale* archetype provides a protection and, finally, an escape from the central problems in the situation. First, the *femme fatale* is granted a Circe-like power over men, relieving them of responsibility for their actions, and, second, the man who can break the grip of that power, like Ulysses, is granted an heroic status [99].

In her discussion of Sue Grafton's Kinsey Millhone and Sara Paretsky's V.I. Warshawski, Johnson stresses how they are made more vulnerable to not only personal, but professional attack as well because of their involvements. Unlike the male detective, who seems bewitched by the woman, the female detective enters the relationship consciously, often deliberately, thereby setting herself up for danger. Even though the detective does ultimately bring the suspect to justice, usually through his death, she is not able to shed completely the "emotional residue" of the connection (102). However, like the male detective, these women adhere to the genre tradition of returning to a solitary life, preferring disengagement to community.

This insistence on retaining the image of the lone female detective requires exploration, particularly as the woman who deliberately chooses such a position runs counter to dominant cultural views of her social positions. As will be discussed more fully in chapter 5, women's public and private lives are generally constructed around the concept of interlocking communities/relationships that shape their moral and psychological development. To create a life that denies the importance of developing a community of others whose experiences and ways of acting in the world replicate her own, marks the female detective in important ways, most obviously leaving her open to the blandishments of a male suspect. Although she rejects this type of intimacy, the detective still desires to create a community to which she can belong and therefore "carefully choos[es] important relationships that do not merely replicate traditional ones— essentially [she] invent[s] new modes of connectedness" (Reddy 1988, 105). The detective establishes and nurtures close ties with another character, of either sex, who will become a surrogate for affection and support. Not surprisingly, the longing of these women for emotional connection is described by the critics in terms of parental care, which precludes the need for developing or sustaining any type of romance.[10] When this quasi-parental bond exists between two women, the specter of the lesbian is raised and must be exorcised. Rebecca Pope's (1995) detailed analysis of the nature of V. I. Warshawski's relationship with Lotty Herschel, in

"'Friends is a Weak Word for It,'" suggests that what prevents the logical consummation of their intimate connections is twofold: the dominance of heterosexuality as an expression of patriarchal control and the desire for a pre–Oedipal union with the nurturing mother (166–68). Since Lotty stands in for V. I.'s dead mother, the merest hint of erotic possibility between them breaks two taboos—homosexual desire and incest. Not all friendships in novels with female protagonists are framed in this manner, but Pope's contention that the possibility of the two women slipping into more than friendship must be forestalled, clearly operates. The detective's friend is often already safely romantically involved with a man or willingly relinquishes her claims on the detective's affection when a suitable romantic partner for the detective is introduced.

Straight female detectives may enjoy the occasional erotic exchange with a male character, but any hint of same-sex intimacy must be eradicated. In lesbian detective fiction, however, the romantic life of the detective moves from the periphery of the narrative to its center, sometimes even disrupting the criminal investigation in favor of the personal one. Palmer (1993) makes this comment:

> The woman who identifies as lesbian struggles to maintain her autonomy in the face of homophobic pressures; like the protagonist of the thriller, she tends to be regarded by her heterosexual relatives and work-mates as an individualist and "loner." Simultaneously, however, she often seeks to become involved in the activities of the lesbian community and, like the protagonist of the romance, places value on love and sexual attachments. In fact, despite the role of loner assigned to her by the dominant culture, she herself frequently envisages her life as a quest for personal involvement and love [67].

Too many lesbian detective novels include the narrative arc of the romance to be ignored; the first question to be answered is why is this story so important to the lesbian text?

While heterosexual romance has a long history, stretching, according to some critics, to Greek and Roman prose works, lesbian romance has a shorter, more problematic history. Historians and critics of lesbian literature will point to certain works, Radclyffe Hall's *The Well of Loneliness* or Virginia Woolf's *Orlando*, as precursors of the representations of lesbian erotic and emotional life, but little continuity can be found in the naming and ordering of texts that are categorized as romantic novels. (The whole issue of identifying such novels as works of the popular genre or as more serious literature is an on-going debate not only in lesbian criticism.) The one moment in lesbian literary history that most scholars agree establishes an important point for the popular articulation of lesbian experience is the period of the pulps.[11] I do not want to divert the direction of this chapter into a detailed analysis of lesbian pulp, but I do feel that some understanding of the content of these early lesbian texts will provide a foundation for my examination of how romance works in detective fiction; after all, many of the character types and plot situations that appeared in the pulps become the template for later romance novels. What separates the representation of lesbian desire in the pulps from earlier texts is their "construction — or signification — of lesbian sexuality in the novels" (Walters 1989, 88). For the first time, lesbians' lives and loves were given concrete representation, however compromised the portrait was. Lesbian readers were able to discover that there were others like themselves and that the characters' stories offered them terms of reference for identifying their own desires.[12] What the pulps did was place sexual and emotional desires at the forefront of the narrative, as the characters move through their worlds trying to make and keep relationships. Ann Bannon's Beebo Brinker novels illustrate the physical and psychological movements as her major characters fall in and out of relationships — both gay and straight. Walters (1989) details this pattern more fully. While many of the pulp romances had to reinforce mainstream social views of the deviant nature of lesbians, they highlighted for their readers that lesbian sexuality "stands as a metaphor for personal autonomy and, openly or implicitly, heterosexuality is posed as inauthentic for women..." (Weir and Wilson 1992, 101). The pulps also gave powerful descriptive form to the butch-femme paradigm of lesbian relationships that still influences the delineation of the couple's physical traits and their interactions. Some contemporary romances, however, play with the expectations of butch and femme in a variety of ways to call into question its prominence within the lesbian community.

Suzanne Juhasz (1998), one of the few critics to address the role and value of the romance for lesbian readers, states that such stories tell of more than the search for love: "the story to be told ... is one of maturation as much as love, for love and self-development prove to be aspects of one another. The complications and difficulties that the relationship occasions provide as well the opportunity for self-development" (74). Without carrying my discussion of lesbian romances too far, some of its characteristics should be briefly described in order to situate the ways in which lesbian detective fiction utilizes them. Like its heterosexual counterpart, lesbian romances aim to illustrate the search for sexual and emotional completion. The main character will undergo a series of trials or tests of her affections for the object of her desires, and the focus of her attentions will often seem unavailable or unapproachable. There are, however, key differences between the lesbian romance and straight romantic novels. The first, of course, is that the object of the main character's interest and pursuit is another woman. When one's romantic needs and desires can only be satisfied through the development of an intimate connection with a woman, the dynamic of the narrative shifts, and the pursuit of fulfillment demands that the main character understand the meaning and implications of her choices. In many lesbian romances the main character comes to realize that her assumption of a heterosexual focus has been wrong, either through society's implicit and explicit coercion of "natural" sexual interest or her denial of same-sex attractions in her formative sexual experience. Coming out remains an integral component of the lesbian romance narrative; what Thomas Wartenberg (1994) says of the lesbian-centered movie *Desert Hearts* is true for the romance novel: "[the movie] depicts how the existence of the "closet" — the consignment of homosexuality to a space of acknowledged invisibility — exacts deep psychic costs to those both within and without it" (194). Where the heterosexual heroine must let go of aspects of her personality that would reaffirm her emotional and practical independence, the main character in the lesbian romance generally retains these attributes and abilities. She brings to the new relationship not only a sense of completeness, but also a sense of reciprocity with the other woman; they balance one another, offering a range of private and public supports that allow them the ability to maintain their commitment and enable them to develop a deeper level of connection and intimacy. Another important distinction between the two romance narratives is that in lesbian stories the couple will be situated — to varying degrees — within a wider community that will reinforce the discoveries of the couple; Juhasz (1998) describes this as the "[m]aternal, sororal, and homoerotic relationships and institutions [that] are both the grid that situates the plot and the network that produces it" (70). This support system will be made up of other lesbians *and* straight friends, and even family, of the couple, and, as is typical in the romance, provide advice, comment, and action to ensure a positive outcome for the couple.

At heart, any romance, whether lesbian or straight, sets its main character a task that is often difficult to achieve — the uncovering of one's desires and learning the ways to articulate and attain them. The heterosexual heroine, however, enjoys the advantage of society's support, indeed encouragement, for her efforts, so long as her outcome meets the approved expressions of the happy ending — acquiescing to her man and accepting the erasure of her individuality. The lesbian romance is audacious in its portrait of two women claiming the same emotional and erotic privileges of the dominant society; like the straight heroine, they seek to learn the truth of themselves, each other, and the developing relationship. It is here that romance shares narrative impulses with the detective novel: a precipitating discovery that sends the main character on to pursue clues that will reveal the truth. Motives must be deciphered, suspects and witnesses engaged, clues interpreted, mistakes corrected, and secrets revealed.

As the previous chapter has discussed, coming out remains a vital component of many lesbian mysteries, and in many nonserial texts this process runs beneath the major investigative narrative, sometimes even overwhelming it.[13] While this particular plot appears frequently in lesbian detective fiction, however, it is not the only format for structuring the romantic story. Just as often, these texts present two characters who are already conscious of their sexuality, have come to terms with the implications of their orientation, and have enjoyed sexual/romantic relationships that antedate the events described in the book. Carlene Miller's *Death Off Stage* (2001), Becky Bohan's *Sinister Paradise* (1993), and Margie Schweitzer's *Courting Death* (2001) represent a small sample of the romance that develops between two lesbians whose sexual identities are well established. Clearly then, what is suggested by such narratives is that lesbian desire and fulfillment can be expressed in terms that expand what is sometimes seen as the only construction of the lesbian romantic plot. I do not intend to underplay the value of the first blush of romantic attraction described in the coming out subplot. Such stories, with their representations of the intensity of discovery for the newly aware lesbian evoke strong emotional responses from the lesbian reader. These texts repeat the same descriptive language as the attraction is felt between the two women: there is an instantaneous recognition of a connection between the two; words like *compelling, being drawn to, intriguing, natural attraction,* and many similar ones appear throughout the texts. Talaran (2001) writes:

> She had made several attempts at reading the pages but each time her mind drifted back to Nic and the kiss they had shared in her car. Leaning her head back against the headboard, she closed her eyes and transported herself back to that moment. *A moment of utter splendor*, she mused. *Where are you right now, Nic? Are you safe? Are you thinking of me, too?* [165; italics in text].

Such expressions tend to repeat the clichés of romance discourse, but the characters' reliance on the conventional should not be seen as a denial of the seriousness of the moment of recognition. For many of the characters at this point are now poised at the tipping point of acceptance of a new identity, and often totally new words are not available to represent the intensity of the feeling. Carly, the woman whose thoughts are presented in the above quotation, has little romantic experience of any sexuality. She can only fall back on the standardized terms of the dominant culture that are available to her. What happens when they are addressed to a woman instead of a man is a radical adjusting of the definition of desire.

To discover that she is in love with another woman, that she wants to posses this woman physically and emotionally, forces this character to reevaluate her notions of passion and to readjust her pervious ideas of gratification. Because in the lesbian detective novel, romance cannot be separated from sex; love as represented in these novels always involves a maneuvering between each woman's knowledge and practice of both types of intimacy. Again, the clichés of romantic description dominate the representation of passion. Winters (2003) puts it like this:

> Denise could feel Sara's eyes on her, even though her own eyes were closed. ...Denise couldn't help but remember how wonderful it felt to have a woman in her life. It had been awhile since she'd had anyone in her life. But women ... with the seductive way they brushed their hair behind their ears, or the way they would tease, licking their lips ... she missed that. Those qualities that women possessed, and used, always made Denise's blood pump harder [43].

But, again, replacing the traditional heterosexual object of the expressed want with a woman reconfigures the notion of normative sexual behavior. Behaviors and speech typically assumed to be the privilege of the male now become the property of the female: "The hard-boiled convention that allows descriptions of sexual encounters is adapted to accommodate the representation of lesbian eroticism" (Walton and Jones 1999, 163). Where before the woman had to keep silent about her desire, the lesbian speaks clearly and openly. Where before women who spoke of their erotic desires were ostracized, lesbians encourage one another to actively and deliberately name their needs. Where before women could be, and often were, threatened with violence for expressing the belief in their right to determine their sexual practice, lesbians support one another as they come to identify and express their positions within the relationship. Of course, such outcomes must be acknowledged as idealized portraits, detailing the fantasy of the perfect erotic and intimate relationship. However, the importance of fantasy in the creation of the romance, whether lesbian or heterosexual, cannot be overlooked; the couple may embody in an exaggerated form the preferred physical attributes and personality characteristics of a particular period, but 'the central issue seems ... to be not so much whether language or even subjectivity is 'free' from culture or constructed by it, as whether that culture, the situation in which language users are embedded, includes the experience and vision of alterity and difference. People do imagine something other than the status quo, and they struggle in various ways to attain and to validate that difference (Juhasz 1998, 80).

To cross the line from an emotional attraction to the acting out of desire through sexual intimacy marks the transformation in the coming out romance of the woman. Having sex proves the power of desire not only to concretize a woman's new identity, but also to reawaken the detective. In many novels, the detective, the object of the other woman's attraction, is pictured as reluctant to instigate any kind of relationship; she has lost a long-time partner through death (Kate Delafield), has been deceived or betrayed by a past lover (Carol Ashton), has a reputation for being sexually aggressive (Denise VanCook), or has rejected any kind of emotional life, focusing only on the job (Tori Hunter). The force of the other woman's desire powerfully impacts the detective's private defenses, breaking them down and allowing her to reconnect with her own and the other's emotions: "Their eyes were locked across the table, as were their hands. Tori wondered what Sam saw in her eyes. Could she see the desire that Tori was trying to hide? (Hill 2005, 244). In the standard criticism of heterosexual romance, sex generally carries a negative burden; Pamela Regis (2003) labels it "distracting" (27) and an "accidental" component rather than an "essential" one (55). Radway's (1984) analysis reiterates the need to defuse the male hero's sexual power, often viewed as potentially violent and one step above rape. Although one would assume the physical consummation of the heterosexual heroine's desire to be a longed for outcome of the romantic plot, actual sex is frequently omitted from the text. The potential to lose self-control, to be too caught up in powerful emotions, must not be fulfilled. For some feminist critics, showing lesbians having sex becomes an intrusion into the main investigative plot; such scenes are unnecessary and border on the pornographic. In her discussion of the Kate Delafield novels, Gill Plain (2001) sees the sex as an "exchange of power," with Aimee Grant (or in the earlier novels a one-time connection) providing Kate with the "strength to return to her 'undercover assignment' as an infiltrator at the heart of the patriarchal state" (186). In a profession where "sex is a viable form of currency," because Kate Delafield remains closeted on the job, she must replenish, in an almost vampirelike manner, her sense of herself as a lesbian (Gallo 2001, 241). While this dynamic has credence particularly for closeted detectives, an increasing majority of these texts present the sexual interaction as mutually beneficial, even when the detective keeps her personal life off-limits while at work.

This benefit appears both in novels that integrate the coming out of a female character when she becomes involved in the investigation and in texts that present the development of a romantic interest between women already out to themselves and others. Two basic variations of the romance plot appear in these texts: in one, the detective, usually a professional or police officer, becomes involved with a criminal investigation, and, during that investigation becomes attracted to another woman connected to the case, either as suspect, witness, or assistant; for example, Schweitzer's *Courting Death* (2001), Jamneck's *Down the Rabbit Hole* (2005), Avenue's *For Pete's Sake* (2001). In the other variant, the detective is, or becomes involved in a relationship. This secondary storyline appears in many of the serial detective novels, and as the development of the main character is charted, so too is her relationship with her lover. The partner may not have any connection to the main character's profession (Lordon's Sydney Sloane or Maiman's Robin Miller) or may herself be part of the investigative team (Clare's Lt. Franco and Chief Coroner Gail Lawless, Radclyffe's Detective Rebecca Frye and consulting psychiatrist Dr. Catherine Rawlings). The movement of the romance obviously relates to the nature of the interaction between the two women. The detective often finds the other to be a hindrance to the investigation's progress or an unwanted diversion; as the search for the criminal continues, the detective becomes increasingly preoccupied with the other woman, but interestingly, not always to the detriment of the outcome. These novels do indulge in some of the standard plot devices, a witness's capture, the intrusion of the other into a crime scene, but, as is typical of both the detective and romance genre, these situations create the dramatic tension — will the detective effect a rescue to bring about the successful outcome as well as the recognition by the previously uncommitted detective of a real connection to the other — that is necessary to meet the generic conventions for closure? When the detective and her lover work together on a criminal investigation, they offer each professional and private support. Such a situation does have the potential to strain the romantic relationship, and with the serial detective this potential is sometimes realized. In nonserial works, the personal tensions are resolved as the case is.

Not all romances in the pages of lesbian detective fiction are successful, of course. As in so many detective novels, the stresses of the investigation counteract even the most supportive partner's efforts to reconcile the private and personal needs of the detective. The trajectory of the detective story, after all, is the solution to the crime and the restoration of some level of order; when personal crises interfere with the detective's primary duty, something has to break, usually the romantic relationship. For example, here is a scene from Baxter Clare's *Bleeding Out* (2000):

> Frank's answering machine indicates she has two messages. ... The other is Gail. She tells Frank she has packed her things in a box and left it in the hall. ...
> Frank has tried not to think about Gail. She's hoped this will somehow

> pass. That maybe time can reconcile them. Frank knows she's wrong and Gail's right. ...
> Frank thinks about calling to offer contrition, but Gail's tone doesn't brook reconciliation. And Frank won't beg. She made her choice when she walked out... [143].

Lt. Franco's relationship with Gail has fallen apart because Frank cannot separate herself from the case, which is not only dissolving her emotional connections with Gail and others, but is also accelerating a slide into alcoholism. By the end of *Last Call*, Frank has come to the moment where she is actually putting her service revolver into her mouth. Other romances collapse in less extreme ways; a former lover suddenly appears and creates fissures in the new relationship that have the potential to split the lovers. Usually, though, a complete rupture is prevented by the realization by one of the couple that what they have developed is essential to their happiness. This scenario is quite frequent in the novels, more often for private detectives than police officers; for example, in *Every Time We Say Goodbye*, Robin's previous lover, Cathy Chapman, shows up connected to a case Robin is working on. In addition to competing for information about the investigation, Cathy also hopes to compete for Robin's affections with K. T., Robin's new lover. As tempted as Robin is, her final commitment is with the future and K. T., not the past represented by Cathy (166). Other sources of anxiety for the romance include the demands of one of the lover's careers (Claire McNab's Denise Cleever), the desire of one to bring the connection to an end on realizing the difficulty of maintaining it (Brett Reece Johnson's Cordelia Morgan), and the preference for belonging to a community that offers emotional intimacy rather than erotic satisfaction (Lauren Wright Douglas's Caitlin Reece). Yet, in spite of the many obstacles for a successful romance, whether from outside forces or individual doubts, even the most adamant loners in lesbian detective fiction are positioned for the possibility of such a relationship.

Of course, no romance in lesbian detective fictions follows a straightforward path since the conventions of each genre often contradict the progression of the narrative. The goal of the romance is to unite two people who seem to be unsuited; the detective seeks to identify the individual who defies social norms and removes that person from any social connection, because crime ultimately destroys such unity. Paradoxically though, the outcomes of romance and detective novels are strikingly familiar: the success of the search, whether for love or perpetrator, drives the main character in spite of threats to her physical and emotional safety. The promise of restoration that both genres offer keeps the reader coming back. Dove (1997) writes:

> The reader moving through the text develops a store not only of isolated recollections of events and impressions but of rules, structures, conventions, ethics, and the like ... which become the reader's perceptions of the genre and which intervene in future expectations of texts.... This influence is especially strong in the reading of a genre like detective fiction, with its conventional usages and its constant reiterations of narrative material like variations on a familiar theme. *Instead of being bored by these almost endless repetitions, the reader feels comfort and security within a framework of familiar expectations* [51; emphasis added].

This repetition should not be looked at simply as the same story being told in exactly the same way; that would bore the reader, who wants familiarity but at the same time desires innovation in the handling of the conventions. The genre must be flexible enough to appropriate and integrate shifts in the cultural environment in which these texts are created. The reader does not want to know too soon if the criminal will be captured or if the lovers will recognize that they belong together. Popular fiction must suspend not only the reader's disbelief, but also maintain a balance between the reader's need for the continuation of suspense and her presumptions about the way the text will work. This helps explain why so many detective novels develop into series, where romances do not. Just as the detective's investigative skills must be continually tested, so must her romantic ones; because the nature of passion is always changing, the detective cannot assume that erotic discovery will be completely resolved. Just as solving one case does not bring an end to all crime, the acceptance of romance does not end the building of a relationship. A brief examination of Claire McNab's Detective Inspector Carol Ashton series highlights the ways romance and crime intersect to maintain the reader's attention to both pursuits.

The investigations of Carol Ashton are detailed in sixteen novels, the first published in 1988, the sixteenth in 2004, all set in Australia except for the twelfth, which takes place in the United States (Virginia and Washington, D.C.). All of the books fall under the category of police procedurals as Ashton and her investigative squad pursue their cases by adhering to the standards of law enforcement. All of the major police characters develop their investigations by the book; there are no daredevils or loose cannons on Ashton's team. Solid police work remains the key to uncovering the perpetrators. The basic narrative pattern is the same in all of the novels: a prologue establishes the initial murder, and the opening chapter generally places Ashton and Mark Bourne, her second in command, at the scene. Carol does not engage in reckless behavior as she follows leads and questions witnesses; in fact, her criminal investigations rely more on an analytical process than brute force; she insists on solid police work from herself and all of her subordinates. Many of the novels develop their plots by showing the constant interviewing and reinterviewing of witnesses and suspects as the team teases out accurate from false information; often Carol discovers the truth during a scene where she, sometimes with Bourke, is hashing out such testimony, a minor discrepancy, a small time gap setting the outcome in motion. However, she does occasionally use the sanctioned violence granted to all police officers; she has drawn her weapon and fired it in *Double Bluff* (1995). She has also been on the receiving end of the criminal's violence as he or she attempts to escape the pursuit, including being struck on the head and suffering a concussion in *Fatal Reunion* (1989), sliced by a knife in *Body Guard* (1994), and having her nose broken in *Inner Circle* (1996). Ashton's success rate, as required by the genre, is high; rarely does the perpetrator avoid capture. Only once, in *Set Up* (1999), does the suspect escape. But as the series develops Carol's commitment to police work wavers; although she never expresses the cynicism of the hard-boiled detective, Carol begins to indicate her frustration with the increasing violence she comes in contact with, with the old boy network that emphasizes political expediency over good police work, with the ever present sexism that stymies her promotion to the upper ranks. In several of the later novels, Carol contemplates severing her ties to the police force, including an offer to work as a private investigator in *Accidental Murder* (2002) or leaving Australia completely and emigrating to America in *Blood Link* (2003).

Weaving through the criminal investigation is the story of Carol's romantic relationships. Over the sixteen novels the reader follows the history of Carol's primary romance with Sybil Quade; during the period when she and Sybil are separated, Carol becomes involved with Madeline Shipley, a television personality, and Leota Woolfe, an FBI agent. That Carol's emotional life is as much a subject for the reader to become connected to as is her professional life has to be recognized since every one of the novels in the series brings this component into the narrative. I think it is important to note that each criminal investigation is treated as a discrete narrative; a crime is committed and the detectives pursue and complete the search by the end of the book. The romantic narrative, however, threads its way throughout the entire series; no clear-cut resolution to Carol and Sybil's relationship is provided. Each new book in the series picks up the development of their involvement, and unlike the criminal investigation, McNab provides no recapitulation of the romance's history. The reader of the series becomes the weaver of this plot, bringing together the known facts and filling in the gaps. By relying on what she expects from the romantic novel, just as the reader of the detective story can fill in the lacunae present in the text, the lesbian reader reconstructs the missing details of the couple's shared experience: "In effect, romance reading provides a vicarious experience of emotional nurturance *and* erotic anticipation and excitement" (Radway 1984, 105; italics in text). Radway refers to the reading experience of heterosexual readers of heterosexual romances, but the same integration of familiarity with the genre and the specifics of the novel at hand work for the lesbian reader as well.

Just as the crime story adheres to a conventional format, the romance is detailed in a patterned way; except for the first novel, *Lessons in Murder* (1988), which introduces the major characters, the other books move from the initial crime to the private life of Carol and Sybil. This repetition allows the reader to anticipate this secondary story as well as reconstruct the entire romance over the series. This placement of the personal against the public links the two; the crime's participants, situation, or motives mirror, although not always as exact duplication, the tensions and concerns that have developed in the romance. For example, in the second novel, *Fatal Reunion* (1989), the murder victim is the husband of Carol Ashton's first lover Christine, and Sybil obviously experiences an intense jealousy about Carol's investigation of the case, fearing that Carol may tire of her and go back to Christine. There are several parallels in the emotional undertones between the three women's situations: like Sybil, Christine is suspected of her husband's murder. Both she and Christine have strong emotional and erotic ties to Carol. Both also place explicit and implicit demands on Carol for assurance that she is committed to them:

> [Sybil] thought of last night and bit her lip. They had been so careful with each other, so cautious not to disturb the peace. When they had gone to bed, Carol had kissed her, said she was tired and turned her back to go to sleep. Sybil wanted to curl around her, to cuddle her and say, "I feel threatened because you're seeing Christine again" [27].

In their first extended interview after the murder Christine reminds Carol several times how much she regrets breaking off their relationship to stay with her husband: "You're the only lover I ever wanted!" (56). During the course of the investigation Carol will remember her's and Christine's shared passion and will also remember its consequences; Carol's husband sued for divorce and took custody of their son, claiming that, as a lesbian, she was an unfit mother. Carol clearly carries the scars of Christine's betrayal, and, unfortunately, those memories interfere with the developing relationship with Sybil. Sybil fears losing Carol's affection because she knows there is unfinished business between Christine and Carol that she cannot compete with. At this point in their relationship Sybil and Carol have only been together for eight months, and this is the first time in her life that Sybil has had and expressed both sexual and emotional feelings for another woman.

Carol, too, is afraid of her inability to sever all ties with Christine despite the harm; she refuses to believe, at least in the investigation's early stages, that Christine is capable of murder, letting her emotions override her professional experience. As the case continues Carol uncovers the truth about Christine's involvement: she does have the capacity to commit murder and to continue killing if it will keep her unsuspected. At the climax of the novel and investigation Christine, after confessing, assumes Carol, because of their shared past, will let her go free. Carol, of course, refuses and her assertion that "No, Chris. It's over" marks the final excision of Christine from her personal life (200). It is no wonder, then, that Christine strikes out at Carol with a poker, trying to murder her as well. The melodramatic quality of the ending — Mark Bourne shoots Christine before she can strike Carol again — should not undercut the importance of the case's impact on the romance. Love must not be static, stuck in memory that denies any possibility of a new expression; both Carol and Sybil must learn this lesson before they can continue to develop their relationship.

The next three novels chart the development of Carol and Sybil's relationship in two ways: the continuing romantic discovery and the integration of identity. The emotional ties between the two women become deeper and more intense; for Carol, Sybil represents a rejection of the kind of romantic possibility projected by Christine. When they are pictured in the intimacy of her home, Carol discovers that she must drop the defenses that have kept her from forming close connections not only with Sybil, but also with others. For instance, Carol tends to isolate herself from her associates; all of these interactions, even with Mark Bourke, remain professional and distant. Sybil's passionate desires also teach Carol to let go of her need to control the relationship, in the daily routines as well as in the bedroom. However, by *Dead Certain* (1992), the fifth book in the series, even though both women are intricately tied to one another, the relationship breaks. But, it is not for reasons the romance plot usually implies.

Sybil's discovery of her attraction to Carol and her developing desire to maintain this relationship have completely shattered her links to heterosexuality; the reader sees Sybil gaining a fuller awareness of her identity as a lesbian, an identity she is proud to claim. In several novels Sybil reiterates this basic challenge: "What is it, then, Carol? Worried that my presence will confirm the gossip? That people will come round to see for themselves?" (1992, 188). Carol, however, remains closeted. Wishing to keep a clear dividing line between her public role and private life, Carol reacts irrationally to Sybil's spoken, and unspoken, criticisms of her refusal to openly acknowledge her sexuality. The irony, of course, is that Carol's hopes of keeping her sexual identity secret are unrealistic. As early as the second novel, Mark Bourke is aware that Carol is a lesbian; when Carol risks telling him of her relationship, he replies: "I know, Carol." He grinned at her raised eyebrows. "At the trial I thought... Well, I'm a detective, remember?" His smile faded as he added, "And perhaps it'll make it easier if I tell you I also know about your relationship with Christine Tait" (1989, 20). Despite Mark's full acceptance and support, Carol will not alter her position. Her justifications for staying closeted are reasonable; as a high profile member of the police force, she risks jeopardizing her position and effectiveness. Several of the early investigations center on crimes against homosexuals (*Dead Certain* and *Cop Out*) or impact homosexual characters or issues in a secondary capacity (*Past Due*) and offer proof to Carol of the continued hostility directed to gays and lesbians. Carol views Sybil's efforts to have her not only publicly acknowledge their relationship, but her own sexuality as well, as an intrusion. Only the threat by a powerful businessman, the father of the murdered man, in *Dead Certain* to out her brings Carol to the realization that staying in the closet poses the greater threat, but while the public revelation can be managed, the personal consequences cannot. At the end of this book Carol "told her what had happened[.] Carol was conscious that Sybil might welcome what she, herself, dreaded. What might represent freedom to Sybil meant loss of control to Carol," and rather than the expected romantic happy reunion, Carol asks her not to come home (188). Carol, it seems, is willing to acknowledge her sexuality for herself at this stage, but to present herself as part of couple remains threatening. From this point in the series Sybil's presence in the novels is greatly reduced, sometimes only represented by others' references. Yet, it is interesting and important for the lesbian reader that Sybil does not disappear completely from the extended romantic narrative.

As the tensions between Carol and Sybil come to the breaking point in *Dead Certain* (1992), Carol is distracted by Madeline Shipley, a television journalist. In previous books, Carol and Madeline's interactions have shifted from being antagonists (Madeline has gently implied that she would out Carol in *Death Down Under*), to acquaintances who use one another to satisfy professional needs. In *Dead Certain* they become sexually involved, and by the seventh novel, *Double Bluff*, after Sybil has left Australia to take a teaching job as well as to give both herself and Carol breathing room, the affair has become intense. At this point the relationship is fueled mainly by sexual desire; Madeline gives Carol a sense of relief and release. When told that Sybil is due to return, Madeline feels confident that she will be able to overcome Carol's reluctance to forget Sybil. Carol's inability to forget Sybil should not be compared to the hold Christine had on Carol; as Carol discovered, Christine's idea of love was superficial, easily broken when their relationship precipitated the collapse of Carol's marriage. Although she expresses anger and frustration with Carol, Sybil's deep commitment to Carol and their emotional connection never wavers. Even when they have reached a mutual agreement to maintain their separation, Carol knows that she can rely on Sybil for support in her private life. She can ask Sybil to take care of her son, David, or to help her Aunt Sarah, but Carol would not ask Madeline, who has been denied access to the most personal aspects of Carol's life.

The most recent novels in the series seem to suggest that Carol and Sybil have reached an acceptable accommodation in the relationship; Carol's liaison with Madeline Shipley has shifted into an easygoing friendship, and she has become romantically involved with Leota Woolfe, an FBI agent she met during her visit to America (see *Under Suspicion*, 2000). Sybil has also become involved in another relationship. But, the reader must ask, if all passionate ties between Carol and Sybil have been severed, why does Sybil keep appearing in the texts? Within the conventions of the romance, this is the key mystery to be solved, and McNab incorporates several clues that suggest that what appears to be final is not. The most important of these is that Sybil's presence in the novels increases not only through the references of other characters, but in her frequent physical appearances in places where Carol will also come. In addition, throughout the series, Carol's Aunt Sarah has advocated for the two to get back together; she has often been the instigator for having Sybil and Carol meet, or to prod Carol about her feelings for Sybil. Even when Carol is involved with Madeline and Leota, Aunt Sarah makes her position clear. Aunt Sarah's efforts become increasingly emphatic in the last two novels; being honored for her political activism, Sarah is having her portrait painted by Yancy, Sybil's new lover. Sarah keeps Carol informed of their relationship as the portrait progresses. She is the first to tell Carol that they have separated, which is confirmed by Yancy herself: "[she] had declared that Sybil had never got over Carol, and "for Sybil, anyone who isn't you is second best" (2004, 125). In the latest of the series, *Fall Guy*, Carol asks Sybil to return to the house they shared to go through photograph albums in order to create a film tribute to Sarah. This reunion is essential if Sybil and Carol's relationship is to recover its emotional intensity; in an earlier book Sybil had been attacked in the house. Carol's job has literally and figuratively invaded the private space that circumscribed their relationship, adding a more compelling reason for Sybil's leaving. When Carol invites her to come, she is surprised at Sybil's agreement, setting the stage for a hoped for reconciliation. At the novel's conclusion, that hope has materialized; the success of the tribute to her aunt, the knowledge that each is no longer involved with others, the growing awareness of each other, compels an unintended suggestion:

> Absurdly nervous, Carol linked her fingers in Sybil's. If Sybil drew away, Carol felt the moment would be lost forever. Sybil didn't move.
> Still gazing down at the lighted windows, Carol said, "Just a thought. We sell our houses, and use the money to buy something that would be ours—not yours or mine."
> Silence. Carol said, "I'm holding my breath, so say something, anything, before I run out of air...." "I believe," Sybil said, "I could become accustomed to the idea" [173].

As in all romances, the lovers' relationship is affirmed; the past trials each undergoes offer the couple insight into one another's understanding of their desires; the complications that seem to destroy any chance of the romance's success prove to be the essential requirement that allows the lovers to give concrete expression to those needs and the courage to act on them. Carol Ashton's reputation as a detective remains unblemished, even her failures to close a case do not diminish her public or professional standing; however, her inability to fully read and interpret the signs that are necessary to solve the mystery of love must be nurtured and honed. Carol has had to discover that keeping Sybil means letting go of her habit of control, that her fear of publicly acknowledging her sexuality and her relationship does not diminish her, that the companionship she sought with Madeline and Leota could not complete her as Sybil can. Not surprisingly, in order to achieve this resolution, Carol must not act like a detective, but like a woman in love.

CHAPTER 3

*Playing the Boys' Game**

> transgress—1. to go beyond the bounds of limits prescribed by (a law, command, etc.); to break, violate, infringe, contravene, trespass against. b. to break a law or command; to trespass, offend, sin. c. to offend against (a person); to disobey.
> 2. to go or pass beyond (any limit or bounds). b. to go beyond limits, to trespass.—*Oxford English Dictionary*

> That's what I thought. Stevie Houston, the Lone Ranger. Let me tell you something. We don't operate that way here. We work together, as a team, gathering evidence one piece at a time in a methodical manner until there is enough to make an arrest and get a conviction. We don't storm in, guns blazing, and round everyone up and haul 'em off to jail like the wild west or something. Do you understand?—Tracey Richardson, 1997, 140

That the earliest appearances of the word *transgress* are in religious and legal works should not be surprising. These sources succinctly frame the values, moral and social, that define the very nature of transgression, since only when a community's sense of shared belief is defined can trespass be known. To transgress requires the breaking of these most basic ideas of what is and is not proper. By pushing beyond these socially imposed limits, the transgressor becomes the target of the community's anger. The group's accepted ideals of order have been violated and opened to questions, and those guilty of such aberrant behavior are quickly identified by this failure to follow social norms. These individuals become the targets of the community's sanctioned retribution. The response will take various forms, but the common purpose of punishment is the defining of the transgressor as outcast. To be identified as different, to be named other, places the offender and the offense outside the group's protection,

---

An earlier version of the essay appeared in Multicultural Detective Fiction. *Copyright (c) 1999 From* Multicultural Detective Fiction: Murder from the "Other" Side, *by Adrienne Johnson Gosselin, ed. Reproduced by permission of Routledge/Taylor & Francis Books, Inc.*

and the institutions devised to serve the group become the wall separating the individual from the community.

The expression of the relationship between society and its transgressors appears with greatest clarity in creative literature. Fictional representation allows these frameworks to be defined concretely, often more accurately, through the requisite literary conventions; fiction enables situation and consequences to be emphasized by creating effective narrative situations, as well as believable characters. The fictional environment draws the reader into the particular situation as a participant. By becoming actively engaged in the story, the reader invests in the projected outcome, which most often reflects conservative, traditional ideals of the dominant society. Nowhere does this expectation dominate the reader's experience more than in genre fiction, especially in mystery and detective fiction. In crime novels the social order suffers temporary breakdown and is reclaimed at the end through the hero's actions. Crime challenges the social norms that define the particular community values described in such works. Order, conformity, and ordinariness characterize the world restored. The hero, whether public agent or independent, represents allegiance to these standards when the transgressor is successfully ousted; no break with communal systems is tolerated in the fictional worlds of the crime novel. Cawelti's (1976) discussion helps explain this appeal:

> Readers of classical detective stories, we hypothesize, shared a need for a temporary release from doubt and guilt, generated at least in part by the decline of traditional moral and spiritual authorities, and the rise of new social and intellectual movements that emphasized the hypocrisy and guilt of respectable middle-class society. For those committed to middle-class values ... the classical detective story offered a temporary release from doubt. First it affirmed the basic principle that crime was strictly a matter of individual motivations and thus reaffirmed the validity of the existing social order [104–5].

Although Cawelti's analysis focuses on the specific subgenre of classical crime detection, this same concern with the reestablishment of a clear sense of moral and social certitude is found in the other types of detective fiction.

One basic paradox inherent in all crime stories is their reliance on the exposition of deviance — murder, fraud, theft, rape, abuse — to establish the moral values that will eventually triumph as the investigation continues.[1] Obviously, for the detective plot to work, a crime is a necessity; in addition to the genre's narrative and character conventions, however, a deeper anxiety operates that draws the reader into the text. Returning the society within the pages of the book to stability, while important, does not totally resolve the doubt noted by Cawelti, especially for the modern reader, where moral certainty can no longer be taken for granted. With the increase in definitions and applications of moral positions that characterize modern society, how does one determine which viewpoint satisfies the demand for order and balance? How can a consensus be reached regarding moral standards and even what determines when such standards have been transgressed? According to R. Gordon Kelly (1998), the mechanism for achieving some semblance of consistency is trust. And trust implies an agreement between one individual and another and between individuals and institutions concerning social interactions, but more importantly that the requisite knowledge and ability is being applied correctly. Relationships, from the most mundane to the essential, are determined by the willingness of the parties to accept their implicit and explicit parameters and the parties' reliance on the tacit and unspoken acceptance of those terms. "Dependency," as Kelly states, "by definition, is an asymmetric relationship of power. As such, it can (and frequently does) create feelings of uncertainty, vulnerability, and resentment in the lay person seeking expert assistance or counsel. It is in the interests of both parties, therefore, to attend to the trust dimension of the relationship, however transitory the interaction may be" (5). This reciprocity becomes particularly vital in the trust placed in the police by the public. In the novels discussed in this chapter, however, this basic premise is overturned as the representatives of the community are also transgressors of its most deeply held values.

It is important to recognize that transgression occurs in a variety of ways, from deliberate to accidental as well as from physical to ideological. Those offenses, easily recognized and understood, receive clear-cut responses: the difficulty for the dominant group comes when the transgressor wears the camouflage of the wider community itself. The greatest perceived transgressive threat to the larger society is the individual who shares in the dominant social codes governing behavior and belief. The person who has absorbed the community's lessons, who accepts these structures, who blends in and is therefore undetectable as offender is potentially the most devastating participant in such a social order. This marks a breakdown in the trust required to facilitate social interactions. Such a person enjoys the protection that allegiance to the larger community brings and at the same time challenges this same community by (ultimately) remaining fundamentally distinct from it. This individual, then, infiltrates the group, thereby representing the potential for dissolution. The presence of such a person also reveals the fragility of not only the institution, but also the shared moral positions seen as its source. The successful infiltrator can pass, and by passing, embody the contradictions that are inherent in such a position. One such figure whose public role contradicts her private life and who captures the complexity of the successfully integrated transgressor is the lesbian police officer. Although her public responsibility demands maintenance of the dominant community standards, her private life severs all connections with them.

Since its inception, the idea of a police force has centered on the relationship between power and authority. Ideally the police system is a formalized conduit for the community's authority to control and regulate its participants. The foundations of the community's authority rest on its definitions of acceptable and deviant behavior. Without the legal and moral determinations of the group, the enforcement power of a police system is nullified. Each depends on the other for security and credibility, in that the police organization exchanges maintenance and enforcement of societal rules for support and tolerance of its organizational actions. Given this mandate, the police system establishes itself through adaptations of larger social institutions that ensure the smooth transfer of its authority into action. The internal structure of the police, while altered to fits its particular needs, retains strong ties to the dominant social framework. Such mirroring guarantees the continuity of the contractual relationship. The "[p]olice," as Kappeler, Sluder, and Alpert (1994) affirm, are

> selected based on demonstrated conformity to dominant social norms and values. They are also socialized into their occupational role and function. Those who become police officers bring to the occupation the perceptual baggage and moral standards common to the working middle class. ... In essence, police are selected, socialized and placed into a working environment that instills within them an ideology and shared culture that breeds unprecedented conformity to the traditional police norms and values [92].

Becoming a police officer, then, requires an expected, deep-seated adherence to society's dominant ideals and practices, as well as demanding an intense, all-encompassing allegiance to the specific communal values of law enforcement. Any deviation, such as homosexuality, cannot be tolerated, let alone accepted, because it would challenge those values. Any crossing of the community's standards can only be met by rejection of the destabilizing force.

The traditional configurations of the police force have been, and continue to be, male defined and dominated. Frances Heidensohn's 1992 study of women in law enforcement sets out as a major premise that "male 'ownership' of social control tends to be taken for granted, leaving women perpetual strangers, invaders in the field" (27). Heidensohn's use of the word *invaders* reinforces the closed worldview held by many traditionally male police forces where the hierarchy of the police system is often a direct imitation of military structures. The stereotypic view remains of policing as an environment restricted only to men because of the continual threat of violence. Even in the twenty-first century, women in the military and police still tend to be kept from the front lines of battle or policing. According to this view, women are not capable of exerting, and more importantly, of maintaining, the force necessary to contain that violence. Typical negative comments point out the tenacity of the stereotypic image of women police officers. As Kappeler, Sulder, and Alpert note,

"...most officers have problems working with female officers and dislike working with them because they believe women don't have the physical stature to do the job."
"Female officers generally cannot back up officers." "Female officers sometimes exacerbate the situation because they feel the need to assert themselves or escalate the potential for use of force" [173–74].

Ten years after this study, such attitudes about women in the police force still influence how male officers view their presence: As Gallo (2001) notes, "A mind-set that allow[s] them to treat the women in the ranks with varying degrees of contempt, or disdain, or blatant and crude sexual overtures.... It happen[s] all the time, ... and [is] so prevalent that the guys accepted it as standard procedure" (44).

Women, however, have always infiltrated police ranks. From the beginning of formalized police systems, the female officer has gained admittance into this closed world by "keep[ing] her mouth shut, accept[ing] the assignments she was given, follow[ing] rules, and maintain[ing] a low profile" (Martin 1980, 9). While still disproportionately represented in many forces, and still fighting social biases and barriers, the female police officer is no longer an anomaly. The female officer gains the approbation of the dominant authority figures when she understands what the rules are, written and unwritten. She is allowed to share in the mechanisms of power and able to wield authority, knowing her actions and decisions have the necessary internal sanctions, when her personal identity is subsumed by the identity of police officer. Gallo (2001) notes that "What was once apprehension has become acceptance.... It's just part of the job, just something I do. What all cops do" (185). Once accepted, the female officer has been transformed from an interloper. She no longer trespasses into the forbidden; she is a fully integrated member of this community.

The essential point of the female officer's acceptance into the police community is her willingness to play by the rules. She will succeed when she subordinates her individuality to the group, taking on its particular attitudes and beliefs. According to Kappeler et al., the authors of *Forces of*

Deviance, this code mixes publicly stated policy, which includes following proper procedures for arresting and processing criminals, obeying the orders of superiors, and maintaining a professional public demeanor, with a frequently unstated set of private expectations dealing with how officers relate to and work with one another. This second, unspoken, set of behaviors asks an officer to maintain a code of silence concerning another officer's questionable or illegal activities; to distrust anyone outside a very limited circle, including superiors in the department; to do anything to protect a partner and oneself, even to the extent of lying, and to take and give physical and emotional abuse when necessary (110–15). There is, then, a seemingly inherent contradiction within the typical police force between allegiance to the system and self-preservation, which is often compounded when this closed system must deal with the broader society it polices. Placing a woman into this situation complicates these interlocking relationships because her loyalty is always open to question. Gina Gallo provides a clear illustration of the pressure to find the right balance of loyalties after being involved in a car accident when she and her partner were responding to a call about an armed robbery:

> "Partners gotta look out for each other," he [her partner] said, "that's what it's all about." ...
> In case I didn't, he proceeded to spell it out. As a recruit, as a woman, I'm under scrutiny. Everybody's watching to see how I handle myself. A car accident's no big deal, not in a cop's life. If I want to be a cop, I have to roll with it. Take too much time off playing sick, and the bosses might think I'm a malingerer, or worse: a whiny, sissy broad who can't take it. Everybody gets banged up sooner or later — it's part of the job. Better take my lumps and get over it. Keep my mouth shut and our collective asses covered [68].

One common point of reference for the acceptance of women as police officers may be the unspoken but assumed agreement that the police community holds the larger society's views regarding sexual issues. Women, whether in the department or not, can be the butt of vulgar sexual jokes, are assumed to be sexually voracious, willing to use sex as a weapon against others or as a tool for advancement, as well as subject to sexual threats and harassment.[2] However sex is referenced within the precinct or outside its walls, women officers' sexual behavior, attractions, and relationships must conform to expected heterosexual patterns. Tracey Richardson's *Northern Blue* (1996) traces the careers of two lesbian police officers from their training to placement and dramatizes the tensions inherent in being out inside the department. Miranda McCauley and Miki Paxton become romantically involved during their training period, and while Miki would like to continue the relationship, Miranda's ambitions to move up to a command position in her town's police department leads her to break off their affair. Once a member of the department, Miranda deliberately disguises her lesbian self; the only acknowledgment she gives to her actual identity is surreptitious trips to Toronto's lesbian community. There she can engage in quick anonymous sexual encounters while "long[ing] for that intimacy — the shared secrets, the private joking, the thrill of imminent sex. Her coworkers and acquaintances all thought she was the lucky one, in love with one of Hooperstown's most eligible bachelors. But only she knew the truth, the longing, of what wasn't. It was at times like this she wondered if she could really go though with this marriage thing" (100). Prepared to go through with the marriage, Miranda's plans are overthrown when Miki is hired as a member of the force. The resulting emotional turmoil forces Miranda to break her engagement; her fiancé, however, threatens to get back at her for the perceived affront and engineers Miranda's denial of promotion.

Susan Martin's (1980) study of the District of Columbia police force in the late 1970s points out the impact that real or perceived questions about female officers' sexuality has on their professional behavior and self-image as women. Here, even the suggestion of being a lesbian can jeopardize a woman's position in the department; as Gina Gallo checks into the Chicago Police Academy, she faces the sexual jibes of the admitting officers who question the reason for her divorce, asking in the crudest terms if she is a lesbian (25). No matter what rank the female officer has obtained, the homophobic responses of male officers remain deeply embedded, and despite the increasing visibility and broad social acceptance of lesbians and gay men in visible positions within the police force in more recent times, these prejudices can still impact working relations within the department.[3] In spite of receiving commendations for bravery, Miranda's application for promotion is rejected because, as a colleague taunts, "I don't think the guys would be too happy about having a dyke in charge. Nor would the brass." (199).

What this deeply rooted negativity to those perceived as outsiders to the institution means is that adherence to the rules is essential to survival inside the system. Miranda, until she has to make the choice between either acknowledging her sexuality or remaining closeted, has been just such an officer. She has fulfilled the requirements of the position and performed well. Even when Micki is held hostage by a suspect, Miranda follows procedure, until the delay in backup compels her to action. Acting properly as a police officer enables the lesbian to pass successfully in the wider social world, and, as a police officer, the lesbian automatically appropriates the privileges of the contract that characterizes her profession. She is given the ability to identify those who obey or disobey social regulations; she is allowed to determine the course of response and instigate the requisite action; she enjoys the support of her peers and superiors when the performance and outcome produce a successful arrest of the criminal or prevention of the crime. The emphasis here rests on the function of the public role of law enforcement. Because the first focus and effort of the officer is to protect the wider community, so long as the lesbian officer upholds that contract, her transgressive existence receives public sanction. Yet her woman-centered life denies the lesbian the right to participate within dominant fields of social interaction.

Outside the closed society of the police station, the lesbian loses the protection of the institution and has no access to the various expressions of power available to her as a police officer, nor does she have the authority to take them on. In fact, she will often become vulnerable to those very forces. Whatever status the lesbian holds as an officer, she relinquishes it when she moves outside the work environment and into the larger community. As mentioned above, Miranda must travel far away from Hooperstown if she wishes to participate in a lesbian life, no matter how limited. She must also be continually vigilant, observing her surroundings closely because she fears possible recognition. In the public sphere the lesbian once again becomes the outcast, the unredeemed transgressor of all social standards. As such she is denied the same protections that, as an officer, she must provide to others.

However, in the fictive world of lesbian police novels, the intersection of the major character's public world and private experience echoes but does not replicate the actual lesbian experience. Sally Munt, in *Murder by the Book?: Feminism and the Crime Novel* (1994), states that "[l]esbian crime fiction provides a site of struggle over the definitions of justice, social status, and sexual identity, positing the lesbian at the center of meaningful dissemination" (140). In the lesbian police novel the transgressive position of the main character is successfully integrated into the development and outcome of the crime plot. The character's lesbian identity, in fact, becomes the fulcrum that enables the transformation necessary to bring about the resolution of the overt and subversive conflicts in a particular novel. As discussed in chapter 1, coming out frees the lesbian detective from the burden of hiding her sexuality; no longer having to pass as straight, she is able to focus her energies on the main goal — the apprehension of the criminal. The lesbian police officer, by doing her job, and doing it well, is able to overcome not only the prejudices of most of her colleagues, but receive full support and acknowledgment of her ability from superiors. Miranda, for example, is promoted to sergeant and has gained the respect of other officers for her bravery in rescuing Micki. In addition, as suggested by Munt, by being open in terms of her sexual orientation, the lesbian officer is enabled to represent a positive outcome to the tensions inherent in her professional and private positions.

Maureen Reddy (1988) states that,

> Lesbian feminist crime fiction redefines the threat lesbian, and potentially all women, pose to men, which is actually threefold: (1) the threat of indifference; (2) the threat of changing the relations of the sexes by placing women at the center of concern, and (3) the threat of radically altering social power relations through a moral vision that does not assume the value of hierarchical order and that does consistently value women's relations to other women [130–31].

Reddy's use of the word *threat* seems at odds with the beneficial outcomes the out lesbian officer achieves in her narrative; however, these threats are felt, not by the lesbian detective (or the lesbian reader), but by those characters who represent the worst of society's prejudice toward women who challenge male privilege. The demands of the fiction alter real social structures to meet the genre's requirements. In the detective novel, the lesbian police officer always succeeds; she is able, through a variety of maneuvers, to be recognized as both a transgressor *and* a supporter of the law. Even though Tori Hunter, Stevie Houston, and Foster Everett, for example, are recognized within their respective departments as lesbians, they ultimately are accepted as full members because they produce results: perpetrators apprehended; cases closed. What happens in these texts, as in all crime novels, is the restoration of social order, and since the police function as the embodiment of that order, the inclusion of the lesbian officer signals her integration into that wider society. More importantly, other officers in the precinct discover that sexuality does not hinder one's performance on the job. However, this recognition is hard won as the lesbian works to achieve this balance of private self and pubic identity.

Reddy's third assertion underscores the problems of claiming an authoritative role in a police environment. As a woman intruding on a male domain and as a lesbian assuming the prerogatives of the dominant heterosexist culture, the lesbian officer is twice suspect. The threat is that by inserting herself into the system and demanding the same access to authority and the ability to wield it as her colleagues, the lesbian officer will dramatically and permanently alter the system itself and redefine that authority. Yet few of the novels discussed here confront this dilemma in a straightforward manner. They either drop the issue totally from the story, or the characters replicate the behavior of the officers described by Martin

(1980) and Wade (1996): keep quiet, do your job, and do it better than the men. Because of the demands of the genre, however, the wider implications of these issues cannot be taken too far; to do so would radically change the basic contract between the reader and the text. While questions can be raised that push the boundaries of the text, the reader must still find satisfaction in the working out of expected techniques. Dove (1997) notes:

> The realization of a book is directed by the synthesis of memories and recollections from past reading with present perceptions and expectations. Thus the reader develops a store of recollections, of not only events and impressions but also rules, structures, conventions, and the like. This store shapes the reader's perception of the genre and intervenes in future expectations of reading [75].

But the questions and variations presented within the texts are also required, not only to keep the reader's interest, but to allow the accommodation and reconciliation of radical ideas and behaviors. One text that examines this tension between maintaining and expanding the conventions of the police novel as it incorporates the experience of lesbians on the force is Catherine Lewis's *Dry Fire* (1996).

Lewis's story follows the cadet and rookie year of Officer Abigail Fitzpatrick, presenting in realistic detail the conflicts still faced by women in the police force even in the 1990s.[4] Fitzpatrick faces strong antagonism from the instructors in the academy, as well as from her male classmates. In sessions on arrest techniques and self-defense, she is often paired with males. Camp, one of the male recruits, becomes Fitzpatrick's particular antagonist, even breaking her rib during a drill. Fitzpatrick, however, contributes to the fracture by refusing to cede to Camp's greater physical strength:

> [Camp is speaking] "It hurts. Admit it *this time*.... Come on, Fitzpatrick, say it hurts."
> "Go to hell," I say [20; emphasis added].

Fitzpatrick fully accepts the idea that a woman must prove tougher and smarter than male officers. This stance impels her to take risks, some of which bring about the desired arrest and some of which backfire. The novel itself shows Fitzpatrick slowly adapting her own ideas of police practice to the department's, but the novel also reveals how she adopts the dominant value system of the police as she becomes an experienced officer.

Fitzpatrick adheres completely to the black and white divisions of society that police officers traditionally create. The times when she questions a supervisor's direction or takes the initiative in a situation are few, and when undertaken, meet with derogatory comments. The harsh reality of police work dominates Fitzpatrick's rookie period: domestic abuse, rape, a suspect who forces an officer to shoot him. Accidents, and the other points when society breaks down quickly teach Fitzpatrick the importance of adhering to policy and procedure. Lewis does present Fitzpatrick reflecting on her role as an officer; she replays situations and examines her actions, but does not place herself in a global context. She is not interested in being a model for others; she is interested in being a good cop. As she becomes a more experienced officer, Fitzpatrick continually takes on the mannerisms and attitudes of her fellow officers. After the arrest of a juvenile thief, Fitzpatrick comments: "In the world according to Abigail Fitzpatrick, he should be spending some time in juvenile jail, but there's not exactly a plethora of politicians beating my door down for advice on rampant crime" (240). Late in the novel, Fitzgerald has completely absorbed the unspoken codes of police society—anyone who is not a cop undermines my efforts—and, at the novel's conclusion, passes these same lessons on to her own rookie.

Surprisingly, Fitzgerald's sexual orientation has little impact on her position on the force. She faces the jokes, and harassment, of other officers for being a woman just as much as being lesbian. Camp taunts her — "is it true you go for the girls?"— but this is more a reflection of the standard view that a woman wanting to be a cop must really want to be a man, and the only women who want to be men must be lesbians (20). This homophobia is apparent in the attitudes of her trainers, supervisors, and peers; a trainer at the academy screams, "You limp-wristed pansy! You wimp!" at a recruit to make him fight harder (19). Homosexuality is equated with not being capable of surviving as an officer, and, perhaps not unexpectedly, it is male, not female, homosexuality that is perceived as the threat. Most of the derogatory jibes refer to gay men and gay behavior, not to lesbians. Fitzpatrick's sexuality seems to be no threat to other officers as demonstrated when one of her supervisors, a woman, even offers to fix her up: "I brought you here for a reason. That cute little server over there is Bonnie, and she'd be perfect for you. She's in my softball league and as sweet as they come" (164). Fitzpatrick's sexuality also seems unimportant in her developing relationship with Morelli, a male officer. Over the course of the novel, the two become close friends, sharing many of the same ideas about police work. Until he asks her to cross the line by lying about an arrest, Fitzpatrick helps Morelli pass examinations and covers his sloppy work. His request marks the collapse in their relationship, but it is Morelli's failure to maintain the integrity of being an officer, not Fitzpatrick's sexuality that separates them.

However, Lewis's novel does illustrate the hostility that lies below the surface for the lesbian officer. Although Fitzpatrick tries to keep her sexuality outside of her professional life, it intrudes in the shape of her former lover, who broke off the relationship fearing she would not make sergeant if it were known: "I didn't understand she said. Two women cops living together would draw attention. Makayla was one of the first female officers on the force, and she remembered the seventies, when women had to sue the department just to hire them as officers.... Now it was her turn for stripes and she wasn't about to jeopardize the opportunity" (38). In addition to dealing with Makayla, Fitzgerald will become involved with a woman who was raped and face the anger of Morelli's wife who blames Fitzgerald for her husband's death. She accuses Fitzgerald of keeping Morelli "fascinated" with policing, not only because of covering for him but for being sexually other and therefore appealing (272). These personal aspects of her life do not, however, distract Fitzgerald from her primary focus; as the novel ends, she is on patrol and looking forward to meeting her new rookie.

Asserting one's right to belong in the police force is not the typical narrative arc in most lesbian police novels. Police officers like Catherine Lewis's Abigail Fitzpatrick or Tracey Richardson's Miranda McCauley must prove themselves to be part of the institution before they gain complete acceptance from their peers. Only then are they allowed to participate in the expressions of power embodied in the badge and uniform. Both recognize that moment of access to power when they are called good cops. The appellation bestows on these characters the right to reflect and use the authority of the system to achieve its ends. More commonly found in police novels is the lesbian officer whose sexual orientation plays either a negligible role in the solution of the crime at the center of the story, or who must integrate her private life more fully into the public sphere. In the first situation, the officer's sexual life is omitted entirely from the text, or is kept on the periphery of events; although the officer may have a lover or initiate an intimate relationship with someone outside of the force, the romance, as discussed in chapter 2, serves its own thematic purpose. In the second, the officer's orientation becomes a touchstone for the successful resolution of the investigation, usually because it offers insight into the motivations for the crime or gives her greater sympathy and understanding of the victim or enables her to discover information that helps for a more speedy resolution to the crime.

Like Abigail Fitzpatrick and others like her, lesbian officers such as Delta Stevens and Kate Martinelli are conservative women, committed to the ideals of police enforcement, and direct all their energies to solving the crime. In these novels, the crime, usually murder, takes place in the world at large, where the task is the restoration of civil order. What this means is that the victims are not exclusively homosexual (if at all) and that the crimes are not specifically directed at homosexuals. Again, like Fitzpatrick, these officers have little authority in the overall hierarchy. Rarely do they instigate action in an investigation nor do they direct it; Stevens is a beat officer, and Martinelli has just been promoted to detective. They understand their part in the whole system and undertake their duties with confidence. Nor does the struggle to reconcile one's professional role and personal identity so common to lesbian crime novels, described by Sally Munt, appear in the investigations carried out by these two officers. They define themselves as necessary components of the law enforcement system; indeed, they are rarely pictured outside of this system. Both women's identity is confined to being police officers.

Delta Stevens, the hero of Linda Kay Silva's series, will deliberately step outside the traditional chain of command, but only when an intimate relationship is threatened. In *Taken by Storm* (1991), for example, Stevens's partner, a straight, male officer, has been murdered by a group of rogue cops. Miles Brookman and Stevens have been partners for several years, and have developed the intense working/private connection typical of police officers. Brookman's murder becomes an invasion of Stevens's private life, and, even more importantly, a revelation of the collapse of the integrity of the police world. Stevens will follow her own leads and go outside conventional procedures to discover who the murderers are. Her insubordination, while technically disavowed by her superiors, is quietly abetted by them, because the focus of her efforts is the restoration of the status quo of the department. Because her goal is to preserve the institution, Stevens becomes the representative of its authority to police itself. She accomplishes this task by utilizing every access point available to her, using standard department channels, and circumventing them as needed. She makes connections with the district attorney and is given full support and leeway for her undercover work.

While it leads to success, such reliance on existing authority structures indicates how limited Stevens's power to act really is; had she attempted any action without the knowledge and implicit approval of her superiors, Delta Stevens would have been forced to leave the department. Such a step is unthinkable to her; being anything but a police officer is beyond comprehension: [O]nce she hit the streets, she fell in love with the job. ... [she] found it incredibly satisfying to collar a criminal after doing her homework on his patterns, motives, and techniques. She never knew life could be so exciting until she became a cop" (2–3). As the novel comes to its conclusion, with Stevens successfully identifying and capturing the rogue officers, she receives the highest level of acknowledgment from her fellow officers:

> "Well, we just wanted you to know that the three of us are behind you. You're okay in our book."
> "Yeah, and if any of the other guys give you any shit, you come to us okay? It's shit like this that gives us all a bad name. We gotta stand by each other" [179].

These statements come from officers who, during much of the novel, have been reluctant to accept Stevens into the brotherhood, especially when her accusations against other officers are still unproven. One cop avenging another, good cops getting rid of bad: Delta Stevens follows the rules of the group and gains the expected respect. Stevens's sexual identity has little impact on the novel's events—her orientation is apparently known in the department. The only reference to her being lesbian occurs early in the story when Miles Brookman physically assaults another officer who makes a derogatory comment about her. That one incident, and its violent resolution, is sufficient to prevent any further discussion of Stevens's sexuality. The officer's sexual orientation becomes incidental to the main plot, or if it intrudes, sexual identity remains centered in the personal sphere.

Romantic involvement between the officer and another woman utilizes the conventional plot devices of the suspect/witness becoming the focus of erotic interest (Delta Stevens becomes attracted to Megan Osbourne, one of Miles's informants) or a relationship of long standing that is put under strain by the investigation (Kate Martinelli's partner, Lee, pushes her so hard to come out that they temporarily separate). As in heterosexual police fiction, however, once she is engaged in direct police activity, the lesbian *woman* becomes a lesbian *officer*. One of the most clearcut representatives of this strategy is Detective Lucia Ramos in Mary Morell's *Final Session* (1991). Here, Ramos appears on the first page confidently in charge of the investigation; she gives the necessary orders to various scene-of-the-crime technicians, interrogates witnesses, and advances the investigation accordingly. So much does Ramos's professionalism dominate the novel's opening scenes that the cues about her orientation—a quick sexual thought about another woman, an allusion to a well-known lesbian science fiction novel—are easily overlooked. For the lesbian reader, though, these small references provide sufficient indication that Ramos is indeed a lesbian, one as comfortable with her sexuality as she is with her investigative ability. Not until well into the second chapter of the novel is Ramos concretely identified as a lesbian. The revelation has no connection to the investigation, and, most importantly, no impact on her relations with superiors or other officers.

When homophobic comments are made, they are addressed to the murder victim and her patients, who are lesbians. While Ramos finds these distasteful, she understands the importance of keeping her emotional responses from influencing her professional ones: "She was not working well with Cowley since his crack about dykes. She needed to relax and get easy. One thing she definitely did not need was the reputation of a ballbuster who threw her weight around" (61). Like the successful officers in Wade's article, Ramos has managed to separate the public and private aspects of her life and to maintain the integrity of each without one impinging on the other. Her immediate commander considers her a capable officer and encourages her to follow the unlikely as well as obvious leads. Throughout the novel Ramos enjoys the respect of the various officers in her department because of her meticulous policework. In this fictional world, at least, a lesbian officer is an integral member of a working community. Ramos can move freely from private, romantic life to a public role. While the exact reasons for Ramos's secure position can only be surmised, it is clear that she understands the regulations. Unlike Delta Stevens, Lucia Ramos is a by-the-book officer. Her authority stems from this allegiance to procedures, and every stage of the murder investigation follows the proper chains of command. Ramos is no maverick. She neither breaks down doors nor goes into dangerous situations solo, even when her new lover is in danger. As such Lucia Ramos inhabits an ideal world, where respect is a given and where one's sexuality is a nonissue.

Not all lesbian police novels, however, present such a complete integration of the lesbian into the law enforcement community. More typical is the lesbian officer who must confront the tensions raised by her sexuality, especially when she appears in an authoritative position. Three such characters—Melanie McAllister's, Elizabeth Mendoza, Katherine Forrest's Kate Delafield mysteries, and Penny Mickelbury's Gianna Maglione mysteries— embody the contradictions of representing the police hierarchy, whose duty is to maintain the smooth functioning of the dominantly heterosexual community, one that includes establishing a smoothly run (or tolerable) working environment while at the same time creating a satisfying personal life. For instance, all three women share a key characteristic in that each functions in prominent positions of authority within her particular force: Maglione is a lieutenant of detectives given command of a special Hate Crime Unit, while both Delafield and Mendoza are detectives with enough years of experience to control more of their investigations than either Ramos or Stevens. All three women have developed a reputation for accomplishment in their particular departments, and each enjoys the support of her superiors, although Mendoza's and Maglione's are more friendly and open than

Delafield's. However, ability does not always guarantee acceptance, as demonstrated by Mendoza and Delafield who both find their investigations hampered by overt and implicit homophobia, in and out of the force. And while all three women are comfortable with their sexuality, each maintains a firm separation between her private live and public role. During the course of their novels, Maglione and Delafield will be faced with the challenge of bringing their orientation out into the open during their investigations. Moreover, the degree to which this reconciliation between the personal and professional will be expressed is determined by the woman's own desire to come out publicly. The consequences of her decision will also have long-lasting implications for her continued relationships inside and outside the police station.

In Forrest's *Amateur City* (1984) Kate Delafield articulates the dilemma which confronts the lesbian — indeed any woman — who desires to become accepted in a mainstream profession:

> She felt the familiar heavy weariness at being reminded of her singularity. The tired knowledge that always she was silhouetted against her background.... She had been the woman reluctantly singled out in her division of the Los Angeles Police Department for one advancement after another as LAPD, in stubborn fighting retreat, gradually succumbed to increasing pressures for change [25].

The most prominent feature of Delafield's and others' relations with the police structure is the reluctance to be anything more than a good officer, a working member of the larger entity, unlike many private detectives described by Munt, Reddy, and other critics of lesbian crime fiction. These characters, by being independent, are able to integrate the political and the personal because they have the freedom to pick the cases they will solve and the luxury to express their views vocally, especially when they go against the majority. None of these women desires any particular notoriety in her position; at the same time, by their very nature as women and as lesbians, they assume that silhouetted position Delafield recognizes. These women cannot help but stand apart from the other members of the force, and their ability to take on the appropriate authoritative posture includes some degree of tenuousness. In each case, it is not that their places in the chain of command deny them access to power, but rather their authority to wield that power that is always open to challenge, particularly from those inside the police system. Moreover, the refusal of cooperation — usually presented in subtle ways— has the potential to jeopardize the successful pursuit of the criminal investigation and as such becomes a threat which each woman must overcome as she works to solve the case.

Each detective carries a double burden during the progress of the investigation: first, each is responsible for the successful resolution of the crime. This, of course, is the basic purpose of the contract between the police and the public, but its success requires that the commanding officer has the respect and trust of those under her command, as well as the public's acceptance and participation. The three detectives examined here enjoy varying levels of respect and camaraderie with their subordinates, and these relationships will be tested over the course of the individual novels as well as the series. In most cases, though, the lead detective's sexuality must become a factor in the development and maintenance of her leadership abilities. This will require the detective to decide whether or not she will come out. The key is if the detective feels she is in control of the time, place, and manner of the revelation. The second burden each detective carries is the knowledge of the impact the revelation of her sexuality may have on the investigation. This knowledge demands a continued vigilance on the part of the lesbian detective, as each attempts to maintain the momentum of the investigation and keep any negative reaction to a minimum. Such responses can come from within the department when supervisors hamstring the detective's ability to function or subordinates let their prejudices overshadow their examination of evidence or interrogation of witnesses/suspects. What frequently opens the contractual relationship to challenge is the introduction of a woman who offers the detective the possibility of a romantic involvement. Such an interruption of her professional life reminds the detective, and potentially others, of the transgressive foundation of her existence. What is brought to the surface, as Reddy notes, is the inherent conundrum of the lesbian police officer:

> the female hero does not experience her sexual and emotional attraction to women as an active, open choice she may make, but does perceive her acknowledgement of, and acting upon, that attraction as a matter of choice with strong political implications [123].

The ability to solve the crime, which Mendoza, Maglione, and Delafield have, is the benchmark for becoming an accepted member of the police community. However, as their professional careers reveal, solid police work and a record of successful investigations can neither eradicate the biases against a female in the ranks, not guarantee acceptance of the lesbian officer's sexual identity. Delafield, Mendoza, and Maglione are self-identified lesbians, although they are not (fully) out to their colleagues. Each reveals a past involvement in the early chapters of her story that indicates an awareness and comfort with that identity, and each becomes involved with another woman during the progress of their current investigations. Still, with the exception of Maglione, the romance for these detectives tends to remain subordinate to the main crime plot. What does surface, however, are subtle tensions and outright hostility toward the lesbian officer, and these attitudes expressed by the public (when orientation is known), as well as by the police community, create an atmosphere that has the potential to thwart their success in apprehending the criminal. Mendoza and Maglione, by admitting their sexuality, will move toward reconciling their private and public lives and find that admission brings beneficial results, especially inside the walls of the precinct. Delafield's fear is of exposure, that someone else will reveal her orientation, and throughout the series, she struggles to retain control of who has access to her private self.

Micklebury's Gianna Maglione's experience represents the idealized version of this situation. She is confident and comfortable with her lesbian identity, and even though her position on the force would suggest otherwise, her sexuality does not prevent a successful working relationship with her special crime unit. This is due, in part, to her selection of a group of officers who represent racial, gender, and sexual diversity. What also helps create an effective working unit is that the members Maglione has chosen are all relatively young, in age and in time on the force, which highlights their openness to change and acceptance of difference. This factor allows Maglione, as the Hate Crime Unit leader, the ability to manipulate the dynamics of the group. Other factors that generate respect among the group are Maglione's sense of fairness and respect for her subordinates, her willingness to do the hard, tedious aspects of police work, and her desire for justice, in both abstract and practical terms. As the series continues, this relationship will move beyond the strictly professional to a more intense connection because of the nature of the crimes the unit covers. Moreover, her professional boundaries are respected by her colleagues particularly Eric Ashby, her second in command. Interestingly, Ashby becomes the impetus forcing Maglione to confront the implications of her identity. Ashby, who knows Maglione is a lesbian, argues early in *Keeping Secrets* that she publicize the homophobic motive for the crimes: all the victims are either gay or lesbian, and as the investigation continues, the motive for the killings is discovered to be the victims' sexual orientation. Ashby confronts Maglione and challenges her: "These people thought they were safe, Anna. They thought their lives were their own. They were wrong and now they're dead and that scares the hell out of me and I know it scares you just as much." Maglione's answer indicates ambivalence in terms of identification with the victims and identification as a police officer. She tells Ashby, "I can't catch a killer if I'm spending time worried about keeping my own closet door locked" (25–26).

Throughout the course of the investigation, Maglione wants to keep her identification with the victims out of the investigation because she believes it will influence her professionalism. When her new lover, a reporter, publishes the story of the crimes and their motivations, the collision of Maglione's allegiances occurs, and their relationship is almost broken by what Maglione sees as a betrayal of her confidence by Mimi. Taken hostage by the murderer and threatened with death for being a lesbian, Maglione articulates for the first time "whether or not it might truly be better for all homosexuals and lesbians to exit the closet.... Keeping secrets is different from keeping privacy" (175). The parallels between the crimes and Maglione's own epiphany are obvious, but do emphasize the difficulty of balancing one's private and public worlds.

Throughout the story Maglione enjoys the mutual sexual pursuit she and Mimi participate in, and, while she is adamant about keeping her sexual orientation out of the paper, Maglione has no fear that she will suffer in the department because of it. It appears that her superior is fully aware that Maglione is a lesbian and has even contrived at introducing her to Mimi, who is a friend of his. Clearly, though, what one knows and what one has the power to do with that knowledge operate on many levels within the text. The outcome will be determined by how the individual chooses to respond to what is known and how willing she is to let the control slip out of her hands.

Were it not for the crime and its victims, Maglione's sexuality would remain an isolated component of her professional life. But because the victims of the serial murderer are all gay and lesbian and because Maglione shares this identification, her struggle to reconcile the public and personal aspects of her life takes on great significance — how her peers and subordinates respond to this knowledge can make the Hate Crimes Unit a success or failure. Moreover, understanding the importance of the Unit (Maglione has lobbied hard for the Unit's formation and to be appointed its head) focuses her attention on keeping these aspects of her personality separate rather than integrating them. Maglione's early preference for drawing a line between her public and private lives, despite the acceptance of her Captain and others, indicates the deep-seated tensions carried by the lesbian who is in a command position. However, the real possibility of her own death simply because of her sexuality compels Maglione to reevaluate the meaning and power of disclosure. She tells Mimi, "I was afraid of myself, Mimi, afraid that I couldn't love you well enough and do my job well enough at the same time. And for the first time in my life I found that I resented the job and that scared me" (187). Giving voice to her fear of having only one choice — career or relationship — allows Maglione to begin working toward finding the right balance of both.

In later novels in the series the reader sees the results of that effort. Maglione, who has been a follower of procedure, discovers that adhering to the rules does not always serve justice. At the end of an emotionally draining investigation, she punches a suspect, an action she would have previously criticized another officer for doing. But she discovers that, "When given the option, [she would] remain a cowboy. She'd adapted well to the free-wheeling life of the elite units and, though she still surprised herself with how easily she'd learned to break rules she'd never have bent before, she was learning to like the freedom" (Mickelbury 1995, 211). This new attitude is reflected in outer changes as well. Before Maglione dressed appropriately for a high-ranking female officer, in skirts and blouses, or the uniform; now she wears "the black jeans, cowboy boots and silk shirt that had become her uniform" (Mickelbury 2004, 16). The most dramatic indication of Maglione's assertiveness is her successful combining of the two strands of her life; at the end of the latest novel in the series she has announced to her chief that she and Mimi have registered as domestic partners and that declaration will be noted in her personnel file.

For Kate Delafield homosexuality is a subtext, an incidental factor to the solution of the murder in *Amateur City* (Forrest 1984), and for Delafield the division between professional and private spheres is instinctive: "I've never pretended to be heterosexual. But I've never made any announcements either, and never will. Why give anyone a weapon? And it *is* a weapon" (180). This view explains Delafield's reasoning for keeping her relationships clearly separated and maintaining strictly professional contacts while on the job. When her partner indicates sympathy for the loss of her long time companion, the sentiment is quietly but completely rebuffed. This distance, however, is bridged as the Delafield series continues. With each new case, up until the fourth book in the series (*Murder by Tradition*, 1993), these two components of her life forcefully, sometimes dramatically, connect. This movement toward reconciliation, unfortunately, is not completely desired or facilitated by Delafield. Any movement she takes toward a more public acknowledgment of her sexuality is carefully calculated; she gives money to the proprietor of the lesbian Nightwood Bar to buy books, but does not often visit; she sits in the bleachers to watch a gay pride parade but will not march. Kate Delafield seems particularly vulnerable to the ambiguities inherent in her position within the police force. Gill Plain (2001) points out the contradiction faced by the lesbian who operates within the confines of the rigid police structure: "Delafield's relationship with and alienation from the structures of law that she also embodies remain in a condition of constant and complex renegotiation. She attains a considerable degree of agency, but this power is contingent and unstable, and, as the narrative develops, we witness neither its consolidation nor its collapse" (170). Delafield's only option for survival in the department seems to be a complete suppression of her lesbian nature; this chameleonlike behavior of redefining herself to fit her environment gives her the necessary authority to pursue her investigations. She takes deliberate steps to keep the two components of her life separate; however, Delafield often finds that, because of the nature of the crime (a gay bashing that becomes a murder), possible suspects (patrons of a lesbian bar), interference by superiors (a memorandum that lists every lesbian and gay officer on the force), the potential for her sexuality to be revealed is increased.

The closest Delafield comes to being outed — and it is essential to note that the choice of revelation is not in her control — appears in *Murder by Tradition* (1993). The case involves the death of a gay man, and during the accused murderer's trial, which takes up the largest amount of the narrative, Delafield's sexual orientation becomes a potential weakness for the prosecution. The defense attorney, who knows that Delafield is a lesbian, attempts to accuse her of bias against his client. During intense questioning, the attorney continually goads her with allegations of conflict of interest and partiality. At this point in the cross-examination the most dangerous implication for Delafield is not so much having her orientation made public as the challenge to her professional position and authority. His questions move closer and closer to a direct confrontation, posing a question that would make her assert her sexual orientation. However, the quick intervention of the prosecutor stops the defense's tactic. Before the trial begins, Delafield, in an effort to defuse the impact of her sexuality, comes out to the prosecutor. While she is concerned with how the defense will use this knowledge, Delafield is more anxious about how any revelation will affect others in the courtroom; the prosecutor tries to assure Delafield that she will try to control how the information will be heard:

> "I really don't think it'll [Delafield's sexuality] fly. It shouldn't get past the objection stage. But the jury will hear the question. And that's all Pritchard really wants."
> "My lieutenant will be in court tomorrow."
> ... "Kate, I can't prevent Pritchard from asking the question" [182].

During the trial, when she is asked if she let anything interfere with her investigations, Delafield answers with an assertion of her commitment to the law and fair play. The defense attorney's constant attacks on her integrity are met by objections from the prosecutor, objections that, more importantly, are upheld by the judge. The jury may guess at Delafield's sexual orientation, but the focus is kept on the victim and the accused. When the guilty verdict is returned, the boundary between Delafield's personal and professional identities has not been crossed.

By *Apparition Alley*, published in 1997, Delafield's sense of boundaries is more concretely threatened when a list naming every gay and lesbian member of the Los Angeles Police Department is rumored to exist and be published. As the plots twists develop, including the death of a gay officer who has threatened to out every closeted member, the shooting of Delafield herself, possibly by another officer, the pressure from the police command to keep the list private, Delafield's investigation forces her to a critical moment of self-determination about her position as an officer and a lesbian. At the final confrontation with Taggart, the instigator of Delafield's involvement with the list, she rejects his demand that she take responsibility for the list and his crusade to out every individual on the list:

> "Taggart, has it never occurred to you that Tony's list is none of your business? You're a straight man. This is a matter that involves the gay community."
> "You're a lesbian cop, your name is on the top of a list of hundreds of other names. That's the reason I involved you in this. It's Ferdie's legacy," he said stubbornly. "And you're now custodian of his list."
> "No, I'm not, Taggart, believe me — I don't have anything to do with this."
> "If you don't have it, you have access to it. *So how can you be a lesbian cop and not be with me?*"
> "*You're no longer a cop of any kind, Taggart, you're an anarchist*" [212; emphasis added].

Although Delafield has by this time in the series become more personally connected to the gay community, she still refuses any connection of her private experiences with her public performance. She insists that her ability to perform her duties does not depend on her being a lesbian, that by upholding the ideals of policing and by maintaining her own integrity as a representative of the system she achieves the best balance possible of private and public identity. As Gill Plain suggests, Delafield's investigations "represent a constant renegotiation of the boundaries of law and disorder, through the appropriately paradoxical assertion that the restoration of order can simultaneously represent a challenge to that order.... This conclusion suggests that lesbian detective fiction is less about maintaining the law than about reinscribing, or even *deceiving*, the law" (189; italics in text).

Unlike Gianna Maglione, whose environment is totally supportive, or Kate Delafield, whose sexuality is always under threat of exposure, Elizabeth Mendoza (McAllister 1994) confronts the overt homophobia of her male colleagues when she is asked to assist in the investigation of a series of rapes. As with several of Delafield's and Maglione's cases, the victims of the rapist are all lesbian. Mendoza must first overcome the prejudices of Steve Carson, her temporary partner for this investigation, before she can pursue and capture the perpetrator. Carson feels threatened on two levels: first as an officer whose abilities are questioned when another detective is brought into his case; second, Carson's blatant homophobia is revealed when Mendoza's own orientation is mentioned. His hostility comes through clearly when he and Mendoza meet for the first time: "I don't need any help with the investigation. You two are here simply to make the victims feel more comfortable.... So make them feel better however you like. Just don't do it in front of me" (*The Lessons* 1994, 37). His outburst suggests that Mendoza will use sexual overtures to comfort the victims. Carson does not, cannot, accept the fact that a lesbian is more than a sexualized person. Mendoza ignores the sexual innuendo, addressing the more important challenge to her authority: "I was a special agent for the FBI for several years.... I have more investigative experience than you and your new partner combined. I wasn't selected to work these cases because of my sexual preference, but because I'm the best my department has to offer" (37). At this point Carson grudgingly accepts Mendoza, because he has checked her credentials, and is willing to "overlook" her gender and orientation. Nonetheless, because of police hierarchy, Mendoza's experience requires that Carson acknowledge her authority over him. Moreover, as the case proceeds, Mendoza discovers a gap in his procedures that could jeopardize the case. Eventually Carson learns to value Mendoza's experience and to respect her leadership in the investigation.

However, while overcoming his prejudice against Mendoza as his commander is more easily done, accepting her lesbian identity is more difficult, even though he can ignore it during the active pursuit of the suspect. The reeducation of Carson comes more slowly over the course of the novel. Besides Mendoza, Carson is give a second partner, Officer Ashley Johnson, another open lesbian. Clearly the novel examines the manifestations of prejudice—from the extreme hostility of the rapist to Carson's more conventional bias: "Steve looked over each case and decided that these were definitely hate crimes. The suspect didn't like lesbos. Steve could understand that, he didn't like them either. Shit, women didn't belong doing it with each other. That wasn't normal. It just wasn't natural" (35). At this moment the two men's views are indistinguishable. However, Carson immediately begins to distance himself from the rapist: "But this guy was sick." He is still unable to recognize that his version of normalcy rests on ignorance. During the investigation Carson will come to realize the extent of his own homophobia. He will begin to compare his views with others' and find his rigid stereotypic judgments being tested. Carson's basic decency comes through as these discoveries drive him to recognize and work to change his perceptions. Interestingly, Mendoza's demand for Carson's professional response (her authoritative demand) acts as a buffer for those, often, intense emotional situations. Acting like a cop enables Carson to become aware: "You know, Tenny [Mendoza's nickname], it was like talking to anybody.... I'm not saying I understand any better why women want to be with other women. But a relationship is a relationship, no matter who it's between" (86). This marks the beginning of Carson's turnaround; he can accept sexual difference at least on an intellectual level. The rape of Ashley Johnson brings this recognition into the personal realm. Instead of Carson turning the attack into a vendetta, it is the finely tuned teamwork of a commander and her partners that brings the rapist to justice.

Whatever her rank, the lesbian police officer's very presence on a force juxtaposes two divergent attitudes. On the one hand, the lesbian embodies all that a society considers aberrant; she flaunts the heterosexual assumptions concerning sexual and emotional attachments. Such behavior demands its practitioner be ostracized from the community because she poses a threat to the traditional definition of community consensus. Palmer (1993) notes:

> The woman who identifies as lesbian, far from occupying a position of power and prestige, is likely to be stigmatized and socially marginal. She is a member of an oppressed minority group, and her way of life is regarded by the general public as dissident and transgressive [70].

As a transgressor, the lesbian is pushed outside the protection society provides; as a transgressor, the lesbian has no power to prevent societal expectations from defining her as deviant. The various institutions of authority that establish a framework of security and stability for a community fail the lesbian in her attempts to function as a member of that community. The implied contract that exists between the individual and society is declared void, and the lesbian has no social recourse.

The lesbian who takes on the role of law enforcement officer also assumes the burden of reconciling the contradictory aspects of her existence. The fundamental duty of the police is to assure that the relationships between members of a community and its authoritative institutions are smoothly integrated. A police officer represents the basic and conservative idea of social control; she embodies the power of maintenance and stasis, and she defends the legal structures that define proper behavior. She succeeds only when she "negotiate[s] the existing system and conform[s] to the organizational and occupational norms" (Martin 1980, xv). For the lesbian officer, however, this support of the status quo denies her very nature. The lesbian, because she stands outside the law, cannot represent or defend the law.

Yet, as these novels featuring lesbian law enforcement officers show, the ability to integrate these opposing positions is possible without compromise. As Sally Munt (1994) points out, "[c]rime fiction is a site for the expression of anxieties about society, and the appeasement of that fear is structurally inscribed in the narrative" (124). Each of the characters considered here has absorbed the ideals of enforcement; each officer is committed to maintaining the laws that hold society together. To return to the idea of the importance of trust between members of society, as articulated by R. Gordon Kelly at the beginning of this chapter, when the lesbian officer is identifiable as someone who upholds the ideals and practices of the police institution she becomes trustworthy; her public actions, which are all the other characters in the text have to judge her by, provide the tangible proof.[5] This allegiance becomes the point of entry into the power systems of the particular police force. Knowing the rules, knowing how to adapt them to her situation, enables the lesbian officer to survive both in and out of that environment. In fact, many of the characters discover that they must bring the personal and professional together or create a mechanism for balancing public and private. Doing this enriches the lesbian's experience in each sphere. The officer gains authoritative stature through her honesty and credibility. Challenging the stereotypic expectations of male officers actually stabilizes her position in the police hierarchy. The lesbian officer does not have to outman her fellow officers, but show that she accepts the limits and expectations of her position. The woman acquires visibility and asserts the right to exist in the police community, not on its margins. The transgressive definition of the lesbian's private life loosens and frees her from the threat of physical and emotional annihilation. Playing the game, when the rules are clear and the play is fair, establishes new points of reference for the lesbian and society.

CHAPTER 4

Lesbian Tough Guys

> If narrative provides the templates of violent identities, contains the visceral horror of killings, and allows murderers to function as social subjects, would it not be better to do without it altogether? The answer, also implicit in the project itself and elaborated in the conclusion, is "no." There is no return to storyless innocence. Human beings are narrative animals, finding themselves only through the lineaments of a tale. The attraction of violence lies precisely in the phantasmagoric escape from the strictures of narrative coherence, into the timeless realm of the sublime. If violence enters culture through narrative, it is also through narrative that it is apprehended and resisted.—Elana Gomel 2003, xivii

> *He grabbed her quickly from behind, had her neck in the crook of his elbow before she even had a chance to turn and see him. Somewhere in the calmer depths of his mind he realized that was a good thing. It bolstered his confidence. She tried to cry, but he quietly told her to shut up or he'd kill her.* He wondered *if he meant that. He didn't know, but it felt good to say it. Holding her against him he dragged her into a thick stand of brush, never letting her see him. And he didn't want to see her. He only wanted one thing.*—Baxter Clare, 2000, 232; italics in text

At the conclusion of Marcia Muller's *Trophies and Dead Things* (1991) a male character comments that "violent women are unnatural" (264). Spoken in a tone of revulsion, these four words succinctly frame the issues to be examined in this chapter. Contained in the statement are basic assumptions about appropriate culturally defined gendered behavior. The exclusionary modifier *violent*, identifying a certain kind of woman, enables the male character to assert expected social norms and approved attitudes. This allows him to support the actions that lead to a successful outcome, but repudiate the practitioner; violence is not the problem; a violent woman is. A violent woman embodies a series of questions and paradoxes that challenge the traditions and ideas about the nature of violence, the focus of that violence, and those who use violence and to what end. Linking violence with women forces the reconsideration of expectations and definitions of proper feminine behavior and attitudes that have infiltrated most societies and colored their perceptions of human interactions.

Women who use violence in a deliberate and calculated manner clearly contradict stereotypic notions of proper womanly behavior. The point of difficulty for society centers on the notion of deliberateness that underlies a woman's use of force. While aggression in women is still considered unseemly, if a woman can justify her actions — to protect herself, her family, or someone incapable of self-defense — her use of decisive and forceful methods can be supported by the wider society. These situations, after all, fall within the conventional images of woman as nurturer and supporter of family. Should a woman exhibit aggressive behavior for other reasons, however, she steps beyond the boundaries of generally perceived notions of normalcy. The representations of the docile woman and how to respond to the woman who refuses to be constrained by them stretch back into history, especially in the Western tradition.[1] She is a figure that still has a tenacious hold on the imagination often in spite of the changes in the political, economic, and social realities of modern women.

When the woman is (or assumed to be) lesbian, these culturally described contradictions of female behavior are magnified and problematized. Women behaving violently or aggressively have always been seen as deviant, breaking down the distinctions between approved versions of acceptable behavior and belief and the actual expression of them. Such women do not match up with the traditional expectations of femininity and are, therefore, viewed as not fitting in with the majority. The aggressive or violent woman becomes marginalized and seen as other — that person who trespasses on the rights and privileges of the dominant community. The area most open to this invasion by the aggressive woman is gender; its definitions and meanings become vulnerable and, perhaps invalid, once notions of masculinity and femininity lose their cultural anchors.

Before looking closely at the ways in which lesbian detective fiction utilizes violence in its pages, however, I need to make some distinctions between the basic terms that will be used throughout this chapter. Words, after all, are malleable and meanings shift according to who uses them and where and when the words are used. Yet, in surprising ways certain words (and the meanings they embody) retain static applications, particularly those that represent concepts of gender. As noted above, it is the appellation of *violent* that calls forth the male character's disgust. That reaction raises a number of questions: is it the violence itself that calls up the response or is it the woman who acts violently? What kind of action is defined as violent? If the same behavior were performed by a man, would the response be the same (the violent woman is unnatural)? What other words could be used to describe the woman's behavior? Would the possible alternative terms include *aggression, toughness, force, brutality*, and the like? Do these words all carry the same meaning? Does meaning depend on the motive for the actions taken or on the recipient of those actions? Can such terms even be appropriately applied to women?

In *Tough Girls: Women Warriors and Wonder Women in Popular Culture* (1999), Sherri Inness examines the history of the representation of tough female characters in popular media. Before discussing the types of tough women and the ways that toughness is portrayed, Inness offers a definition of what being tough entails:

> A super-fit physique is a common attribute of toughness, but there is much more involved, including self-presentation, attire, setting, and attitude. All these attributes go into making someone "tough." Toughness, in many ways, is a performance of a certain demeanor and image, an act that might be more or less successful according to how many tough signifiers are adopted and how convincingly they are presented as "real" [12].

Being tough must first be a self-generated physical and emotional construct; the individual cannot project toughness—and its accompanying actions—until she has developed the necessary personal qualities and mannerisms associated with it. And, as Inness suggests, the hallmarks of toughness are open to variable formulations, usually based on a particular set of cultural norms and values that also reflect a particular time and place. Once the person determines which qualities to assemble to project toughness, she will then create a corresponding public "performance" of that idea. In order for this image to be seen as credible, the individual must balance her private interpretations and expression with the public's. Should the balance tilt toward an excessive or insufficient representation, the person becomes suspect and therefore open to criticism.

Toughness calls up both positive and negative responses; I admire a person who is confident and capable, who is willing to take risks that she has prepared herself for. I enjoy watching the sheer physicality of the athlete who has trained and honed her body. I appreciate the courage of someone who is not afraid to challenge the status quo, who puts her reputation on the line for her convictions. On the other hand, toughness can also describe an individual who is hard and inflexible, one who is willing to use force, whether brute strength or intimidation, to achieve her ends. Someone who is tough can easily become a bully, imposing her views and desires on others whether they agree or not with her positions. In popular fiction, especially in the detective genre, both aspects of the tough character are portrayed: the hero embodies all the positive qualities of toughness, otherwise the readers would not applaud her efforts. The villain represents the undesirable attributes since readers are meant to distance themselves from identification with that character. However, even in the twenty-first century, toughness remains the prerogative of men; when women "adopt the characteristics stereotypically associated with men ... they place themselves as outsiders in relation to a culture that assumes that women should strive to act and appear feminine" (Inness, 1999, 19).

At the center of many discussions of gender lies the question of what qualities represent appropriate behavior; after all, the first indication of one's gender is how that person behaves; most importantly, how that person behaves in the public realm. Human interactions and relationships depend on the ability to decipher the signs of an individual's appearance, speech, and attitudes and place them within recognizable categories.[2] An individual who decides to cross gender boundaries and force a reframing of what is and is not suitable for proper gender identification and placement faces a wide range of responses; she may be applauded for defying convention and seen as a model for others to emulate, or she may be ostracized, laughed at, or threatened. When a woman deliberately takes on the characteristics of toughness, she "disturbs society" and "challenges the notion that there is a 'natural' connection between women and femininity and between masculinity and men"(Inness, 1999, 21). The assumption, when women take on the aggressive stances and behavior of men, is that they want to be (like) men, and popular cultural representations of this assumption of masculine privilege often illustrate the negative consequences of the attempt. Sara Crosby (2004) calls the process by which an aggressive, tough female hero confronts those consequences the "snapping point," that moment when she recognizes that her efforts are, ultimately, futile; she cannot carry the implications of her heroic position to their logical outcome, because she does not want to. Crosby (2004) identifies three factors that push the female hero to the brink:

> Tough female heroes feel guilt *because* of their heroism. Their agency, their toughness, is their sin. Second, ... the patriarchal community ... make[s] women want to alienate their power. Because of their guilty criminality and because of their passive "nature," female heroes do not want their trangressive toughness.... Third, the only stable or pragmatic possible community is the patriarchal community [155; emphasis in text].

The limitations of traditional gender roles remain difficult to break through, but within the confines of genre fiction, like detective fiction, the point at which the female hero "snaps" is placed further and further beyond the limits of the narrative.

Whether it takes the form of the police procedural or the hard-boiled detective story, aggression and violence have belonged to men. Men are attracted to violence because it provides a "combination of moral, aesthetic, and psychological values" that allow its use to be justified (Cawelti 2004, 158). As an embodiment of those values, the detective, particularly the lone private eye, is sanctioned not only to use violent means to achieve his goal, but also to understand the implications of such use. The detective, in a sense, carries the burden of responsibility for his own violence and becomes an implicit critic of the wider society for its demands that violence be the method of achieving a resolution to the crime. This knowledge puts the detective outside of ordinary society, giving him the ability to pursue the investigation without having the restrictions of the legal system hindering his efforts. If the detective is a police officer, he will flout the rules, at the risk of his career, in order to pursue justice. The women who enter these characters' stories are incapable of playing dominant roles in the crime's resolution; the standard view of a woman is that she is weak in terms of her physical and intellectual abilities, is easily swayed in her moral positions, and is more interested in superficial issues such as appearance, economic worth, and social position. When female characters do appear in these narratives, they become the faithful secretary who provides logistical and emotional support, or the femme fatale who often instigates the detective's pursuit through false representation and who will become the enemy to be destroyed (literally killed or imprisoned or figuratively diminished or rejected).[3]

Once women began to write within the detective genre, the ways that female characters are drawn and the positions they take in the narratives are obviously revised. Most importantly, the attributes and behaviors once seen as drawbacks become strengths: "While the traditional hard-boiled novel demonized and punished the female character who contravened conventional ideas about feminine submissiveness by desiring and acting, the feminist hard-boiled novel makes that role a heroic one, a gesture that would have been inconceivable to the early practitioners of the genre" (Walton and Jones 1999, 195). Placed in the center of the narrative and given the dominant character position, the female detective reconstructs the practices and development of the genre; while maintaining its basic parameters, she demonstrates that crime and detection are open to modification in how the investigation will precede and who is capable of conducting it.[4] Once women became accepted figures in crime fiction, they began to appropriate the methods and stances of male detectives in a number of ways. Some are amalgams of force and femininity, able to solve the crime depending more on intuition and their sexuality, but often relying on a male counterpart for the final, usually physical, capture of the villain; for example Agatha Christie's Tuppence Beresford, Carolyn Hart's Annie Laurance, or Gilliam Roberts's Amanda Pepper among them. Others become extreme practitioners of stereotypical masculine behavior, supercops who could outrun, outshoot, outmaneuver even the most exaggerated criminal. Many times this type of female detective is presented as a parodic figure, found in satires of the detective or thriller genre — Modesty Blaise, Emma Peel, or Honey West.

The majority of female detectives, however, appear in their narratives as focused, dedicated professionals, whether they are private investigators or members of a police force. The names of such figures — Warshawski, Millhone, McCone, Carlyle — are well-known, and their continued appearance illustrates the ways the self-directed female detective has become integrated into the standards of the genre. Like their male counterparts, these investigators exhibit the intensity, ability, and morality needed to accomplish the task of finding a solution to the crime committed. But, the very fact of their gender alters their perceptions and evaluations of the crime, suspects, investigation, and outcome; their gender also impacts the methods and progress of the investigation. Women detectives approach crime differently from the typical male perspective; they will redefine their positions in and outside of the actual investigation. In many novels, for example, the detective's political beliefs are tested or reevaluated; a detective will, in fact, take a job for an ideological reason or pursue the investigation beyond its original scope when the abstract issue takes precedence. Cathy Cole (2004) writes:

> In crime fiction with a left-leaning female private eye as protagonist, the reader is absolutely sure that good, however tainted, will prevail. And in reaching the novel's denouement the protagonist will expose the reader to some unpleasant social truths: poverty and racism contribute to crime; damaged children can become damaged, transgressing adults; domestic violence can push women to murder; corporate criminals destroy workers' lives [140].

While much of the actual investigation will be done alone, female detectives are more likely to have a circle of intimates who offer assistance in some form. A male detective may have a partner, but the relationship usually stays professional; the relationships formed between the female detective and other characters tend to move into the personal arena. Besides offering assistance that will help in the solution to the crime, these intimates provide the detective with emotional support that extends beyond the investigation. Most importantly, this circle of friends offers the detective affection, a complex combination of love, trust, criticism, and concern that allows her the opportunity to recoup once the investigation is over. Although Sharon Ross's (2004) essay examines the television series *Buffy, Vampire Slayer* and *Xena, Warrior Princess*, her assertion that "[e]motional connections ... demonstrate the value of female friendship and female bonding in providing a space where women can express themselves and resist the self-doubt and lack of confidence they may have about their identities and purposes" holds true for fictional female detectives (248). The reliance on talk, in fact, marks an essential difference between female and male detectives. For the male, "the flat, tough-talking voice denotes a certain sense of distance from its subject matter; its bluntness and often cynical tone give a feeling of straightforwardness and authenticity. The tough-talker's language tells us that he shoots straight from the hip, both literally and figuratively" (Walton and Jones 1999, 123). Through their appropriation and reinterpretation of language, even if the style replicates the "tough-talking" male, women "readdress and redress power imbalances," by giving voice to those who cannot speak for themselves, by articulating the "truth" about the outcome of the investigation, by expressing alternative viewpoints regarding the crime and the investigation (Walton and Jones 1999, 148).

The tough female offers readers a reimagining of the concepts of the hero and heroism. The conventional figure of the male detective, solitary and self-contained, who departs from the crime scene, is altered to fit the woman's articulations of aggression and engagement. While the female hero may also remain solitary at the novel's conclusion, throughout the narrative she has shown by her commitment to achieving a just outcome and her willingness to use violence that all women have the potential to perform similarly. Heroic women strip away the traditional notion that only men have the ability and prerogative to behave aggressively: "By [adopting characteristics stereotypically associated with men], they place themselves as outsiders in relation to a culture that assumes that women should strive to act and appear feminine" (Inness, 1999, 19). Gender roles are seen as deliberate constructions that are, therefore, open to challenge and change. In typical crime novels, after all, female characters are passive or acted upon; when they do take a more active position, they are usually the villain or a distraction. This passivity is denied once the woman becomes the actor in the narrative, "creating pleasure by disrupting and revising both gender and genre codes" (Walton and Jones 1999, 155). There will, of course, be variations in the ways authors illustrate the female detective's manipulations of genre and gender expectations: the type of case, the methods of investigation, the empathy shown towards client and/or criminal, the response to the investigation's outcome. Most importantly, it is the detective's articulation of her role as detective and as a woman that shapes the manner in which her toughness is represented in the text and responded to by the reader.

For many women readers, the aggressive female hero becomes the focus for fantasies of freedom, respect, and accomplishment. Because she can protect herself and others, develop the means of solving the crime, and bring about a successful resolution, the female hero elicits from the reader a sense of shared involvement. There is a perceived sense of the woman detective replicating the experiences of the female reader. Like her audience, the detective may have a husband and/or family that require a careful balancing of the demands of the case and home; if the detective is part of the police force, she will face the condescension and criticism of superiors, to the point of being denied career advancement; attempts to develop or nurture romantic relationships are often tested or ruined by the demands of the investigation. While the woman reader looks to the narrative of the female investigator for fantasy, she also reads to find an acknowledgement of her daily routines and desires which male writers neglect.[5]

The one area where female detectives in heterosexual crime novels most clearly differ from their male counterparts is their responses to the use of violence. Again the distinction between aggression and violence must be stressed. Aggression represents the approach taken by the detective to the various mechanisms used to investigate and achieve a solution to a crime. By mechanisms I mean the strategies—identifying suspects, interview tactics, forensics, tactical operations, etc.—used by the detective to facilitate the desired arrest. The detective must focus all her efforts toward that end; this may mean that the ordinary requirements of life are ignored—regular meals and sleep, balanced relationships with friends, lovers, partners, physical injuries, paying attention to noncrime related events. All of the detective's actions must be applied and every possible opportunity taken to produce a successful outcome. If this demands confronting hostile commanders who wish to derail the investigation, the detective will do so; if this means going beyond legal methods to get results, the detective will do so; if this calls for the use of extreme measures to prevent further actions by the criminal, the detective will use it. Violence represents a specific action, usually involving a physical challenge or confrontation between the detective and the criminal, which, while centered on the particular situation, transforms the violent act into a moral imperative. John Cawelti (2004) calls this the "myth of regeneration through violence," where "the justification of moral violence derives from its treatment as a necessary act of purification and regeneration" (169). The threat of its use or the actual manifestation of the threat, according to Cawelti, performs a purgative function in its removal of the evil embodied in the crime and its perpetrator.[6] The other dominant view of violence in crime novels is based on a range of psychological theories, whether the source is Freud or Foucault. Here, the major topics deal with the dissolution of the body and therefore one's identity, obviously for the male detective at least the threat of the loss of masculinity, and the subordination of reason to baser, instinctual behavior that challenges the notion of free will.

Fictional female detectives must participate in the violence created by the crime and the pursuit of the criminal although they express ambivalence about the necessity for using violence. Only because the narrative of the crime demands it, can the female protagonist use violence in culturally sanctioned ways— to save herself, protect her client, or stop the criminal. To use violence outside of these boundaries suggests that the female detective has compromised her sense of identity not only as a detective but also as a woman. After all, violence is the signature of the criminal who deliberately flouts the principles of law and order, thereby threatening the stability of society: "The assumption of 'making sense' is an ideological assumption propped up by fear of its being otherwise. The function of the detective is to ally this fear" (Gomel 2003, 69). The fear is that, despite her best efforts to bring about a semblance of order and balance, those efforts are only temporary; the law operates from a consensus of the community, and as all detective fiction reveals, that consensus is easily overturned. The female detective constantly faces challenges to and doubts about her abilities to function as a valid representation of the law and that consensus.

Violence is also the signature of the male, whether pursuer or pursued, and becomes an essential attribute of his way of responding to the progress of the investigation. As Maureen Reddy affirms, "[h]ard-boiled characters glory in violence, and it comes naturally to them, but their female counterparts have more mixed emotions..." (113). The immediate, forceful response — the punch, chokehold, shot — becomes the symbol of male physical power and of the authority to use it. For a male detective not to respond with force calls into question his ability and his own identity, not only as the person who is capable of solving the crime and restoring social order, but also his very sense of himself as a man.[7] The woman who assumes the prerogatives of masculine power and authority sets herself up for feelings of doubt — is she able to use violent means to bring about the desired resolution, will she be tough enough or ineffective should she decide to use violence, what will her final response be to having used violence, and will she still be considered a true woman once the need for violent action is over? Sherri Inness (1999) quotes Myra Macdonald to highlight the importance for the straight female detective to retain the social signals of femininity: "The body's traditional centrality to feminine identity can be sub-divided into a variety of codes of appearance.... It is not the body, but the codifying of the body into structures of appearance, that culturally shapes and molds what it means to be 'feminine'" (21–22). Relishing the power of violence, enjoying the privilege of command, and asserting the right to be in this situation only emphasizes the unnaturalness of the woman who advocates using violence. Such assertions marginalize the heterosexual female detective, even though she may ultimately understand the value of violence. Many of the most prominent mainstream female detectives, Kinsey Millhone, V. I. Warshawski, Kaye Scarpetta, rarely maintain long-term romantic relationships; they tend to be isolated from family and even coworkers; they seldom are shown in settings beyond the scope of the investigation; their homes are sparse and strictly utilitarian places.

Being assigned to the margins further problematizes such a woman's naturalness by calling into question her sexuality; these detectives are frequently stigmatized as dykes, perverts, or lesbians. In *Hardboiled & High Heeled: The Woman Detective in Popular Culture* (2004) Linda Mizejewski describes the reluctance of mainstream representations of women detectives to even suggest the possibility that the main character might be a lesbian.[8] In mainstream heterosexual mysteries, the female detective is provided with narrative opportunities to contradict any suggestion of deviant sexual orientation. A male lover or husband (whether dead or divorced) will be included in the story or alluded to, thus reassuring the reader, that, although the detective is behaving inappropriately, she is still a "real" woman. Although this detective shows her ability to be tough, she must often be rescued at the novel's conclusion by a male character. Many times she has placed herself in this position by refusing the assistance of the male or by misjudging her ability to control the violence in the situation. While the character is not usually described in idealized terms, the detective's physical appearance also falls within accepted standards of feminine beauty. The assumption is that if she looks like a real woman she must be a real woman.

The detective's appearance attests to the importance for the female detective to maintain her bodily integrity especially when she is herself vulnerable to the harm that violence can do to the body. The body, after all, is society's reference point for the person's identity and for how others respond to that identity. Since the female body is traditionally not seen as literally or figuratively fit for violence, it becomes vulnerable to assault.

Female detectives, just like their male counterparts, are regularly shot at, beaten, chased, and physically damaged, and like male detectives, the women will often overlook bodily pain in the pursuit of the criminal. Not until the resolution will she pay attention to the need for medical care. The damaged body is a sign of weakness; maintaining the health of the body is tantamount to retaining her image as self-sufficient investigator. However, the female body is more easily violated than the male body. Biology determines body mass and stamina, and the woman detective must take appropriate measures to improve her physical abilities: "The obsession with self-defense and physical fitness is ... a symbolic possession of the object of violence, making it an active subject — taking control of the gendered body itself, vulnerable as it has traditionally been to being (literally and figuratively) overpowered by patriarchal figures" (Walton and Jones 1999, 178–79). Yet, at the same time, heterosexual women investigators do not wish to transform their bodies beyond the limits of acceptable feminine strength; to bulk up beyond them is to cross the line: "women fear that such behavior might make them appear too tough — too masculine" (Inness, 1999, 23). And if the female detective alters her appearance to the point of gender ambiguity, she faces the possibility of being identified as lesbian. As noted above, the straight female detective must confront the implications of being sexually other by asserting her claim to heterosexual normalcy.

The dilemma for the straight reader centers on how to justify her attraction for the female hero without calling the character's (or her own) sexuality into question. Throughout *Tough Girls* (1999) and *Hardboiled and High Heeled* (2004), Inness and Mizejewski illustrate this paradox of identifying with the detective's toughness, "finding it sexy and alluring" (Inness 23) while at the same time insisting that "this spunky, independent woman doesn't *have* to be gay" (Mizejewski 9; emphasis in text). Some writers will insist on the detective's heterosexuality by references to her femininity; the detective's own body becomes the focal point for asserting her possession of the signs of acceptable sexuality. Her clothing will be recognizably feminine, dresses and suits with skirts; if she wears pants, they will be suitably female, even jeans, by highlighting the shape of her buttocks and legs. Her hair will most often reach her shoulders, and she will wear make-up to accentuate her femininity. The private or amateur detective, particularly, will often use her sexuality to further her investigation, either as a deliberate ploy or as her natural self-expression; she will flirt with suspects, witnesses, or the police as a way to gather information or create situations to facilitate the investigation's progress. She may also emphasize the traditional female qualities of physical helplessness or an inability to reason or lack of seriousness. The reader's level of identification with the detective will determine how willing she is to accept these uses of stereotypic behaviors. While the reader sees through the tactic to the tough woman, in the end, however, the reader expects to find that the female detective remains a clear-cut embodiment of the conventional cultural markers of gender.

When a self-identified lesbian enters the mystery text, she drastically realigns these issues of toughness, aggression, and violence. The lesbian is already suspect. She contravenes cultural notions regarding natural feminine appearance and behavior; she is readily placed on the margins because she looks and acts too much like a man. The outward signs of gender make the lesbian detective unrecognizable. She will be mistaken for a man because she looks and acts like a man; yet her sexualized body is the body of a woman and her sexual and emotional desires are directed toward women. Since the lesbian detective is able to slip across gender lines, she has greater freedom in choosing the methods she will use to build the investigation of the crime she has been asked to solve. Assuming the look of masculinity allows the lesbian to blur the previously believed clear distinctions of what kind of behavior is suited to each gender. Such blurring can be seen in the names given to lesbian detectives, names that provide little, if any, clear sense of gender: Maris Middleton (Kay Davis's forensic expert, Cassidy James (Kate Calloway's private investigator), Cameron Roberts (Radclyffe's FBI special agent). When the detective has a recognizably feminine name, her physical description often undercuts the linking of traditional attributes with the character: on first meeting Detective Sergeant Rebecca Frye, like Dr. Rawlings, the reader sees "the gold shield clipped to the pocket of the officer's navy-blue blazer and ... the tailored fit of her pale shirt and gray gabardine trousers. Tall, blond-haired, and blue-eyed, the woman moved with a degree of assuredness that suggested she was rarely intimidated. She was slender, but there was a suggestion of power in the sleek lines of her shoulders and narrow hips" (Radclyffe 2002, 2). The lesbian detective tends to be taller than average, keeps her hair short, wears androgynous clothing (pants/jeans, man-tailored shirts, boots, leather jackets), drives muscle cars or trucks or motorcycles, speaks in a lower register, exercises to develop/maintain a muscular, well-toned body. She rarely cooks, and then only the most basic meals, does not keep her home/apartment spotlessly clean, prefers to distance herself from emotional attachments, ignores social obligations, pursues nonwork related activities like body building or camping or boating, and sometimes engages in potentially self-destructive behavior like excessive drinking.

Looking and acting like a stereotypic man enables the lesbian detective to perform those tasks also associated with the stereotypic male, unlike a straight female investigator who must consciously be alert to overstepping these boundaries. The lesbian's outsider status

> reveal[s] the paradox of sexual identities. For on the one hand, heterosexuality secures its ontology by constructing the homosexual as external and foreign, and hence implicitly hostile. On the other hand, the homosexual is intrinsic to the constitution of the heterosexual — the "other" *within* — the "perversion" always only comprehended as a deviation from "normality" [L. Hart 1994, 16; emphasis in text].

The lesbian's destabilization of strict gender identification allows her to engage in the practices of toughness more readily, because she does not worry about appearances. Appearance, in this context, operates on two levels: how one looks and how one behaves. The lesbian looks out of place, and since she does not match the expectations of the majority, her out of place behavior may be more easily named. Yet there exists a real and perceived threat to the dominant heterosexist society; by challenging the dominance of a two-gender society and by denying dominance to the authority of the male, the lesbian refuses to be limited by the straitjacket of such attempts to define her. And instead of being the object of the majority's violence, the lesbian turns that violence outward.[9] Refusing to be the projections of male fantasy or fear, the lesbian detective assumes the power of definition, not only of her identity but of the way she will articulate the narrative of that self-creation.

Directing her own narrative, the detective is able to establish the relationship between the telling of the story and the listener, and, more importantly, to separate herself from the influences of male response. As Marilyn Farwell states, in *Heterosexual Plots & Lesbian Narratives* (1996),

> It is the tension between the ideologically determined traditional narrative roles, along with the subsequent reader expectations, and the particular woman or lesbian who occupies the space that creates the energy in contemporary narratives by women and lesbians. The tension between function and the character permits disruption and a shift in the narrative paradigm itself; for the woman, and especially the lesbian, is by definition a figure marginal to society.... Thus, when a woman occupies the space of the hero or lover she is differently aligned to power but not necessarily either devoid of it nor necessarily absorbed by the maleness of the binary structure [59].

Applied to the hard-boiled detective tradition, these narrative strategies allow the lesbian hero the freedom to negotiate the representations of the crime, its participants, and resolution in ways that give her complete control. These strategies then frame the development of the lesbian detective's appearance in the text; she is the agent who situates not only her role in the story, but the reader's as well. As Walton and Jones (1999) attest, "[w]omen who take advantage of a typically masculine genre like hard-boiled detective fiction are, in a sense, generic outlaws, who, in appropriating powerful linguistic conventions, resituate and redirect power" (195). In the interplay between the detective and the need for and use of violence, this power can be seen in the conscious articulation of the reasons for using violence and its value, the careful selection of the appropriate methods, the controlled application of violence, and the required negations over the outcomes of such use.

By taking over the telling of the story the lesbian obviously (and symbolically) gives voice to a community normally displaced from social conversations, because the terms used to present lesbian and gay reality have generally been the property of the dominant heterosexual institutions. When, like any female detective, the lesbian asserts the power of speech, she becomes aware "of her own position of subjectivity—a self-consciousness about the grounding of the private eye's racial, cultural, and gender perspective. The private "I" of the narrator becomes a point of identification through which the reader can investigate both internal self-positioning and externalized alternative realities..." (Walton and Jones 1999, 173). I would add sexuality to Walton and Jones's list; while gender plays a key role in the lesbian detective's approach to how she will frame her story, the intrinsic nature of desire, private and public, does impact the lesbian's construction of her specific place within the female gender.[10] Many critics of the detective genre have commented on the use of the first person narrative strategy, especially for the hard-boiled detective — whether male or female; the basic issue is that by telling of her own investigation, the detective moves from the passive subject position to the active one. This gives the detective control of the selection and ordering of the details of the investigation, as well as directing their meaning.

As already noted, the simple fact of a woman's presence "works to destabilize and denaturalize" the frames of reference that determine her behavior in the text (Walton and Jones, 102). Her appearance implies that the privileges of toughness and aggression are not the sole property of men, and if even a woman can behave in such a way, the accepted protected status of men as the only ones able to express them is open to challenge. If she can act like a man, the possibility that she can become a man seems credible. But, since the straight woman detective takes pains, ultimately, to maintain the traditional definitions of proper gender behavior, only a deviant woman would want to be like a man:

> In patriarchy, woman is presented as having a split nature, the façade of the nurturer masking her dangerous sexuality ... This split nature ... is represented within patriarchal (and hence, heterosexist) perspectives as dangerous to dominant, masculine order because appearance is a façade under which the "true" nature or spirit of a woman or a homosexual is hidden [Wilson 1995, 153].

Ann Wilson's homosexual is a gay man, who like the female detective, challenges cultural definitions of masculinity and proper male action. Since the lesbian expresses no interest in or desire for masculine qualities or behaviors, she is not burdened with the obligation to mimic them. Toughness, aggression, and violence, in and of themselves, are not gendered: society has linked them with men, but this linkage is finally always tentative. The lesbian may *seem* masculine, but only because society has restricted the categories of gender to male and female.[11]

Adding sexual orientation to the female detective's makeup complicates the way aggression and violence will be presented in the text. Already banished to the margins because of her preference for women, the lesbian's social and professional status are frequently challenged. As noted in the preceding chapter, the lesbian police officer confronts, often on a daily basis, comment and criticism of her abilities to uphold the law. When the crime being investigated by the lesbian officer centers on the lesbian and gay community in some way, she must decide if she can or should introduce her own orientation. The consequences of such a revelation will have a direct impact on the investigation and longer lasting ones on her position within the department. The private detective's sexuality sets up two contradictory reactions; since the victim of the crime or the instigator of the investigation is frequently lesbian or gay, the detective enjoys easier access to information and support. If the crime is rooted in the perpetrator's homophobia, the detective will be forced to deal with the same hostility and, sometimes, violent confrontations. The lesbian detective, therefore, must constantly maneuver the borderlines between straight and gay communities and establish her credentials not only in her role as detective, but as a member of the larger community. The lesbian character always negotiates the definitions of acceptable and unacceptable behavior. Continually viewed and judged through the filter of the dominant heterosexual culture, the lesbian detective must position herself as the instigator of action or face the consequences of inaction. In specifically lesbian authored texts this awareness creates an understanding and acceptance of the expression and intention of violence.

Violence works in two directions within the crime novel: there is the wider environment of violence that operates as the framework within which the particular crime will take place. This backdrop comprises an abstract quality of a world where the rule of law has either been corrupted or proven inadequate to contain the irrationality of violence: "evil has become endemic and pervasive; it has begun to crumble the very pillars of middle-class society, respectable citizens, the modern metropolis, and the institutions of law and order" (Cawelti 1976, 156). The other frame of reference for violence in the text is the restricted, concentrated crime and its victim(s), which occurs in a concretely identified place and requires the services of a particular investigator. Murder, of course, represents the ultimate form of violence: "we are seeing bodies like our own being cut open, pulled, apart, bleeding, suffering, in pain. The spectacle of violence reminds us of our own mortality; reminds on a basic, visceral level that circumvents all the justifications and explanations of discourse" (Gomel 2003, xxii). In addition to the physical dissolution of the body, violence also appears in the breakdown of social institutions—family, marriage, government, religion, even the law itself—as well as personal relationships. The detective's task, even if only possible through the conventions of the mystery narrative, is to restore some semblance of order, balance, or normalcy to the community.

This moment of restoration marks a key distinction between the straight and lesbian detective; even if the lesbian investigator manages to solve the crime, a disconnect exists between her position at that outcome and the dominant society. Although the disruption caused by the crime has been stabilized, the lesbian is, in the most basic sense, unable to participate because her sexuality has not been fully reconciled with the community standards she has worked to restore. In those stories that provide the lesbian with either an intimate relationship or supportive community, it is important to note that these relationships remain separated from the wider society; after all, the lover is a woman, the community made up predominantly of lesbians and gay men. This withdrawal can be found whether the detective is a member of the police or an independent investigator: Caitlin Reece, Mickey Knight, Cassidy James, Lt. Maglione, Sgt. Delafield, Det. Supt. Carol Ashton, all establish residences that allow them to maintain the privacy of their personal lives and relationships. A frequent occurrence in these novels is the intrusion of the values and behaviors of the dominant society; the detective's public duty intrudes into her desire to create a separate, private life, preventing a developing relationship from becoming permanent: Carol Ashton's lover Sybil Wade eventually leaves because she cannot deal with the constant threats of harm to Carol and because she can no longer accept the confines of Ashton's closeted work life. The women engage in temporary, mainly physical connections: Emma

Victor and Nell Fury both enjoy their sometimes relationships, and while regretting their disruptions or ending show no interest in establishing more permanent connections. The woman detective many express no interest in pursuing any kind of personal relationship: Jane Lawless, in the early books, seems content to maintain an unattached life.

Such interference with the lesbian's most private experiences must be recognized as a violation, if not comparable to the physical violence of a crime, of her basic sense of self and of belonging. I do not believe that violence is too strong a word to apply to such a denial of the lesbian's recognition as part of the whole community her efforts support. As a lesbian reader, I know that below the surface of the praise and commendation for a successful resolution to the investigation, the lesbian detective will, in the end, still be unwelcome as a full participant in her society. Although many straight detectives, female or male, may suffer the same kinds of intrusions, their very heterosexuality always ensures them that, should they decide to pursue the private, their efforts will be accepted, even applauded.

The crime that instigates the investigation, however, is more overt than the unspoken ostracism of the lesbian detective described above. The violence that explicitly appears in the pages of lesbian detective novels replicates the traditional forms found in the genre: murder, understandably, the most common starting point for an investigation. The victims of murder also fall into the standard categories: those killed for deliberate reasons (to cover up some malfeasance, a contract killing, the falling out of conspirators, hate crimes, economic gain/loss, or gang related) and those killed for more intimate motives, such as greed, fear, jealousy, and other passions. Serial killers have become more frequent in these texts, as they have in mainstream crime stories. Some deaths occur because of ideology, the murderer usually belonging to some fringe or strongly political organization. Conspiracies, national security, terrorism, infiltration of the enemy provide the motives for the deaths that appear in thrillers, which has become an increasingly popular narrative form for lesbian mystery writers. While neither the crime nor the motives for them are unique to the lesbian crime/detective novel, they are often realigned to represent the precarious nature of being lesbian or gay in the wider world. A homosexual orientation still faces the ignorance and often grudging tolerance of the dominant community; the lesbian is seen as an unknowable other and, therefore, kept to the margins of social interactions and discourse:

> Why is it so difficult to see the lesbian — even when she is there, quite plainly, in front of us? In part because she has been "ghosted"— or made to seem invisible — by culture itself. It would be putting it mildly to say that

the lesbian represents a threat to patriarchal protocol: Western civilization has for centuries been haunted by a fear of "women without men"—of women indifferent or resistant to male desire [Castle 1993, 4–5].

Placed on the edges of society, outside of the purview of its institutions, the lesbian becomes vulnerable to the bias and hostility of those who refuse to see her as an equal member of and participant in the community. The lesbian is doubly marginalized by the majority view because she is a woman, therefore less than the male standard, and a sexual deviant, not even comprehensible as female. This double-bind is seen in those mysteries that involve the rape or murder of lesbians. The event that has acted to bring about the rapist/killer's crimes may involve rejection of his overtures for a relationship or be purely sexual or stem from the woman's coming to realize her sexuality and putting an end to the initial connection. Whatever the impetus, the perpetrator's anger quickly escalates to extreme measures; the rapes, if the woman survives, are vicious and include anal, vaginal, even oral penetration as well as brutal beatings. The sexual assault becomes a way to "teach" the lesbian a lesson: "Women who stole other women from men" must be punished for crossing the line and taking over the prerogatives of men (McAllister 1994, 4). The types of intimidation lesbians confront include professional and personal blackmail, threats to family, lovers, and friends, and smear campaigns in addition to physical violence.

Many early mysteries developed plots that emphasized issues of particular importance to the lesbian and gay community: HIV/AIDS often became the motive for the crime, directed at a gay man because he was seen as the source of the killer's own infection (Jaye Maiman"s *Crazy for Loving*, 1992) or the disease became a signifier of homosexuality for the infected individual or family and attempts to publicize it needed to be prevented (Claire McNab's *Dead Certain*, 1992). Homophobia, which takes many forms, is the underlying motive used by many lesbian writers: gay panic in Katherine Forrest's *Murder by Tradition* (1993), fear of outing or being outed in Pat Welch's *Fallen from Grace* (1998) and Julia Lieber's *There Came Two Angels* (2004), male anger at a lesbian for real or perceived sexual rejection in Gerri Hill's *Hunter's Way* (2005) and Diane Davidson's *Deadly Rendezvous* (1996). The threat of violence does not only strike from outside the lesbian and gay community; the lesbian detective also discovers that her community is not immune to acts of aggression and violence, including murder. Mary Morell's *Final Session* (1991) and Jean Taylor's *The Last of Her Lies* (1996) deal with same sex-abuse, both physical and sexual. Mary Wings's *She Came by the Book* (1995) and Elaine Beale's *Murder in the Castro* (1997) show how leaders of gay/lesbian organizations can be willing to manipulate the homophobic attitudes of society to advance their own agendas—usually self-promotion or advancement.

More recent mysteries have moved away from the victim's sexuality as the prime factor in crime or homophobia as the dominant motive for the perpetrator. This suggests that the lesbian detective need no longer be seen as a specialist, called into the scene of the crime only when her "particular" skills will benefit the investigation. Of the sixteen books in the Carol Ashton series, for example, only three have specifically gay/lesbian-centered plots. This does not mean that the hostility faced by lesbians and gay men has disappeared from these stories: the most recent Penny Micklebury mystery featuring Lt. Gianna Maglione and Mimi Patterson, *Darkness Descending* (2004), deals with the death of a black lesbian who lives the life of an A/G (Dominants and Aggressives—women who take on male dress and behavior to the point where they are often unrecognizable as women). This also is not meant to suggest that the lesbian detective is no longer the subject of derogatory comments or physical threats because of her sexuality. Yet, as the victims of the crimes she investigates move into the realm of the dominant society, the lesbian's outsider status often gives her a vantage point from which she can pursue the investigation. This position is particularly effective for the amateur or private detective because it allows her to bring an unbiased (either because of explicit or implicit prejudices about the victim or because of the limitations that following procedures can impose) approach to the crime. In Ellen Hart's *Hallowed Murder*, for example, Jane Lawless's understanding of the emotional tensions and social and academic pressures that work within sororities enables her to understand the motivations and actions of those involved in the case.

Because popular fiction can more easily respond to shifts in the culture's interests and concerns, the nature of the crime, the type of victim, and the level of violence will adjust to those demands. Domestic violence, particularly spousal abuse, was a dominant narrative focus in novels of the 1980s; the lesbian detective could sympathize with the wife or lover of the, usually male perpetrator, but remain dispassionate enough not to accept, perhaps not understand, the need to defend him nor the victim's desire to stay in the relationship (Sarah Dreher's *Stoner McTavish*, 1985). In the late 1980s and early 1990s crimes against children, abduction, child pornography, sexual abuse, and abandonment became the plotline for crime novels. Although the detective sometimes develops close ties with the child, she maintains an emotional distance to prevent the investigation from failing (Laurie King's *With Child*, 1997). By the late 1990s and first years of the twenty-first century, serial killers become prominent villains, and many lesbian detectives find themselves confronting such malevolent figures:

since the victims are typically female, the lesbian detective confronts the most horrendous forms of violence against women. Extreme violations of the female body are the preferred signature of the serial murderer, and, as a woman, the lesbian detective identifies with that reduction of the person to a thing. Rather than be diminished by this recognition, the detective, even if she herself becomes the serial killer's target, separates her inherent acknowledgment of similarity to the victim from her professional obligations in order to allow her professionalism to take charge (Claire McNab's *Chain Letter*, 1997).

No matter the crime, both victim and detective come face to face with varying degrees of violence that eventually lead to death, "which expose[es] readers to their greatest fears. None of us know how we will die and how those final moments will feel" (C. Cole 2004, 72). By showing the violated body, the reader experiences a paradoxical fascination with its condition, but at the same time recoils from the portrayal. Even though the violence is contained within the pages of the fiction, the reader must deal with the realization of the basic premise of crime novels: the "view of violence as a necessary and inescapable component of any subjectivity" (Gomel 2003, 94). The pervasiveness of violence, then, demands that someone make the attempt to limit the presence of violence within society. All detective fiction makes this the task of the detective, and the community within and outside of the text's pages allows the detective whatever methods will reduce the fear of violence escaping, even if they replicate the very violence that precipitated the investigation. The detective's own violence, then, becomes the mechanism of retaliation, what John Cawelti describes as "the oldest and simplest human conceptions of justice, the lex taliones, or 'eye for an eye' (2004, 162). However, the detective's use of force, whether directly physical or with weapons, is engaged in for more complex reasons; the decision to respond with aggression is not undertaken lightly, particularly by female detectives. This hesitation illustrates the conflict for the woman between expected social behavior and the circumstances of the situation. As is typical of most crime novels, the climax places the female detective in an often perilous situation, having to defend a witness or innocent bystander or herself from the final frenzied attack of the criminal. Although she may be tough enough to take the necessary decisive action, including shooting, using physical force, or devising some trick to bring down the criminal, in the end the female detective tends to distance herself from the implications of being/becoming violent. Toughness may be a desirable quality, but it is a troubling one for both the woman herself and her culture, neither ready to accept totally a woman capable of embodying the full meaning of being tough. Most popular media, including mainstream female detective novels, according to Sherrie Inness in *Tough Girls* (1999) illustrate

> how the toughness of even the toughest women is limited, confined, reduced, and regulated in a number of ways. In some cases, the femininity or maternity of a tough woman is emphasized, suggesting that the toughness does not significantly change what is considered to be a woman's essential nature. In other cases, the sexuality of a tough woman is stressed. In a society where a woman's sexuality is often associated with her subordination, this emphasis reduces the threat of her toughness. In yet other situations, tough women are not as tough as their male cohorts, often needing to be rescued by men [178–79].

Unlike her straight counterpart, the lesbian detective always negotiates the definitions of acceptable and unacceptable gender behavior. Continually viewed and judged through the filter of the dominant heterosexual culture, the lesbian detective must position herself as the instigator of action or face the consequences of inaction. Since she need not worry about matching the expectations of femininity and its restrictions on aggressive action, the lesbian detective becomes a free agent when confronted with the choice to be tough enough or not; this awareness, and ability to choose, allows her to create an understanding and acceptance of the expression and intention of violence.

Violence, placed in a narrative situation that does not question the intrinsic nature of the detective's sexuality, becomes an accepted and acceptable form of response. A clear pattern of the lesbian detective's decision to use violence as a means to achieving a successful outcome to her investigation can be traced in the novels. The most essential characteristic of the decision to take direct, violent action is that there *is* a choice. The issue of choosing from a range of violent responses, of course, is found in those novels that present the lesbian professional private detective. Police officers, even if they are lesbian, do not deal with violence in the same way. In fact, excessive use of force by a member of the force is severely regulated and rarely condoned in detective fiction; it often becomes the justification for dismissing the officer. Amateur detectives, lesbian or straight, since they most often fall into their investigations, may use aggressive tactics, but the use of violence is most likely impulsive, an immediate, uncalculated reaction to the situation. However, for the professional, violence is not simply a reaction to the events surrounding the crime, the situation of the participants, or the means of achieving the resolutions. The detective makes a deliberately calculated and directed choice of action, evaluating the situation, examining the requirements of the situation, and selecting the appropriate methods for succeeding.

A detailed scene from Lauren Wright Douglas's *The Always Anonymous Beast* (1987) illustrates this key point:

> From a locked cupboard in my study I took a tape recorder, telephone attachment, earphone, and after a moment's deliberation, my Smith and Wesson .357 Magnum. Feeling a little chilly, I changed clothes quickly, into a pair of tan corduroy slacks and a white wool turtleneck. I clipped the gun to the back of my slacks and put on a tweed jacket that hung nicely, concealing the bulge. I do not have a license to carry a concealed weapon — they are almost impossible to obtain in Canada. So I try to forget that I'm breaking the law. As the wags say, better to be judged by twelve than carried by six. I also have a Colt .45 automatic, but I prefer the reliability of a revolver. There's nothing to jam. Critics might say that the .357 semi-wad cutter load is a bit of overkill, but friends of mine in the police department have told me a sufficient number of hair-raising tales of bad guys who get up after taking four or five .38 rounds, that I prefer to have an extra edge. If I have to shoot someone, I want him to go down and stay down [24].

Two factors need to be stressed regarding this scene: its position in the narrative and Caitlin Reece's (Douglas's private detective) professionalism. Reece is preparing to record the blackmail demands directed against her clients. This takes place early in the text on the same evening of her receiving the case. Reece prepares methodically for the assignment, on the professional end — the electronic surveillance equipment — and on the personal end — dressing comfortably and making sure her illegally carried weapon is concealed. She has also evaluated the value of her pistols, weighing the advantages and disadvantages before selecting the one to carry. Reece is also conscious that her actions have placed her in almost the same position as the blackmailer; by carrying the firearm she is breaking the law. However, as the last portion of the excerpt indicates, she is prepared to face the legal consequences rather than the alternative. At this point in the novel there has been no kind of physical attack against Reece or her clients, nor has there been even the threat of violence, only the threat to reveal the secret if the blackmailer's demands are not met. Nothing has happened yet to require the use of deadly force, yet Reece prepares for the possibility. The sense of overkill — the powerful caliber of the pistol — cannot be interpreted merely as insecurity or female overcompensation since nothing has happened yet. Reece is simply functioning in the appropriate manner, being prepared for whatever may occur. The final sentences indicate that Reece is drawing from her previous experience as a detective as well as the experience of other law enforcement officers. This anticipatory stance means that Reece intends to stay in command of the situation and is clearly willing to use whatever means allow.

Reece, here, is the consummate professional; there is a deliberate, matter-of-fact quality to her speech. She evaluates her options and chooses the weapon that will keep the balance of power in her hands, rather than let the situation determine her actions. Reece's tone also conveys the seriousness of her action — "If I have to shoot someone, I want him to go down and stay down." She understands the potential that the weapon carries by it physical presence; in fact, throughout *The Always Anonymous Beast* (1987), Caitlin Reece acknowledges the reality of her weapon. As the blackmail turns into murder, her reliance on the pistol's ability to do damage is demonstrated again: "Although I didn't intend to use it, I wanted no surprises. I loaded it with the brand new .357 ammunition — full wad cutter load this time: it makes a bigger hole — and slipped two speed loaders into my pocket" (171). Here, too, is an almost dispassionate appreciation of the potential injury the gun is capable of producing and a serious intention to be fully prepared. Ironically, Reece has returned the gun to its place when she most needs it; surprised by the murderer, she cannot reach her weapon and is severely beaten before he is subdued by another character. Relinquishing the means of violence has made her vulnerable to violence.

It is important to note that Reece, and other lesbian detectives, prefers not to engage in violent action if at all possible. However, they will take on the role of aggressor when circumstances require, and when violence is the proper response, they apply it in, for them, the most judicious way. Reacting with violence simply for revenge is rarely seen in the lesbian detective's investigation, although it does occasionally appear (e.g., Jean Marcy's *Dead and Blonde*, 1998).Not wanting to use violence does not indicate the lesbian detective's reluctance to be violent. Early in her investigation of the blackmail, Reece tells her client, "But I do have the will. And the power. And it has nothing to do with physical strength or proficiency with weapons. It's a ... determination (30; ellipsis in text). A number of lesbian detectives share Reece's belief that violence is the proper response when its use is judged necessary. Implied in Reece's statement, however, is the belief that if you use violence you must be able to shape its expression; uncontrolled violence undercuts the very reason for using it, setting the detective up for potentially disastrous results. Determined action demands control of both the situation and one's emotional response; if the detective loses that restraint, she knows that her efforts will be wasted. Randye Lordon's detective, Sydney Sloane, puts the point more succinctly (1993):

> I needed my rage. At that moment, there was no room for pain or grief. Grief would only dull my senses, and though the pain was there and real, it's sometimes confusing for me as to what really hurts. No, I needed to get angry enough to see past the blood and the waste so that I could focus [86].

Emma Victor, Mary Wings's hard-boiled private detective, loses that focus at the end of *She Came in Drag* (1999) when she discovers the callousness of her client's blackmailer regarding the damage she has deliberately and tangentially caused:

> I am not a violent person — or I like to think that my anger will not take a violent form — but this time, I failed. My hands reached out and shook Bevin Crosswell. Her headset sprang off her hairdo. Her head snapped back and forth like a doll.
> "You idiot! You monster!" I was out of control, but I didn't care." [313].

Scott Christianson (1995), in a study of Sue Grafton's Kinsey Millhone mysteries, identifies a characteristic of the female hard-boiled detective, which he calls "posture promising violence" (131). He defines this as the ability *and* the willingness of the detective to back up the performance of toughness with the actuality of violence. As noted earlier, tough talk is a hallmark of the private detective, and straight women have taken this language and reframed the conversation, using words, tone, and interpretation to deflect and defuse the hostility directed at her. Words alone, however, are insufficient to bring about the desired resolution of an investigation.[12] The detective must be able and, most importantly, willing to back up any verbal assertion with action. And she must be able and willing to control the force with which such actions are used. Both Reece and Sloane direct, as much as possible, the development of the investigation, particularly at the narrative's climactic scenes: Sloane has orchestrated the confession of the murderer, and, although he smashes her cheek with a pistol, her precautions prevent further violence (chap. 17). After her client has used a typewriter to bash the skull of the murderer, Reece provides her with the justification that violence is sometimes the only response (204). Knowing that uncontrolled violence is possible both detectives hope to redirect its force away from themselves and their clients. While total command of the situation is impossible, after all the suspect disturbs any calculation of complete control, the aim is to minimize the effects of the perpetrator's efforts.

The lesbian detective negotiates a sometimes razor thin line between gesture and action. Various factors in the investigation — escalating threats by the criminal, hindering of her efforts by the police, a developing romantic interest in one of the participants — exert pressure on the detective's ability to manipulate the progress of the investigation. The detective is constantly reevaluating her position and making choices based on these determinations. While her desire is to contain the violence for its greatest impact, the detective must stay flexible enough to adjust the methods of achieving that outcome. To be too rigid in confronting violence reduces the detective's ability to manipulate it and its effects. The detective must be able to make split-second decisions during violent episodes; anything less jeopardizes her and her client. Even the most aggressive of these characters, J. M. Redmann's Mickey Knight, does not haphazardly engage in physical encounters simply because she can. *Death by the Riverside* (1990), the first in the series, does present numerous scenes of increasingly intense violence, and Knight's involvement in them becomes more complicated, affecting her response. From the position of observer and facilitator (the case begins as a search for a missing person), Mickey Knight becomes the center around whom the violent actions of others operate. Pulled into the atrocities committed by a cartel of drug dealers and corrupt police, Knight refuses to remain an accidental participant. She becomes not only more determined to solve the major crime, but she also takes on more conscious responsibility for her efforts. During the course of the novel Knight's level of response develops from the traditional, instinctual reaction to a more carefully negotiated action. At the end of the narrative, and severely wounded, Knight manages to devise an appropriate retribution:

> I walked carefully toward the plane, trying not to jostle the bag [which contains a rattlesnake and a pygmy rattler], trying to ignore the pain in my leg. I concentrated on what I had to do.
> A needle, a pin prick in Korby's thick, lizard hide. A small message to him and all the men like him that they weren't always in control. That if they bent and broke enough people, someone would fight back. One snake in the plane could be an act of nature, but two was an act of vengeance [224–25].

While Knight's actions are more typical of the hard-boiled detective in his quest for real and abstract justice, and do not match the consistent, cold deliberations of Caitlin Reece, both women take control of the situation. Knight, however, illustrates a typical contradiction in the detective's display of toughness: while she asserts the privilege of aggression, she has to be reminded to carry her gun; while she knows how to use firearms, in the beginning of the novel she has never fired one.

The ability to reconfigure the need for and use of violence is more often seen in the thrillers that feature a lesbian as a current or former government agent, either for a recognizable law enforcement agency or a fictional office. In these instances it is the mission — discovering the head of a drug cartel (Sharon Bowers's *Lucifer Rising*, 1999), the infiltration of the CIA (C. Paradee's *Deep Cover*, 2004), or the membership and funding of a paramilitary group (R. S. Corliss's *Conspiracy of Swords*, 2001) — that drives the investigation. Like Caitlin Reece, these agents are trained in the techniques of force and have no problem in elevating it to extreme levels. This willingness to expand the level of violence is even more apparent in the novels that describe the efforts of former agents to put their past behind them; the plot requires them, however, to depend on their training to achieve this end by taking on one more mission:

> Nora caught the motion of the Russians moving fast toward the back of the cabin. Making a judgment call, she sighted on the figure in the lead and squeezed the trigger. She did not watch the figure fall out of her view but instead resighted on the second target. She fired again and turned the weapon on the front door. Three came out. Two going left and right, one crouched in the door, waiting. She fired again and the figure to the left went down [Roselle Graskey 2002, 156–57].

Such scenes, due to the conventions of the thriller, exaggerate the violence and the capability of the agent; they become practically superhuman in their ability to use their skills in killing and destruction. What is important to note here, though, is how easily the lesbian fits into the role.

Like her straight male and female counterparts, the lesbian detective exists in an environment that encourages violence. This profession creates and supports the varied circumstances that produce the crime and its aftermath. However, the lesbian benefits from her outsider status as she traverses this landscape. Society's demands for accommodation to its expectations of proper gender behavior and definitions of toughness can be ignored because the lesbian has already been rejected by the very system that calls for such a compromise. Since it is no longer necessary for her to obey the laws of the larger society, the lesbian detective gains the ability to pursue violence as an acceptable means to solve a crime.

Heterosexual detectives, both women and men, frequently attempt such a disengagement from cultural norms; the image of the solitary detective is a staple of the hard-boiled story. However, they are often forced to reconcile their separate position with the dominant culture's expectations of agreement. Their position as outsiders is tempered by the ease with which they can move into the mainstream when necessary or desired. While not fully supported, their deviations from social norms are recognizable by the public at large. The straight detective's use of violence may be criticized, but she will still be considered a full member of the group and be able to enjoy its prerogatives. The lesbian, even after the crime has been solved and the social order of the dominant community restored, is not welcome; she is still too perverse to be integrated into it completely. What community does exist at the conclusion of the lesbian detective's investigation is self-determined. Often the narrative ends with the promise of a romantic connection between the detective and another character

(Lordon); or she returns to a specifically defined homosexual community (Redmann); or she retreats to her solitary environment (Douglas). To integrate, in fact, would be to disappear, and for the lesbian detective such a position is unacceptable.

Inhabiting the margins grants the lesbian detective the freedom to take on the habits of violence without losing its privileges. Being labeled as deviant, the lesbian can safely determine the ways in which violence will play out in her investigation. Her unnatural sexuality allows her the ability to maneuver between gendered behaviors and expectations without having to answer for that movement. Since she's not a real woman anyway, society can accept that the lesbian will be outrageous and do whatever it takes to solve her case. As Caitlin Reece says, "Violence works" (30).

Chapter 5

Marginal Values

> In crime fiction we learn as we read: we form opinions, judge, reshape our views about good and evil, test our liberalism or conservatism. We do this with fictional narratives as actively as we do when we respond to an account of the real-life child pleading with the Moors murderers, or to the discovery of the corpse of a murdered woman in a field of cows that have licked her wounds clean. These stories move us in ways that have more to do with religiosity and a kind of excruciating compassion than any depiction of the violence that ended their lives ever could.—Cathy Cole 2004, 120

> It *was* a victory, and it felt good. She knew, though, that such triumphs were short-lived, and the beast would rise again. That's what police work was—a series of battles in a war that was never won. She learned to take satisfaction in each small success.—Radclyffe 2003, 292

Value is a loaded term. It is mercurial, slipping in and out of different contexts that change its application and meaning: I can own a material object—a Rembrandt portrait, a First Folio of Shakespeare, a Revere silver cup—that is acknowledged as valuable because it meets certain recognized and accepted criteria established by experts. My ownership of the object also grants me a certain social value; my economic status, which enables me to purchase this object, my aesthetic knowledge, which allows me to identify and appreciate such an object, and my altruism, which lets me place the object in a way that gives others access to it, all express a set of ideas and behaviors that are viewed as positive and beneficial. I have become a good person through this intersection of private action and public perception. However, *goodness*, like *value*, is a flexible term that is attached to material objects and tangible events as well as abstract beliefs and behaviors. Its meaning, too, changes continually as the points of reference for what constitutes goodness shift over time. Both concepts become focal points for determining how I perceive my position in the world: I use my understanding of them to establish core principles that will help create and maintain the various public and private relationships necessary for a successful life.

Value and goodness rest on shared assumptions and specific interpretations based on those assumptions, although, in my interpretation of Colin McGinn (1997), establishing a clear definition of these concepts is difficult: "The property of goodness is part of plain common sense, not a piece of speculative parascience or religious metaphysics. It is also unanalysable in any non-moral terms..."(31). Given this seeming paradox that goodness is and is not based on a set of moral ideals, understanding what comprises moral/ethical behavior requires linking the conclusion — this is good — with some individual action or observation. If I have earned, through hard work and fair dealings, the money to purchase the valuable object, then I gain society's approbation; however, if I have possession of the object through illegal means, my moral position is weakened. If my knowledge is based on years of study and practice, I am seen as worthy of ownership, but if I purchased someone else's expertise, I drop in the public's estimation. If I donate the object in order to enrich others' enjoyment, I become a supporter of culture; if I donated it simply for a tax break, however, I lose the community's respect. Recognition of what is moral or immoral comes about only when I put myself in a situation where my actions are open to others' interpretations.

Positioning oneself within an ethical framework generally requires the articulation of a set of shared beliefs and the expression of them through recognized and recognizable behavior. Ideally, a community functions smoothly when its members accept the implicit standards it uses to define the various public relationships expressed through legal, political, economic, and cultural institutions. Typically, the assumption has been that an ethical position reflects certain universal traits. Everyone, regardless of sex, race, or status, it is asserted, can agree with the identification of right and wrong, that concepts such as justice, responsibility, and freedom have clear and constant meanings, that the methods of establishing moral positions are equitable, and that the applications of moral judgments are consistent. Unfortunately, these assumptions do not reflect actual experience; abstract definitions and expectations are constantly undercut by everyday behavior. Tensions often exist between the belief and the practice and can influence the degree to which an individual will adhere to certain moral positions. For example, I will complain about the absence of the police when someone tailgates me or drives in what I call an aggressive manner; however, my habit of driving five, even ten, miles over the speed limit is acceptable because I am a good driver. I will also excuse my driving by noting that every other driver is doing the same. Such rationalizations reflect the limitations and biases of the particular time and place in which these ideas have been articulated. Most of us, however, are less interested in theoretical discussions of good and evil, morality and immorality than in the immediate, concrete representations of ethical systems. While we may reference certain religious principles or philosophical concepts as the source of our ethics, we prefer to find more easily understandable ways to illustrate and interpret those beliefs.[1]

In their preface, Todd Davis and Kenneth Womack (2001) identify what, for the majority, provides the most accessible means of engaging with questions of morality:

> Part of being human involves the daily struggle with the meanings and consequences of our actions, a struggle most often understood in narrative structures as we tell others and ourselves about what has transpired or what we fear will transpire in the future. As creatures driven by story, we find ourselves immersed in narrative in almost every aspect of our lives. The act of telling stories—the gesture to represent what all too often is unrepresentable, ineffable — grounds and distinguishes human activity [ix–x].

Literature, particularly fiction, through its creation of character and plot, encourages a reader to identify with the various personal and social dilemmas represented in the text. The text allows its reader to experience what happens inside the narrative, permitting sometimes intense emotional connection to events; at the same time, because of the fictionality of the text, the reader is also able to judge the thoughts and actions of the characters and to compare their behavior and beliefs to her own.

The ways in which the fictional work engages its reader's moral sensibility vary depending on the type of text, the technical apparatus of the work, and the ability of the writer to present them. Drama and novels are the two literary types most effective in embodying moral issues due to the reliance on the creation of characters who literally and thematically play out the ethical tensions captured in the narrative. Not only do fictional characters pull the reader into the moral situation of the text, but the specificity of the story also adds to the effectiveness of the presentation:

> It helps enormously to have a particular character in a specific context with whom to raise and test ethical ideas. Without this specificity the discussion is apt to become lifeless and unmoored, the moral generalities hanging limply in the air. The strength of an ethical idea lies in its applications, in how it *plays out*. In fiction, we can put an ethical idea through its paces, testing its ability to command our assent. We can also explore it alignments, limitations, repercussions. We can face moral reality in all its complexity and drama [McGinn 1997, 175–76; emphasis in text].

Given these two components— specificity and character — one would expect that the most compelling fictional presentations of a narrative's ethical tensions would be found only in those works considered great — Sophocles'

Oedipus trilogy, Shakespeare's tragedies, Toni Morrison's novels. While such works clearly deal with essential ethical questions, literature considered canonical is not the only vehicle for offering its readers the experience of moral engagement.

Throughout *Pulp: Reading Popular Fiction* (1997) Scott McCracken emphasizes the trangressive nature of popular genres; despite these texts' reliance on conventional plots and stereotyped characters, McCracken holds that such works are able to break through cultural notions of class, gender, and race by placing contradictory situations and relationships within the same narrative space. This allows the tensions inherent in such confrontations to be made explicit during the course of the novel. While the outcomes of such situations will not necessarily bring about social revolution and transformation, what does occur is the recognition of "popular culture's role in struggles over meaning. [Trangressive theory] argues that the popular text is successful because it operates at the borders of what is socially acceptable; and, in order to provoke a widespread interest, the text must, at some level, breach the bounds of that acceptability. It must, in other words, challenge social standards and norms" (158). The reader, therefore, becomes engaged in a process of discovering similarities and differences between the story and its actors and the world outside of the text and will work to develop a sense of identification within these fluctuations. The constraints of popular fiction's conventions require the progression of the narrative to move toward expected conclusions, but, at the same time, reconfigurations of assumed shared beliefs and the potential for new outcomes are projected in the text. Paradoxically, popular fiction balances two contradictory impulses: maintaining the status quo and challenging that conservative idea: "In the best examples, the text will signify ... the potential that lies beyond the limitations of the reader's present position. At the very least it will signify a lack which stimulates the reader's desire for a better world" (180).

The detective novel most readily incorporates this mediating of traditional social viewpoints and their revisioning. Since its initial thematic and plot premises concern the breaking of the law, the detective story traditionally focuses on the moral conflicts present in the investigator's pursuit of the crime's resolution. Regardless of the nature of the crime committed, a rupture in the interactions of society has occurred; the daily routines of people have been broken by the criminal's desire to circumvent the particular standards the rest uphold. This refusal to abide by social codes of behavior marks the criminal as no longer a member of that community. Except for those seen as truly mentally diseased, most perpetrators are viewed as deliberately choosing to contravene social norms.[2] This emphasis on an individual's choice of action becomes one of the ways in which readers will evaluate the detective's behavior during the investigation. Since the detective operates simultaneously as the representative voice of the community as well as the mediator of that community to the reader, how she or he carries out the investigation clearly impacts the level of the reader's response: "'Morality,' 'ethics,' and 'social responsibility' are terms more likely to be equated with didactic religious tracts, yet they form a significant subtext to a genre whose very purpose is to examine the moral and ethical, the difference between good and evil" (C. Cole 2004, 86). If the investigator, whether professional or amateur, presents herself as a person who operates according to an understandable set of ethics, the reader will applaud her efforts. Even if her pursuit of the criminal may circumvent legal formalities, her interest in justice overrides any bending of the law and wins the reader's approval. The process of the investigation pulls the reader in with its red herrings, its suspense, its complexity; however, without an insistence on the possibility of some kind of moral certitude, whether it is an assertion of traditional, conservative values or the expression of a personal, idiosyncratic morality, the reader may feel uneasy at the idea that the potential for anarchy that exists in the novel will break through into her own. On a deep level, the reader hopes the detective and the assertion of moral value in the text will offer strategies for survival and preventative action.

At its heart, after all, the detective novel insists that there is no longer a link between illegal and immoral action and clear-cut punishment. Whatever motivates the crime, its effects permeate the social fabric described in the text and lead the participants to question previously held views about the world in which they live and the various relationships they have formed. Crime has always forced a community to attempt to control its meaning and contain its influence; criminal behavior threatens the stability of the community by destroying the sense of safety and trust among its inhabitants.[3] Whatever form they take, the methods for responding to those who attack the community often prove unequal to the task of maintaining social order. The disruption caused by the crime in the pages of the detective novel requires that the investigator represent, at least, a temporary restoration of ethical norms. Margaret Urban Walker (2001) uses the concept of "moral repair," the methods people must use "to decide how to respond to wrongdoing, whether to ourselves or to others, and whether by ourselves or by others" (112). Walker describes a variety of approaches to creating not only the behavior, but the attitude necessary to bring about such reconciliation:

> These responses address wrongs as wrongs, that is, as something that should not have happened, and for which someone is, more or less, responsible. ... The damage done is always specific to the particular wrong; but all wrongdoings are occasions when trust in our moral understandings, and the hope that we are trustworthy in honoring them are threatened or broken. Moral repair aims at reinstating moral terms and replenishing our trust and hope in them and in ourselves [115].[4]

Crime stories are especially effective in presenting narrative situations that call for characters, particularly the detective, to articulate, and perhaps instigate, this reparation.

Traditionally, though, the role of moral exemplar or evaluator has been given to the male detective. Ever since Raymond Chandler's famous definition of the detective in "The Simple Art of Murder" as a man "who is not himself mean, who is neither tarnished nor afraid, ... a man of honor, by instinct, by inevitability, without thought of it, and certainly without saying it. He must be the best man in his world and a good enough man for any world," the ethical burden has been placed in male hands (1944/1995, 219). The male detective carries the responsibility for upholding the ideals of a credible moral position even when other characters in the text deny its possibility: "Society and law exist not as a fountainhead of what is just, but as a set of rules controlling the action of individuals who are the true source of morality and justice as well as of injustice" (Cawelti 2004, 175). Such a stance makes him a marginal figure, since the detective is typically portrayed as confronting his society's moral corruption as he works to solve his case. In fact, the detective's incorruptible morality often puts him at odds with the very systems that provide him with a livelihood and with which he must engage if he wishes to solve the crime. This outsider position also permits the male detective to use whatever means he feels will bring about a solution and, perhaps, even justice; for the private detective, whether professional or amateur, this includes violence. When the legal institutions cannot or will not perform their required function of punishment, the detective's anger is often transformed into the arm of righteous vengeance. The hard-boiled detective has often been viewed by the critics in such a role and gains a mythic status.[5] The male detective's use of violence also exposes him to violent retaliation, and his physical danger and damage add to his heroic stature because he refuses to succumb to the pain. Nothing interferes with the detective's pursuit, and he will only stop when the investigation is complete.

In spite of his assertions of distance and stoicism, the male detective also represents a belief in and allegiance to the ideas of "[c]ompassion, the sense of decency, community bonding, the sense of equality before the law and events of life..." (Browne 1986, 3). No matter how these ideals are expressed, the detective acts from a moral foundation and works for its survival. This position is usually not concretely expressed by the detective, although his behavior indicates the degree to which he upholds them.[6] Such a sense of responsibility helps to explain not only the social isolation of the detective, but also his inability to form lasting emotional relationships and his tendency to engage in some kind of addictive behavior, usually alcohol. Yet, in spite of the male detective's ethical sensibilities and his difficulties connecting with others, he must still be seen as a representative of a patriarchal system that continues to privilege his interpretations of moral people and behavior. In his worldview women are incapable of achieving or expressing clear moral positions; women are still classified as either Madonna or whore and are expected to adhere to the stereotypic behavior associated with these images; women's morality remains rooted in the personal and emotional, rendering them incapable of achieving a higher understanding and expression of social interactions. These views have become the focus of feminist revision; since 1980, feminist theorists in philosophy, psychology, and sociology have called for a reexamination of "traditional moral theories [that] have implicitly excluded and silenced women and their moral perspectives" (Cole and Coultrap-McQuin 1992, 2).

A brief outline of some of the more important aspects of the reinterpretation of ethics that brings in women's experience helps clarify and defend the adaptations women writers of detective fiction make in their female heroes. The work of Carol Gilligan, particularly in *In a Different Voice* (1982), describes what is now almost a cliché in discussing the sources and articulation of female and male ideas of moral behavior. Her basic premise, "that men's social orientation is positional while women's is personal," establishes the reason for the separation and diminishment of women's moral decision making and its expression (16). Partially due to biology and also to their acculturation, women's lives center on interpersonal connections as the hallmark of their ethics. Gilligan uses the metaphor of the web to distinguish women's way of relating to others and to the world. Men, on the other hand, project their ethical thinking and action in a straight-line trajectory that ultimately moves away from intimate interactions. Traditionally, the male model of achieving full moral development by shifting from the concrete to the abstract, from the personal to the public, has been viewed as the most mature and desirable, and therefore applicable to all. However, as Gilligan states, "the moral judgments of women differ from those of men in the greater extent to which women's judgments are tied to feelings of empathy and compassion and are concerned with the resolution of real as opposed to hypothetical dilemmas" (69). Through a series of studies Gilligan illustrates that male moral choices tend to emphasize legalistic analyses of situations and behaviors; typically men concentrate on the abstract principle involved and often narrow the range of interpretation to fit. Women often seek accommodation of a variety of viewpoints and actions, so that their moral positions appear relativist rather than principled. The clashes in female and male morality result from these contrasting approaches: women aim to recognize the validity of others' needs and intentions as they work through an ethical question where men discard those viewpoints that are perceived to dilute their sense of certitude.

"It is precisely this dilemma — the conflict between compassion and autonomy, between virtue and power — which the feminine voice struggles to resolve in its effort to reclaim the self and to solve the moral problem in such a way that no one is hurt" (Gilligan 1982, 71). Female detectives often express this tension during their investigations, especially in their confrontations with the police and legal institutions still largely controlled by men. Like her male counterpart, the woman private detective has the ability to control her contact with those institutions; she determines the level of trust she can place with the men who work there. This, of course, becomes complicated when the female detective develops a romantic interest in one of these men, as often happens in heterosexual mysteries. Yet, even romance is relegated to the sidelines when the detective confronts the social, political, or cultural inequities that have impacted the crime's victim(s) and suspect(s). The detective's goal, then, is not only to solve the case, but also to attempt some recognition of such forces:

> The hard-boiled genre inscribes a contestatory position for its hero, offering the precedent — indeed, the necessity, as far as the genre is concerned — for representing not just an eye that sees but a voice that speaks from the margins, a voice originating in a character who both talks and behaves in an insubordinate manner [Walton and Jones 1999, 194].

It is, perhaps, not coincidental that many of the cases taken on by the female detective deal with the ways in which society has continued to abuse its weakest members — women and children. Part of the detective's duty, then, is to become the means of exposing these abuses to a wider audience.[7]

Of course, the detective's desire to affect some kind of positive change rarely comes to a fully satisfactory outcome; she is, after all, only one person combating entrenched systems of power. Since the private detective, especially, has little access to or influence on those systems, her efforts can be seen as futile and perceived as little more than a personal crusade. The conventions of the genre itself appear to collude in the detective's ultimate failure to bring about systematic changes; after all, the moral vision that compels many investigations rests on supporting those same institutions that harm a society's marginalized members. The initial crime — murder, theft, fraud — signals a challenge to an ethical position shared by the detective; it is during the progress of the investigation that she may discover a more serious ethical collapse that reveals the true extent of the crime's or criminal's intentions. At this point in her investigation, the detective must decide how to proceed, whether to support the system (following the male pattern of a "hierarchy of power" and abstract values identified by Gilligan) or to move to creating a personal interaction with her client (Gilligan's "web of relationships") (32). The detective must also recognize what R. Gordon Kelly (1998) calls the costs of the investigation:

> [T]he fictional investigator usually pays a price for his or her skill in pursuing truth. These costs are deeply "social" in nature, being reckoned up in the form of cultural goods that tend to occur as opposite or mutually exclusive pairings. ... Hence the "cost" of success in the public sphere may be reckoned in terms of the sacrifice or loss of satisfactions afforded only, or best, in the private sphere, since important cultural goods are associated with both, but the separation of public and private makes it difficult to achieve them simultaneously [118].

When the detective expresses her willingness to accept those costs, she has repositioned herself within the public realm, moving from the center to the margin and often sharing the same negative status of her client, even of the criminal.[8]

The moment the female detective decides to reject the moral standards of social and cultural institutions, she assumes a new moral agency, one that shifts their definition from patriarchal control. Building on the work of Carol Gilligan, other feminist philosophers have expanded the ways of describing how women make moral choices and create a moral sense and life. The ability to choose, the importance of relationships, an emphasis on the individual's emotional character, and a developed sense of self are common threads within feminist ethics. The movement from the woman recognizing her autonomy, and then acting from a position of knowledge, allows the individual to know the distinctiveness of others while at the same time recognizing the importance of making connections with those others: "Ways of knowing oneself are inseparable from ways of knowing others and being known by them" (Tomm 1992, 102). Once the woman has come to know and understand her self, according to Tomm, she is able to construct an ethics that enables her to express social relationships built on "respect, sympathy and autonomy" (102). Tomm stresses the importance for the woman to realize the value of her own autonomy; she must first recover her own sense of agency and cultivate the personal power to express that self. Once the woman has accomplished this, she can then move into relationship: "Self-knowledge includes knowing that one's self-determination is inextricably tied to that of the other. Social justice depends on such knowing" (103). Justice, for the female detective, becomes the preeminent motivation for her pursuit of the criminal; she will continue an investigation even if she is not paid and often at the expense of her own safety.

Such choices against self-interest are typical of the detective, and while male investigators do exhibit this ability to push selfish motives from their decisions, women find this behavior more common. Usually, though, this placing of others before the self has been ascribed to women in a negative way; always thinking of others infringes on her desire and ability to develop an autonomous self, keeping her dependent on others' identification of her self. When the truly self-knowing woman moves into a community, she does not disappear into others' expectations and demands: "If we incorrectly construct an object with our perception, that will be a relatively minor problem; but if we incorrectly construct another human being, we can do her very severe damage indeed" (Fox 1992, 114). Female detectives, while constantly struggling to maintain their private lives in the face of the pressures in their public ones, find it increasingly difficult to keep the borders between them intact. Once the detective opens her professionalism to the intense emotionality of the situation, whether involving the victim or the suspect, she figuratively shifts her status in the investigation, becoming more intimately connected to the underlying forces that have instigated the narrative. Since many of the victims and suspects in the novels with female detectives are themselves women, the investigator's recognition that the situation could be easily reversed, that she is just as vulnerable to the abuses of power by a patriarchal system, solidifies the connection she makes with these other women. This understanding also contributes to the female detective's reliance on the assistance of others, especially other women, to assist her and assure the success of the investigation. The creation of a network of relationships and emotional connections (what Maureen Reddy calls "preservative love") is as much an outcome of the female detective's investigation as the identification and capture of the perpetrator (1990, 183).[9]

Typically, the detective's emotions get in the way of the investigation, especially for the male. His anger quickly turns into vengeance; his romantic feelings are turned against him. This unwillingness, or inability, to become emotionally engaged with others identifies his strength of character and devotion to the abstract issues of truth and justice. Cathy Cole, however, stresses the important function of emotional connection; quoting Sandrine Berges, Cole agrees that "novels become morally valuable when they succeed in engaging our emotions in an appropriate manner" (119). The key word here is *appropriate*; the exaggerations of the detective's emotional responses—rage, lust, greed—must be controlled. Otherwise, the detective reflects too closely the motives and feeling of the criminal or his increasing commitment to violence reaches, sometimes, an apocalyptic force, destroying even those his pursuit was meant to save. Women's emotional lives have traditionally been seen as a limitation, their feelings entangling them in unnecessary complications and interfering with the required rational thinking that will produce the successful outcome. Feminist philosophy, however, urges the recognition and importance of women's capacity for feeling; the ability to acknowledge their own and others' emotions, and to integrate feeling into action, becomes a source of self-awareness and provides women with the power to act. It is usually, after all, such a lack of emotional connection that motivates the crime initially; the criminal, whether an individual or corporate entity, no longer sympathizes with the condition of those whose lives are impacted by decisions made or actions (not) taken. As Winnie Tomm (1992) asserts,

> Sympathy is shared awareness. It motivates ethical conduct. Sympathy (moral sensitivity) with the expression of others is very often undermined by selfishness, a lack of sympathy with others (moral callousness). Injustice occurs when there is a lack of sympathy toward the other. Lack of sympathy is not merely indifference, it entails ignorance, fear, and hostility. ... They are intrinsic to the desire to dominate others... [105].

By aligning herself emotionally as well as professionally with the victim or suspect, the female detective bridges the legal, economic, and sexual gaps in human interaction that have instigated the criminal act. Instead of confusing the situation, the detective's emotional connection frees her from being confined by one limited and biased view of the crime and its participants. She figuratively, and sometimes literally, has repositioned herself in relation to events and gains a new perspective on their progress. While a complete reversal of the attitudes and processes that have generated the breakdown reflected in the crime are not always seen as possible at a novel's end, forcing a reinterpretation of what has occurred and why indicates the potential for correction.

The most important moral question for the detective is whether or not to take the case. Unlike police officers, who usually have no input into cases they investigate, the private detective enjoys the luxury of choice; even the most marginalized detective has the ability to say no. Once the case is accepted, however, the initial act opens the investigation to a more complex series of choices, ranging from the relatively straightforward technicalities of the investigation to the more intricate subjective decisions concerning attitudes and responses. This second set of options requires the detective to deal with the moral implications of the crime and the actions taken. The male detective is able often to disengage from extensive consideration of his moral position: Cawelti highlights his " disinterested morality ... [which] rests primarily on a personal sense of honor and rightness, which is outside both law and conventional morality and, being primarily concerned with the individual's own image, does not contain a clear conception of the social virtue of justice" (2004, 187). His moral agency (the ability and desire to act based on self-knowing) is not so much compromised as limited to a small circle of those who are immediately involved in the investigation. Once the solution has been offered, the male detective separates himself from any continued relation with those participants. His choice is to remain apart until his services might be needed again.

Choice, for women, has not always been something to be assumed; the social and cultural positions have and continue to actively work to prevent their exercise of self-determination. Without the ability of freedom to choose, women face the domination and control of their desires by others, which act to diminish their capacity to move into self-knowledge and social action. These restrictions take forms in both the private and public spheres, from abusive spouses to glass ceilings; whatever choices a woman has have traditionally been narrowed to acceptance of the dominant institutions that have defined her being and abilities or to be rejected by them. The woman is granted no agency, even in being pushed to the margins. As women begin to recognize the importance of determining their own desires, they move from being controlled by others to controlling their own being.[10] Making choices signifies a woman's fully realized sense of self and of her agency, and this awareness enables the creation of new relationships and communities that offer the possibility of personal and social change. For the female detective this means realizing the limitations placed on her by the very system she believes in, at least at the beginning of the investigation. Not only is the detective confronted by the criminal's manipulations (a scenario many male detectives also face) but she also confronts the explicit and implicit sexism working behind such actions. And it is not only the criminal, but the law creating and abiding society that denigrates her efforts and abilities as well. Even professional women detectives must continually affirm their own agency during the course of their investigations. It is not surprising that when she does (re)gain her independence from male definition she is attacked, whether verbally, physically, or professionally. To achieve the positive solution, the female detective needs to "be familiar with male ways and, while challenging them, move within male spaces to decode male ways of doing things" (C. Cole 2004, 139). However, in moving in and out of male spaces and terms, the female detective must be careful not to become trapped in the ways of being in the world and relating with others they create. If she is simply a male detective in drag, she loses much of her moral authority.

However, the conventions of the crime story require the writer to reconcile the character's desire for complete self-determination with the narrative's progression to completion — of the story and the thematic issues. This tension between genre demands and reader expectations allows for an expansion of both, "suggest[ing] a continuity between the social order portrayed in the book and the social order in the world in which the book is read ... that the plot's resolution is somehow *meaningful* to the reader in more than simply a formal sense. Yet the degree to which the narrative is meaningful also depends on its *lack* of formal closure ... (Walton and Jones 1999, 219; emphasis in text). The murder, or other crime, must be brought to a conclusion that reinforces basic principles of law and justice; if not, the worldview presented in the text becomes nihilistic. This is not to suggest that the detective story totally negates the reality of crime, that its conclusions promise an end to societal corruption: "Whether the crime is regarded as a banal, normal event or as a shocking incident, it supplies a narrative event through which questions about the self and society can be worked" (McCracken 1998, 66). McCracken and other modern critics of the detective novel emphasize the role of the detective in expressing a contradictory ethics. In exposing conventional ideas of moral belief or behavior for the reader's consideration by showing, through the investigative process, that these positions are, first, human constructions and, second, that they are subject to, and sometimes need to, change.

If any detective, male or female, serves as a critic of conventional moral codes, does the lesbian detective offer anything new to the reframing of their assertions? In what is perhaps the first explicit discussion of lesbian ethics, Sarah Hoagland lays out a process of identification and action that allows lesbians to develop a sense of self, in terms of knowing and being, to create personal and community relationships that encourage a full experience of these connections, and to discover the means of moral agency that encourage a continual critique of patriarchal systems: "What I am calling Lesbian Ethics focuses on enabling and developing individual integrity and agency in relation to others—I mean to invoke a self who is both separate and related, a self which is neither autonomous nor dissolved: a self in community who is one among many, what I call *autokoenony*" (*Lesbian Ethics* 1988, 12).[11] Hoagland's analysis of the ways by which this state can be achieved rests on the individual's recognition of the strategies that co-opt lesbian agency, strategies that assume the view that social interactions reflect a consistent interchange of dominant and submissive postures, even if the terms are couched in positive sounding notions of protection or responsibility or acceptance. No matter how it may be glamorized, oppression by the majority has the potential to influence the various choices— moral and intimate — made by the lesbian minority, going so far as to deny the very existence of lesbians as distinct people.

To develop moral agency the lesbian, according to Hoagland, must recognize that it

> is the ability to choose in limited situations, to pursue one possibility rather than another, to thereby create value through what we choose, and to conceive of ourselves as ones who are able to and do make choices— and thus as ones who are able to make a difference for ourselves and each other in this living [231].

The ability to choose freely despite the limitations placed on her provides the lesbian with the status of moral agent, and she is able, then, to determine the order of her life. This is particularly necessary because most of the limitations experienced by lesbians are grounded in their oppression. Being able to maneuver through this oppressive environment encourages lesbians to transgress by forming supportive communities. Recognizing and dealing with the differences experienced within these communities, lesbians can learn methods of interaction that will help them move successfully in the wider realm of patriarchal domination. Hoagland identifies a number of these in her analysis, each setting up an inclusive involvement rather than a selfish one; for example, she calls for lesbians to develop "intelligibility ... both of us trying to reach each other, to connect, at some level. Thus it involves, minimally, a presumption of cooperation..." rather than "accountability [which] encourages a one-way process. ... The problem is with the arrogance of perception — that to make a judgment, I need consider you only within my framework" (227). Working to embody those behaviors that support community and relationship, the lesbian acquires the ability to maneuver through the larger society (Hoagland references Maria Lugones's notions of flexibility and playfulness in this description of how lesbians can reside successfully in straight society [242].) Being flexible incorporates Hoagland's concept of positive choice because, despite the lesbian seemingly being confined, she exercise her choices, an expression of her power and based on her ideas of value. The essential component, Hoagland (1992) reminds lesbians, is that these choices do not require a sense of loss, but rather instill an awareness of gain:

If we regard choice as creation not sacrifice, we can regard our ability to make choices as a source of enabling power rather than as a source of sacrifice or compromise. As a result we can revalue female agency, developing it independently of the manipulation and control from the position of subordination to heterosexualism [163].

The lesbian detective novel, although not formally addressing Hoagland's theories, shows strong connections to her descriptions of the ethical situations and dilemmas faced by its main characters.

The lesbian detective's moral position in these novels is framed by the nature of the crime, the particular situation of the victim/suspect, the methods used by the detective to reach a solution, and the implications of the outcome of the investigation. It should not be surprising that in some of the earliest lesbian detective novels the stories centered on crimes against lesbians and gay men or social issues affecting gay and lesbian life, nor should it be surprising that these concerns remain the subject matter of more recent works. Forrest's Kate Delafield deals specifically with two murders that reflect the homophobia of the perpetrators and the wider society that implicitly condones such acts in *Murder at the Nightwood Bar* (1989) and *Murder by Tradition* (1993). The political activism of gays and lesbians is threatened, internally and externally, as Maggie Garrett investigates accounting discrepancies in Jean Taylor's *We Know Where You Live* (1995) or when Alix Nicholson becomes involved in the politics of AIDS funding in Sharon Gilligan's *Danger in High Places* (1993) or that outing a gay or lesbian has served as the motive for murder from McNab's Carol Ashton's investigation in *Dead Certain* (1992) to Loy Lombard's in Julia Lieber's *There Came Two Angels* (2004). What these particular storylines suggest is that the very existence of people whose sexuality does not fit the rigid categories of male and female threatens the dominant society's sense of entitlement; what the crimes against gays and lesbians posit is that one can be stopped, by death if necessary, from claiming the right to be acknowledged and to share in the cultural, economic, and political life of the community.

No matter how reluctantly the recognition comes, the lesbian detective comes to identify that her sense of belonging to the majority and the privileges she enjoys are only tentative. Like the victims she is just as vulnerable, and even though she may not immediately espouse radical separatist ideology, the lesbian detective comes to understand that she must move beyond the limited vision of the wider society if she is to succeed.

The narrative situation that most strongly illustrates the lesbian detective's moral shift deals with sexually based crimes, usually rape, but also sexual sadism that leads to the death of the victim, the sexual abuse of women and especially children, and attacks on prostitutes. Conditioned by hundreds of years of male dominance, women have accepted characterizations that reduce them to reproductive machines, that have claimed them unfit for intellectual pursuit, and that deny them moral agency: "Heterosexualism is a particular economic, political, and emotional relationship between men and women: men must dominate women and women must subordinate themselves to men in any of a number of ways. As a result, men presume access to women..." (Hoagland, 1998, 29). Throughout these novels women are punished for attempting to break free from these limitations and claim ownership of their individual being. Many villains attempt to reassert control over what they perceive as personal property, to exercise their moral claim to act as they see fit. Violating the woman's body becomes the most concrete expression of this assumed right. The lesbian investigator must be able to identify with the victim but not to the point of paralysis; knowing she is subject to the same violence (fictional private detectives are especially prone to being physically attacked or shot at) requires the lesbian to create emotional distance in order to affect a satisfactory outcome. This does not mean, however, that she denies the victim sympathy or accuses her of being complicit in her own abuse. That view duplicates the imbalanced power relationship that advantages male privilege, which the detective becomes engaged in overturning with the capture and punishment of the perpetrator. This becomes particularly difficult when the victims of sexual crimes are themselves lesbian, since the attack on the lesbian body can be read as an attempt to "normalize" her sexual practice: "He was going to show these women that they couldn't steal power or women from men. He thought they would all get the message when he left this symbol [a labrys] on the raped and dead body of Elizabeth 'Tenacity' Mendoza" (McAllister 1992, 218). The detective's efforts often take on an urgency due to the assault not only of the victim's, and because she shares her sexual orientation, the detective's physical body, but on their shared autonomy. This connection, whether concretely expressed through the detective's actions or more subtly recognized by her reactions to others' behavior, marks the redirection of the moral positions embodied in the investigation.

Whatever the crime, the lesbian detective balances two sources of technical and emotional support in the pursuit of the criminal—the formal investigative institutions and an informal collaboration of friends and associates. As noted in the references to Delta Stevens below, many lesbian detectives, whatever their professional affiliation, develop communities or relationships to assist them. The detective will circumvent open channels within a department to uncover needed information or evidence, usually calling on the computer/surveillance expertise of a friend inside the station or forging relationships within the district attorney's office. If such assistance is not available in-house, the detective may turn to outsiders, most often individuals who skirt the law (FBI agent Samantha Skellar relies on the ability of Lucy Spoon to hack the most sophisticated computer systems in Lynne Jamneck's *Down the Rabbit Hole*; Caitlin Reece often calls on the electronic skills and devices of Lester Baines). Professional private detectives make use of the same extracurricular support services in their investigation, especially if they are a one-woman operation; for example, Cassidy James will turn to her friend Maggie, a police officer, for particular help as well as for emotional support. In addition to specific investigative assistance, the detective will widen this circle to include those whose knowledge or abilities can further her pursuit; Carol Ashton makes use of Madeline Shipley's media presence and contacts to air information or entice the criminal to self-exposure. That most of those whose assistance proves valuable to the investigation's resolution are lesbians should not be unexpected:

> If we perceive our selves as autokoenonous, as selves within community, then the process of acknowledging our boundaries is a process of becoming aware of our limits and hence of our need for others who have different limits and so who have the capacity to help us expand. Lesbian community is a rich source of diversity and offers up access to a multitude and variety of differences virtually not available elsewhere... [Hoagland 1988, 241].

Typically the detective at the beginning of the novel embodies the dominant, heterosexualist version of morality; as she discovers others like her, not only in their sexuality, but also in their shared moral vision, the detective realizes the negative impact of the restrictions within which she has previously moved. By the novel's end, the detective has come to value the tangible assistance as well as the new moral possibility.

Also figuring into the detective's moral stance is whether she operates as a member of the police force or as an independent private agent; in each case, the detective must integrate public and private codes of behavior in pursuit of the criminal. Within the text, these ethical positions will often clash as public expectations—about the disposition of key evidence, for example, or whether the perpetrator will be captured or allowed to escape—butt up against the detective's personal sense of values. The amateur detective will also find her personal ethical code challenged during the progress of an investigation, but since her involvement is usually inadvertent, the confrontation is often unexpected. Professional detectives understand the implications and requirements of confronting the shared, normative expressions of morality; they are also willing, when circumstances of the case demand, to separate themselves from any allegiance to them. To accept that she must distance herself from the dominant moral positions is an important step in the lesbian detective's moving to a new moral perspective. While this seems contradictory to the notion of building relationships even with those in power, this new perspective is both literal (at times) and figurative; the lesbian may need to sever all practical considerations — reporting to superiors, limiting her involvement, following standard procedure — and strike out on her own.

Delta Stevens, for example, is a police officer who frequently breaks the rules to pursue the "real" justice of a case. She has a hair-trigger temper and will turn to sometimes, excessive violence as the tension of the case builds. Violence also becomes Stevens's means of meting out the "right" punishment for the criminal; however, she has no moral qualms about the value of her approach to solving the case. As she tells her rookie partner in *Weathering the Storm*, "Carducci, let me spell this out for you in plain English. We've broken the law. We have withheld information pertinent to the investigation, we have obstructed justice, and worse yet, we've killed two suspects in this case. It wouldn't be wise for us to run to them showing them all of the evidence we have. Not if we value our freedom" (269). Stevens and her small group of like-minded friends have been conducting a parallel investigation during the course of the novel, finding the evidence to insure conviction; the authority figures, unfortunately, do not approve of these efforts, and when important information is produced, they only reluctantly follow through, demanding that proper investigative procedures and administrative channels are maintained. At the end of *Storm Shelter* Stevens's renegade tactics have broken through the administration's tolerance; she has flouted all authoritative restraint, and at the end of the novel is facing suspension, an intense Internal Affairs investigation of her behavior, and, her ally the district attorney implies, dismissal from the police force. Delta's response illustrates her belief in separating approved reaction from essential action:

> Delta locked eyes with Alexandria and inhaled slowly through her nose. "Look, my best friend is alive, her lover uninjured, hell, even Aphrodite pulled through. I'd say we won this round against the bad gays, wouldn't you? If we're scolded and reprimanded for saving lives but not following the rules to do so, then it's not worth it" [291].

What follows in this last chapter is a discussion of the ethical dilemmas that result from the collision of authority and its support of public standards and the individual's assertion of personal affiliations. Delta understands the seriousness of her situation, but refuses to accept what she sees as a limiting of justice: "I'll take whatever consequence comes my way, knowing that I'd do it all again if I had to" (293).[12]

Many private lesbian detectives also have uneasy relationships with law enforcement: Micky Knight, among many, has a close friend, Danielle Clayton, who is an assistant district attorney, and periodically, Micky will take advantage of her resources. However, Micky does not always reciprocate as her investigations develop. Separating gives the lesbian the necessary perspective to stay alert to efforts to coerce her allegiance or force her to assume an undeserved moral burden:

> By separating ourselves, at least from the illusion that we are equal participants in these events, we can avoid claiming responsibility for something over which we have no control. Thus, we can go on to make choices as best we can with others who share the same values. Viewed this way, separation is not a matter of hiding from reality by pretending it doesn't exist. It is a way of acknowledging reality. Nor is it a way of avoiding struggle. It is a way of struggling [Hoagland 1988, 214].

Private investigators' sense of fair play and justice, in fact, regularly collides with the views of the police and legal institutions: Caitlin Reece, Micky Knight, Cordelia Morgan, Emma Victor carry unlicensed firearms, manipulate crime scenes, withhold information, delay the involvement of law enforcement, break and enter, and commit other illegal acts that place them in ethical jeopardy. Such behavior reinforces these detectives' connection to the hard-boiled male tradition, but unlike their male counterparts, who share the basic moral perspective of the dominant society, these lesbians cannot wholeheartedly accept an ethics that denies them agency. What prevents the lesbian detective, even if she is a police officer, from fully participating in a presumed universal set of ethical precepts is her sexuality.

Whatever ethical position she may articulate, the lesbian detective, by simply being a woman-identified and loving woman, must straddle competing and conflicting ideas of identity and agency. As noted in chapter 3, even lesbian members of law enforcement do not always receive the respect of their colleagues, even though the police hierarchy demands that the chain of command serves both as an organizational and moral authority. If you have earned your place in the chain, you can expect the corollary positive attitude from your subordinates. Yet, as shown through the experience of Lt. Mendoza or Lt. Franco, despite records of accomplishment and commitment to the system, the lesbian officer must be constantly alert to subtle insubordination or open hostility from coworkers. The dominant moral authority of the detective genre, even in the pages of lesbian authored texts, reflects a conservative, masculine oriented perspective, and since it is based on heterosexualist constructions of individuals and personal interaction, as well as defining the ways social institutions will work, the lesbian cannot be fit. The tendency of the majority is to position human relationships in binary and oppositional situations: domination/suppression, male/female, black (brown, yellow, red)/white, rich/poor, straight/deviant. Those who do not (or will not) adapt to the configurations of the majority face ostracism, denial, and violence. Yet the lesbian who represents components of these public systems impels a reevaluation of them by the very fact of her presence within the institution. She invites a rewriting of the duality that lies at the heart of traditional morality. This is accomplished through the detective's recognition of the strictures she works under, and despite the threat of co-option by the system, developing a set of moral principles and actions that grant her moral agency and allow her to extend its influence. The series of crime novels chronicling the investigations of Det. Sgt. Rebecca Frye illustrates the process by which the traditional masculine qualities of policing embodied by the lesbian detective are translated into a new paradigm that reflects a self-conscious lesbian ethics.

Radclyffe's Rebecca Frye represents the stereotypical by-the-book, intensely committed police officer; she enters the first book in her series, *Shield of Justice*, fully intent on getting the information she needs from Dr. Catherine Rawlings about a patient of hers who has been severely beaten after witnessing a crime. Frye's tone is clipped, her movements controlled, her attitude toward Dr. Rawlings sharp; she wants the doctor to share details about her client even though it would break the confidential relationship of doctor and patient. When Dr. Rawlings demurs, Rebecca's internal reaction is swift and typical: "God, how she hated dealing with these ethically rigorous types, when all she needed was a little assistance" (3). Throughout this first meeting Frye is described as barely containing her anger and frustration — at the lack of cooperation from the doctor and, more importantly, at the escalation in the violence attached to a series of rapes that have stymied the Special Crimes Unit of which Frye is a member. Rebecca's desire to catch the rapist illustrates two levels of ethical conduct; the first is her belief in the abstract idea of justice. Rape, like other crimes, breaks the social contract that holds society together, and as a member of the police, Rebecca feels obligated to pursue and catch the perpetrator. While she regrets the harm done to Janet Ryan, the witness, Frye is more interested in her ability to help solve the crime: "I mean, Doctor, is Janet Ryan likely to fake this amnesia thing — for attention, or a thrill, or to fuck with the police? Until I know, my hands are tied" (7). However, her harsh attitude masks the second layer of Frye's moral sense; her commitment to finding this rapist represents her deep personal belief in the importance of restoring the balance that crime disrupts. Frye has all the characteristics of the detective who assumes the responsibility for restoring order to the entire community: she gets little sleep, eats haphazardly, pushes herself to her physical limits. Rebecca for much of the novel is physically and emotionally exhausted, yet she will not relinquish control of the investigation, even to her partner Jeffrey Cruz. She expects perfection and blames herself when she or others do not meet those expectations:

> If she allowed herself to hear the victims' cries, feel their fear, experience their helplessness, her own anger and revulsion and pity would paralyze her. She would never be able to do her job, and she would never be able to help them. It was a lesson she had learned early in her career, and the emotional detachment came naturally to her now [27–28].

Rebecca's detached moral position impacts the way she conducts her cases but also affects her few personal relationships; her partner, for instance, has learned to keep his concern for Rebecca out of their interactions. Rebecca Frye has built a wall that prevents her from developing any kind of intimacy with others, and over the course of *Shield of Justice*, this will be breached as Rebecca realizes she must acknowledge that she cannot control events or predict their outcomes, that she cannot be held responsible for failing to apprehend the rapist sooner, that building new relationships is not a rejection of old ones. The murder of Jeffrey Cruz becomes the first impetus to Frye's expanding moral perspective. Cruz is killed after he meets with an informant about a child prostitution ring operating in the city. (This is a secondary storyline that will become prominent in the two later novels in the series.) The loss of her partner pushes Rebecca over the brink emotionally. She goes to a bar after being sober for several years; she begins to question the sincerity and commitment of the officers assigned to the case: "This was not the razor-sharp, controlled detective. ... This was a woman on the verge of collapse" (75).

Most importantly, in spite of her superficial rejection of the idea, Rebecca desires the sympathy and emotional security represented by Catherine Rawlings. As discussed in chapter 2, a romantic attraction between the detective and another character in lesbian mysteries offers her the opportunity to break out of emotional isolation, and while the death of her partner contributes to Frye's personal crisis, she has already experienced an intense physical and emotional attraction to Dr. Rawlings. Rebecca believes that, although she is attracted to Catherine, she can control the level of her feelings. Over the course of the novel, however, Rebecca comes to accept not only their connection but to understand that she must accept its implications as well: "Intelligibility, thus, means being able to offer explanations for our choices and being able to assess the energy between us, including our abilities, defenses, intentions, goals, and needs.... The idea is not that we make no mistakes or that we never hurt another; the idea is that we understand the full dynamics of our interactions" (Hoagland 1988, 223). After her epiphany that she wants and needs a connection with Catherine, the novel moves to its conclusion along rather traditional lines; Rebecca reluctantly agrees to Catherine's involvement in the case, especially when the rapist continues to contact her as a way to taunt the police. This leads to the rapist abducting Catherine with Rebecca and her new partner Watts following to prevent her from coming to any harm. The novel's climax replicates a standard plot device, a stand-off between Rebecca and the criminal who is using Catherine as a shield. Both have guns drawn and with the split second distraction of the rapist, Rebecca and Watts her partner fire simultaneously; the perpetrator is dead and Rebecca critically wounded. More typical of romantic novels, when Rebecca wakes up to find Catherine at her bedside her first thought indicates that her defenses against connection and feeling have crumbled: "Dying wouldn't have been so bad, but losing Catherine would have been unbearable" (185). Although *Shield of Justice* does not explore the full implications of their relationship, Rebecca's moral vision and practice will expand in the two novels that makeup the series.

In the two subsequent novels in this series, *In Pursuit of Justice* and *Justice in the Shadows*, the moral issues become more prominent. The child pornography subplot in *Shield of Justice* moves to the narrative center, and Rebecca increasingly widens the circle of those who will assist her investigation. On the professional side Rebecca and Watts are assigned to work with a federal task force on breaking an international child pornography ring. The tensions between the local police force and the federal agency are exacerbated with the inclusion of a private computer firm, headed by J. T. Sloan, in the task force. Resenting being included only in an administrative capacity because she is still recovering from the gunshot, Rebecca feels slightly out of place; she accedes to reassignment because she hopes it will help in her private commitment to finding those responsible for the death of Jeffrey Cruz. As the investigation unfolds, each of the main characters reveals personal agendas that have the potential for ruining the primary investigation. Yet, it is in these tensions that Sloan, Frye, Rawlings, Watts, Jason McBride (Sloan's assistant), and Officer Dellon Mitchell, who has been assigned as support staff for the task force, will discover a shared sense of purpose and vision. All become committed to breaking up the pornography ring, but, more importantly, they forge a new community that will act independently of federal oversight when they see fit. Throughout *In Pursuit of Justice* the reader learns what motivates each character, particularly the two main women who share more than a moral passion for justice.

A former federal agent, Sloan has left the government under a cloud and established her own intelligence gathering firm. (Radclyffe had presented Sloan's own story in a separate novel — *A Matter of Trust*, 2003) She shares Frye's frustration with the rigid adherence to regulations and chains of command and is willing to bend the law to further a successful outcome. Like Frye, Sloan has been emotionally isolated and during her case has discovered the freeing effects of romantic love. Tentative at the beginning of their shared assignment, Sloan and Frye develop a relationship that moves beyond the simple expedient of each having skills and access the other needs. Each sees in the other traits that will bring out the best in both; during the sting operation at the center of *In Pursuit of Justice*, the leadership of the task force shifts between Sloan and Frye as each woman comes to understand that being flexible about the nature of control will improve the operation's chances of success. Suspicion becomes respect; control becomes cooperation. The importance of developing this cooperative stance is proven when, at the end of the sting, federal agents take over the case, blocking Frye and Sloan from information and evidence that will help them in their personal concerns: Sloan's lover has been injured by a car intended for Sloan, and Frye is convinced that the pornographers are implicated in Cruz's murder; however, neither submits to the government's demands to drop their involvement. In the last pages of the novel, all of the major participants are expressing dismay at the loss of the case, but also promise to work in concert to stay involved:

> Rebecca blew out a frustrated breath. "I've still got some leads."
> "You've got more than that," Sloan responded with a hint of her usual fire. ... "I've go the download of tonight's video." Sloan lifted her laptop. "All of it. There's information I can get from that. ... It's a place to start. [Rebecca then reminds Sloan that Clark, the federal agent, will push Sloan away from any further connection to the case.]
> "I told you before," Sloan replied evenly, "I don't work for Clark. Someone behind this pornography operation, or someone working *with* whoever's running it, tried to have me killed. Instead, they put my lover in the hospital. I'm not done with this yet."
> "No," Rebecca agreed, thinking that this *someone* was probably the same person who had her previous partner killed, "neither am I" [215–16; emphasis in text].

As Frye and Sloan work toward creating a mutual respect, they bring several other characters into the task force, each with specific talents and different perspectives that will play off against each other as the group pulls the sting operation together. Catherine will be brought in to profile the men who make and distribute child pornography. Jason McBride, besides his computer expertise, will go undercover to meet with a low level distributor. Dellon Mitchell's contributions remain limited in this novel, but will be given full reign in *Justice in the Shadows*. All of them come to the same understanding that Frye and Sloan reach: that each member has distinct abilities which, when integrated, will enable them to succeed. Working beneath this professional accommodation, however, is a reinterpretation of sexuality that stretches the boundaries of the personal identity.

As the series develops, an expanding examination of gender identity and the expectations of proper gendered behavior becomes intertwined with Frye and Sloan's search for the source of the child pornography, especially in the third novel, *Justice in the Shadows*. The idea of clear gender assignment is destabilized through several characters' growing ability to slip in and out of their surface gender affiliation. Jason McBride, a straight man, is also a transvestite, whose alter ego Jasmine is so naturally portrayed that Sloan finds herself attracted to her: "Most of the time she was able to balance her affections for Jason and Jasmine, but there were times, like now, when she looked at Jasmine and saw only a beautiful woman" (114). Dellon Mitchell finds herself attracted to the world of drag kings, and with the help of Jason, transforms herself in order to gather information about the location of a studio that films the pornography. Mitchell does not drop the "disguise," however. Sandy, a young prostitute, and Mitchell have become involved, and Sandy has been the instigator of Mitchell's adoption of drag. Placed within the plot of finding and disrupting a child pornography ring, Radclyffe's disruption of gender acts as a counterweight to traditional constructs of morality. One can no longer rely on surface appearances as definitions of deviance begin to shift; the sexual abuse of children, after all, is performed, packaged, and distributed by heterosexual men. The traditional assumptions about appropriate feminine and masculine behavior fall apart as the signs of gender merely become changeable attributes in its performance.[13] If gender can be changed at will, the majority's use of predetermined expectations of gender to dominate social interaction is shown to be hollow. Jason and Dellon reveal the inconsistencies and limitations of rigid assumptions of gender, and by the novel's end even Watts, Frye's stolid partner, is able to play with gender:

> Watts picked up the champagne bottle and gestured to Jason. "Come on, I'll buy you a drink." He cocked his head as Jason rose. "Although I kinda wish you were wearing that little red number."
>
> Jason's perfect eyebrow arched. "And you think *Sloan* is scary" [294; italics in text].

What *Justice in the Shadows* emphasizes is the growing network of all levels of support among these characters; by the conclusion of this novel they have established degrees of intimacy none would have thought possible. By recognizing the commonalities, but not at the expense of their specific strengths, Frye, Sloan, and their companions achieve their desired outcomes: even though the pornography ring has not been completely broken up at the end of the third novel, Rebecca and Sloan have done it serious damage. More importantly, Rebecca has convinced her superiors that the task force should be maintained. On the personal side, each member of this particular community has discovered strengths and acknowledged and responded to their weaknesses with the help of the others. A disparate group—computer experts, police officers, prostitute, and psychiatrist—have merged in ways that promise the continuation of a new ethics:

> Again, what I am suggesting is not an individual endeavor, for meaning emerges from a context. But the context is one we create by means of our interactions, from the patterns we respond to, participate in, and create by our living. The kind of choices we make both reflect and create the community we live in. Lesbian meaning arises out of lesbian context as a result of lesbians interacting as lesbians [Hoagland 1988, 300].

CHAPTER 6

Real Time, Gay Time

> "We arouse and arrange our memories to suit our psychic needs. Historians on the left are surely correct in referring to "the social production of memory," and in positing the existence of dominant memories (or a mainstream collective consciousness) along with alternative (usually subordinate) memories. Such historians are equally sensible to differentiate between official and more spontaneous or populistic memories."—Michael Kammen 1993, 9

> "Perry kept his eyes on his teacup. "Last year I wrote a complete history of the castle which credits the positive lesbian influence of the Ketcham women, Mercy Hayworth, and Olympia Swan. Their contributions to this town were considerable. I wrote the history primarily for the gay community, but if I have to, I'll use it to block Seascape or any other attempt to tear down the castle."—Vickki P. McConnell 1984, 20

Liberty Square, Katherine Forrest's 1996 Kate Delafield mystery includes the following disclaimer: "This novel and its characters are the product of the author's imagination. Certain locales, historical events and situations are factual in basis, but are used fictitiously." On the surface the statement provides the necessary legal notification that the text's historical background has been integrated into the fictional requirements of the novel; history provides the foundation for characters and plot. Since the motive for the murder depends on the characters' shared experiences in Vietnam, Forrest has researched the times and lives of soldiers, nurses, and doctors who served there. In fact, only by recovering and reinterpreting that shared past is Kate Delafield able to solve the crime. The reality of the war and individual experiences in Vietnam, then, must be brought into the imagined world of Forrest's fiction not only to lend credibility to characterization and scene, but to establish the truth of the emotional lives of these figures—who, after all, are not real.

I must make a clear distinction here between the two major ways that history appears in the texts to be examined: history as setting, the literary convention of time and place, and history as the subject matter of the narrative. There are two more ways that history enters a narrative; one is the personal life story of the major character(s), particularly in serial fiction, where each subsequent novel expands on their biographies. The second is a more focused and limited tracing of the history of the crime in detective fiction. In each case the type of information and how it is embodied/represented in the narrative will change. David Cowart, in *History and the Contemporary Novel* (1989), describes what he terms as four paradigms for the integration of history into the text:

1. The way it was—fiction whose authors aspire purely or largely to historical verisimilitude.
2. The way it will be—fiction whose authors reverse history to contemplate the future.
3. The turning point—fictions whose authors seek to pinpoint the precise historical moment when the modern age or some prominent feature of it came into existence.
4. The distant mirror—fictions whose authors project the present into the past [8–9].

In each situation, history becomes the means by which an author examines the relationships of the (re)created society and, perhaps, engages the reader through an implied or explicit comparison to the present. Cowart's (1989) paradigms rarely appear in pure form in historical fiction; there will be a variety of combinations and reconfigurations to present the story.

Inherent in historical fiction is the essential paradox of combining factual material with a creative reimagining that manipulates the material to achieve a specific outcome; the collapsing of time, putting real-life people into fictional plots, altering the progress or outcome of events, all are common genre strategies.[1] The process of selection and interpretation is common to both fictional and nonfictional texts and opens the discussion to a consideration of wider philosophical and theoretical issues centered on the telling of history: "That the historical record is itself a discursive entity made up of signs means that it offers a *re*-presented, thoroughly selective account of what actually happened" (Cobley 2001, 30; italics in text). The means of deciding what to include and how to organize the material calls for the examination of the processes of selection themselves as well as the motivations behind such choices. Where historical records were once considered a truthful representation, they have lost that status because of the intrusion of an individual perspective and purpose. As Michael Kammen and other critics note, the content of the historical records often reflects a particular agenda, and they are frequently used to project a deliberately devised national or cultural image.[2]

These issues also appear in historical detective fiction, which is the focus of this chapter, as well as the broader category of historical fiction:

> Historical fiction generally covers adventures of all kinds and deals with all aspects of culture. Historical *crime fiction*, though more narrow in its thematic treatment, is concerned with the major drives of human life. ... crime fiction becomes the official judging of the actions of the persons as they interact one against another in illegal ways. The role of such fiction is to catalogue, measure, and adjudicate the actions, point out infractions, and bring to penalty those who do not act according to the rules. Historical crime fiction registers the actions of the people of the past, recording how they influenced, both good and bad, their future — and our present [Browne and Kreiser 2001; emphasis in text].

Like nonfictional historical records, fictionalized history reflects the subjective interests of its authors and the particular issues of its moment in time. On the surface history offers a point of contact for the reader's expectations and understanding of the novel's events. This historical framework provides place names, political situations and outcomes, and commonly shared experience. Yet, choosing a historical setting also seems to provide the opportunity for the writer to explore an unfamiliar world and "demonstrate the value of the fiction of everyday life of the past in adding a new depth and warmth of understanding to the world long gone. We see those people faced with the same problems and hoped-for solutions that we face today" (Browne and Kreiser 2001, 10). By bridging the past of the text and the reader's present, these authors offer two very different views of how to interpret those connections; either humanity is incapable of improvement, since the same depravity toward others and disregard for order exists in all times and places, or the lessons of history can be learned and used to develop a better society.

Unfortunately, detailed analyses of historical detective fiction appear to be very limited. My research has relied on the numerous *histories of* the detective novel, but I have found little discussion of *history in* detective fiction. To my knowledge only the Browne and Kreiser collection discusses this topic, but the essays in this collection tend to concentrate on examining the accuracy of the texts' representations of time and place rather than providing full discussions of the rationale for selecting a historical framework or the implications of the intersections of history and fiction. In *Hard Facts* (1987), Philip Fisher, using the idea of Georg Lukacs, sets out his view that the historical novel enables the homogenization of major cultural situations that have the potential for catastrophe (he examines the removal of Indians, slavery, and impact of the city): "[The historical novel] brings a certain abstractness and blankness into character in order to make the choices and temperaments comprehensible as products of a given society and moment" (15). While I agree with Fisher that there is a process at work in popular forms that makes the unacceptable palatable, I also believe that this is a process that develops slowly and seemingly at random; in his discussion of Cooper, for example, Fisher notes that novels like *The Deerslayer* and *The Last of the Mohicans* established narratives, characters, and themes that later writers of the dime novels and westerns would duplicate, beginning the work of justifying the removal of Indian from the American landscape. Not until the last decades of the twentieth century, however, did a reinterpretation of dominant popular representations of Indians appear. Many marginalized groups—based on race, ethnicity, ability, gender, sexuality—have experienced this same process of historical and cultural disappearance until concentrated efforts are undertaken to reassert their right to exist. The success of these efforts results from the formal engagements with and the integration of those results into social institutions; success also comes when the controversies raised when the status quo is challenged become, to use Fisher's term, *ordinary* experiences capable of appearing in popular culture.

For many mainstream women mystery writers who incorporate history into their novels, the selection of the particular historical moment may rest on interest, training, or other personal reasons. Once chosen, however, the writer is then able to incorporate that time period as fully as she wishes. History offers a *particular* place, at a *particular* time, with a *particular* set of cultural ideas and behaviors, which give the writer free reign to develop the story. Once the realism of the work is established, the reader can concentrate on the main purpose of the fiction. The resolution to the crime, after all, is the essential goal. The question these writers most likely do not have to answer is, do I have a legitimate claim to this history. Whatever period they choose, that they have an accepted past to use and the right to use it is never doubted. This is not intended to undermine the struggles women have faced throughout history to be recognized and for their demands for equality to be taken seriously. Nor is this to suggest that these struggles are finished or that these goals have been achieved. What it does indicate, though, is that the idea of a women's history has gained general acceptance, that the exclusion of women from political, economic, or cultural representation can no longer be taken lightly, that the recognition of the contributions women have made across time and place are increasingly recognized and celebrated.[3] For the lesbian mystery writer, however, these very assumptions become the central dilemma. What constitutes lesbian history—or indeed, is it the history of lesbians? Simply placing the terms *lesbian* and *history* together opens up a complex debate.

Is it the same history that is available to mainstream mystery writers? Can the lesbian writer place the story and characters in a time when the "idea" of lesbian identity was unknown? Questions such as these only touch the surface of what history lesbian writers have access to.

Even asking such questions sets up the problem of determining if there is a specifically gay history? The debate over inclusion is not unique to the gay and lesbian community; as with other marginalized peoples, the battle for recognition and documentation of homosexual experience has extended over many years and faced denial and hostility. The importance of such efforts cannot be downplayed, although, as is often the case, hostile critics of the study of gay and lesbian history constantly denigrate its validity. But history, as Michael Kammen suggests, is a mechanism by which a particular group defines its character and its place, and the efforts taken to identify and construct that history are essential to how the group will then transmit its representations ("Introduction," 1993). Of course, the process of selection carries potentially negative, as well as positive outcomes: the image created can often impose a distorted version of the material, usually denying the existence of those who fall outside the accepted limits. This tendency to frame history to suit ideology contributes to the ongoing marginalization of those considered to have no place in the dominant group. However, since the last decades of the twentieth century, gay and lesbian activists and scholars have begun the task of recovery and dissemination of information on their history. Their efforts have ranged from foregrounding the homosexual context of historical figures like Gertrude Stein and Walt Whitman, of describing the social and cultural influence of gays and lesbians throughout history (1920s Paris or early twentieth century New York or post-World War II San Francisco), of reframing the debates on gender and identity. By filling in the blank spaces, "gay history helps constitute the gay community by giving it a tradition, helps women and men validate and understand who they are by showing them why they have been" (Duberman, Vicinus, and Chauncey 1990, 12).

However, gay history is not a monolithic subject; like other communities what constitutes the totality of gays and lesbians is constantly being challenged and redefined. Once the legitimacy of the history is accepted, the concern becomes to articulate the range of meanings and purposes to which this knowledge may be put. Scott Bravmann (1997) poses the issue this way: "[W]e need to look at how the images of the gay and lesbian past circulating among us animate the present and to read lesbian and gay historical self-representations as sites of ongoing hermeneutic and political struggle in the formation of new social subjects and new cultural possibilities" (4). Nonfictional historical texts perform these functions in ways outside the scope of my study. Fictional texts, whatever the genre, that use history to retell the lives of gays and lesbians, provide a way for their readers to make a series of links between the present and the past, between oneself and others, between isolation and community. The history presented in these texts operates on the technical level of providing accurate detail that enriches the descriptive and plot experience as well as establishing a thematic context that encourages the reader to lay claim to those experiences.[4] The reader discovers that, whatever the time or place, others have undergone not only the same experiences, but have also overcome the personal and social obstructions to the happy ending required by the genre text.

Mainstream historical mysteries written by women, while presenting their main characters as feeling alienated from their particular society, do not seem to question the assumption that the characters can embody the particular time and place. In fact, it is more likely that such characters feel trapped by that very time and place, and their efforts in the mystery are directed not only at solving the crime, but at solving their own dilemma of fitting in as well. Elizabeth Peters's Amelia Peabody, Anne Perry's Charlotte Pitt, Carole Nelson Douglas's Irene Adler and others, all struggle with reconciling the restrictions placed on them by the worlds in which they live, and as their series show, one of the implicit outcomes of these characters' actions is to offer a critique on the attitudes toward and expectations of women of those periods. That is, such novels illustrate Cowart's fourth paradigm of projecting the present onto the past. That many writers select historical periods that present momentous shifts in women's lives cannot be accidental. There is a series set in1840s Seneca Falls during the beginnings of the American suffrage movement, during the reign of Elizabeth I, during the labor unrest and settlement period of early twentieth century Pittsburgh, during the early English Renaissance of Chaucer. In every situation previous ideas about women are in the process of changing, and the main character illustrates the tensions caused by these shifts. Genre fiction, however, requires that the contradictions of the character's behavior and the actual possibilities available for women at the time be elided to allow the conventions to work; this means that these characters will be able, ultimately, to reconcile these contradictions and feel at home because they have been able to prove the value of allowing old notions to be replaced by the new. These characters also have successful (heterosexual) relationships in which the husband or companion, while at first skeptical, comes to accept the woman's viewpoint. Despite her potential radicalism, the main character in mainstream historical mysteries retains her allegiance to the dominant social order and still enjoys its privileges. After all, the goal is to restore balance to the community as it is currently established, not to overturn it.

Unlike her mainstream counterpart, the lesbian detective begins each story in an isolated position, disconnected from the various social institutions and, most importantly, from any personal community. Having no relationship with the immediate world, the lesbian character's major concern is to establish such links during the resolution of the mystery. Any past this character confronts is severely restricted, mainly due to the character's ignorance of a shared historical connection with other individuals or a larger experience. More common to the lesbian mystery is the need to discover, or more likely recover, the particular past of the figure at the center of the crime. This is more than just a question of finding out a suspect's or victim's personal history, for often these figures are gay or lesbian themselves. The search for *their* past is also the search for a gay past. Lesbian detectives do not start out looking for their place in history, but often they find it as it becomes integral to the resolution of the crime. The outcome of this dis(re)covery is that such a past exists. Unlike mainstream mystery writers, lesbian authors cannot take their history for granted. The writers examined here deliberately appropriate a particular set of historical references in the novels used for my analysis. This appropriation functions not simply to carry the narrative or provide accurate setting, but to establish essential links between the detective's and reader's experience. Each text explicitly asserts the identification and acceptance of a shared role in and relation to that experience which bridges the fictional and historical worlds. By identifying what particular historical situation is appropriated, how that past is incorporated into the fiction, and what that appropriation offers the reader, this chapter will attempt to answer the questions of how lesbians find themselves in the historical world as well as the fictional one.

All of the novels used here are set in the twentieth century, ranging from a 1929 cross-country air race (ReBecca Beguin's *Hers Was the Sky* (1993), to 1936 Houston (Deborah Powell's *Bayou City Secrets* 1981, and *Houston Town* 1992), 1949 New York City (Lisa Davis's *Under the Mink* 2001), the McCarthy hearings of the 1950s (Katherine Forrest's *The Beverly Malibu* 1989b), the end of the Vietnam War (Forrest's *Liberty Square* 1997b), and the first years of the gay liberation movement (Mary Wings's *She Came by the Book*, 1995). Vicki McConnell's *Mrs. Porter's Letter* (1982) and *The Burnton Widows* (1984) will be included because they represent, to my knowledge, the earliest mystery novels to incorporate the uncovering of a specifically gay history as the driving force of the narrative. The mysteries by Beguin, Powell, and Davis recreate the historical periods in which the narratives are set; in each text the author has worked to achieve accuracy through attention to descriptive details—of such things as clothing, houses, various physical setting—to replicating the language of the time, having characters use the appropriate slang and cultural references. The other texts to be discussed are set in the detective's present-day existence; the investigation's success depends on the ability of the investigator to learn, understand, and connect the past to the present.[5] Unless the detective is able to see the relationship between past and present, she will not be able to bring about a total resolution to the investigation because that understanding provides the motive for the crime. In the world of detective fiction as much time is given to discovering the motive for the criminal's behavior as to determining the means and opportunity. The requirements of the detective story enable the investigator to apprehend not only the criminal, but the reasons for the crime as well. We cannot ignore the fact that too many mysteries end with the detective's explanation of why the perpetrator acted in such a way and for such a purpose. This typical ending allows the reader to believe that evil and violence can be comprehended, although, as Elana Gomel (2003) reminds us in her analysis of the writings of real-life serial killers, "these narratives, the representational molds of the criminal self, always fail to explain and thus to contain the excessive and irrational violence whose unruly opacity constitutes their reason d'etre" (34). When the lesbian detective finally grasps the importance of linking the past to the present, she achieves the same level of comprehension; however, in addition to gaining insight into the motivation for the crime, she also gains a new understanding and recognition of her own place in the world.

Vicki McConnell's texts, *Mrs. Porter's Letter* and *The Burnton Widows*, focus their stories on Nyla Wade's pursuit of the past. In order to solve the present mysteries—who killed Val and Joan, how to find W. Stone—Nyla must uncover and reconnect the individuals' personal history with a larger community experience. McConnell's narratives make use of the traditional detective fiction convention of "temporality ... tell[ing] two stories simultaneously, that of the investigation (present) and of the crime (past)" (Dove 1997, 81). What Dove describes is the ability of the detective story to layer past and present as the investigation conveys two stories in the same time. The solution depends on the detective's ability to merge the two stories; as the detective proceeds to uncover clues and interview suspects and witnesses, she must find the points where time slips and events and people inhabit two places and times at once. In *The Burnton Widows* McConnell adds a third layer of time by having Nyla learn of the history of Druscilla Ketcham's house as well. This house, built in the last century by lesbians, has nurtured a continuous heritage of lesbian life. As the investigation progresses, Nyla's pursuit becomes twofold; she must find the murderer and save the house, which is threatened with demolition to make room for commercial development. Saving the house will also offer Nyla the opportunity to discover her own place in that past; in the first Nyla Wade novel, *Mrs. Porter's Letter*, Nyla recognized her own lesbian identity, and it is not coincidental that throughout this second book Nyla becomes more secure in her sexuality and romantically involved. As in *Liberty Square*, the motive behind the mystery becomes entwined with the personal background of the victims. The women were killed not only to remove an obstacle to developing the property, but because, as lesbians, their deaths would not instigate sufficient community outcry, as this exchange between the police chief and Lucy (Nyla's lover) demonstrates:

> "Two people were brutally murdered..." "Members of this community."
> "I'm not sure the widows were members of this community." Lucy's temper flared. "Didn't they shop at the market? Walk the beach every day? Pay their taxes like everyone else?"
> "That's not what I meant," the Chief said, knowing his offhand remark had been a mistake. "You just need to know there's a difference between people who live here and members of the community" [179].

For Lucy, the denial of Val and Joan's being lesbians is only possible because they are seen as outsiders on a literal and figurative level. Like its occupants, the house itself is constructed of nonnative materials and therefore suspect. Just as the house does not fit its surroundings, the stereotypic view of homosexuals as unconnected to the values of the history of the community places them in a questionable position; the majority's unspoken question, where do these people come from, is answered during Nyla's dual investigations.

Who ultimately owns the property rests at the center of the investigation, and whoever gains possession of the Ketchum house also gains possession of its history and how it will be remembered. The legal ownership of the property is in doubt due to challenges to its disposition: Val's will leaves the property to Perry Truman, an activist committed to restoring the house's gay past, but the family of Joan have begun legal action to prevent Perry from inheriting the property. The murders complicate the inheritance issue; since Joan's will leaves everything to Val, who died first becomes important to the case. The other complicating factor is the refusal by Joan's family to recognize her relationship with Val and her right to leave the property to whomever she wishes. The battle throughout *The Burnton Widows* centers on who has the legitimate claim and the right to represent what the house embodies. The town's straight community would rather the property be torn down to allow the development of the resort complex, to literally pave over its lesbian associations. Since the house can easily be integrated into the resort's plans without its being demolished, the refusal to compromise must be seen as the denial that lesbians or gay men have any claim to recognition. The small homosexual community in Burnton hopes to turn the house into a museum which will maintain and assert its gay past.

McConnell's novel forces the reader to consider not only the conundrum of who "owns" the past, but whose past is owned. Throughout the novel Nyla keeps challenging the Chief to accept that, "The widows were killed because they were lesbian lovers adamant about keeping the castle standing. Lesbians built that castle and lived there together and everyone in this town knows it. Perry himself told me he couldn't get any government or agency support for the same reason, because of the castle's suggestive history" (178). This continual affirmation echoes through the book, and by placing lesbians in the middle of the investigation, Nyla guarantees the survival of the house and its memories. During her investigation Nyla reads about the Ketcham family, a history written by a gay man whose efforts to save the castle compel her to become involved in solving the murders. A gay man, writing lesbian history, has pulled the newly out Nyla Wade into multiple discoveries of the possibilities of lesbian community and continuity. Nyla's discovery and recognition of her connection to the Burnton widows underscores the pressing need to save the house and what it stands for. Nyla needs the house to stand as a symbol of the existence of an actual lesbian history, and her calling on the entire gay community, from Oregon to California, indicates the depth of her commitment. In the closed world of detective fiction, Nyla's hopes for securing the continuance of the house are realized as the castle will, in the end, be integrated into the resort complex that will be built on the property.

Nyla Wade's compulsion to discover her connection to a specifically lesbian past becomes a metaphor for the impact of the absence of such a history. Throughout *Mrs. Porter's Letter* Nyla believes she is chasing ghosts, since her efforts to find W. Stone, the writer of the letter, are thwarted by the Porter family and friends. Until her discovery that W. Stone is a woman, Wade has read both the letter and her efforts to deliver it as a traditional heterosexual romance. When she learns the true gender of W. Stone, the impact is intense: "I was taken totally by surprise at her revelation. It had never occurred to me to see their eloquent exchange as other than heterosexual. I knew in that nearly painful moment what a victim I was of an ordinary and limited perspective" (198). The discovery that Cybil Porter and Winona Stone are alive, and still together, brings the ghosts into the light. Nyla gains a new perspective on her own identity (it is during her search that she claims her lesbian identity), and she recognizes her own participation in that lesbian continuity: "I am alive and will be alive in a new way for the rest of my life because of them, understanding a season that is a part of nature and human love. We've been around since time began and we're still ahead of our time" (209).

Nyla Wade's ghost is the lesbian past that slips between the pages of mainstream history texts. Although she is referring to literature, Terry Castle's (1993) definition of the lesbian as apparition defines the difficulty of positioning lesbians inside the historical record:

> The literary history of lesbianism, I would like to argue, is first of all a history of derealization. ... lesbianism, or its possibility, can only be represented to the degree that it is simultaneously "derealized," through a blanching authorial infusion of spectral metaphors. ... One woman or the other must be a ghost, or on the way to becoming one. Passion is excited, only to be obscured, disembodied, decarnalized. The vision is inevitably waved off [34].

Just as in literary texts, the lesbian appears in the margins of history only to be rejected or renamed. The ability — the willingness— to look for evidence and not to distort its interpretation determines whether the tenuous position of lesbian achievement becomes concretely expressed. Because the lesbian's (and gay man's) identity is so closely tied to sexual behavior, a particular community's position on sexual expression colors the ways by which the lesbian will be acknowledged and accommodated. As Lillian Faderman notes in the introduction to *Surpassing the Love of Men* (1981), intimacy, whether genital or not, between women was generally accepted, even encouraged. Two factors influenced the relegation of love between women to the margins: women who assumed the aggressive sexual position and power of men and the late nineteenth-century sexologists' reshaping of same-sex attraction as a disease (17–19). At the same time as such attempts to describe and contain lesbians were undertaken, the legal system refused to admit their existence; both Castle and Lynda Hart reference the refusal, in 1921, by the British Parliament to establish sanctions against lesbians, promoting what Hart calls the "perform[ance of] the paradoxical double gesture of prohibiting 'the impossible'" (3). If the lesbian cannot be identified, she is easily dismissed. The success of Nyla Wade's investigations asserts that lesbians have a history worth remembering.

The emphasis on evoking the lesbian's historical position rests not only in the factual record, but also in the acceptance of it. Only then is there the possibility of including that existence in a culture's public record. History, after all, is what a particular community decides to remember.

The actual selection of people and events represents only a portion of this communal recollection; the arrangement and emphasis of the chosen history is just as important. The purpose for establishing a socially approved past will vary according to place and time, but the outcome is the creation of a supportive, idealized construct of that community, presenting what Roger Bromley (1983) calls "cultural mediation" (3). Mainstream society has always chosen to eliminate the record of lesbian presence and achievement. Such deliberate excision serves as a way to protect the imagined portrait the community determines to present. The omission of differing viewpoints on events and outcomes becomes an attempt to prevent challenges to the dominant group's authority. Control is established by a calculated deletion of an historical record to preserve and protect that particular vision. For example, John Boswell's study of same-sex marriage in the Middle Ages and the several studies of lesbian nuns during the same period have received much negative criticism because they challenge the accepted position that homosexuals did not exist until the late nineteenth century. If alternative memories of the past are encouraged, the nature of a community's identity can be questioned. As Bromley states,

> Part of the struggle against cultural power is the challenge to forgetting posed by memory. What is "forgotten" may represent more threatening aspects of popular "memory" and have been carefully and consciously, not casually and unconsciously, omitted from the narrative economy of remembering [12].

Other perspectives call into doubt not only the idealized image of the dominant society, but the values and behaviors often based on them. American history, alone, has many examples illustrating this process of selective forgetting and remembering, from the controversy surrounding the 500th anniversary of Columbus's landing to the canceled Hiroshima exhibit at the Smithsonian in 1995.[6]

While this process may represent a "romantic desire for political stability," a community's selective memory has extensive repercussions for a marginalized group: the most damaging is the willingness to sacrifice its very existence for political expediency (Kammen 1997, 204). The power of any hegemony remains pervasive in its influence, by denying access, recognition, and acceptance. This exclusion produces what the historian Michael Kammen calls the "heritage phenomenon," filtering the past to create a "highly selective, sentimental, and sanitized version" of history (214). This reimagined golden age smoothes out the contradictions and tensions that contain the reality of the past. Anything that has not been sanctioned cannot be historically true, and any attempts to correct the record are met with denials—the records questioned, the interpretations challenged.

The standardized versions of history attempt to exorcise the ghosts of marginalized people and their accomplishments and leave unreconciled gaps in the idealized narrative. These gaps, when examined closely, reveal the inconsistencies in maintaining the mediated record. Lesbians, for example, *are known* to have been nonexistent before the late nineteenth-century when the sexologists described female sexual inversion. Once defined, the lesbian suddenly materializes throughout the twentieth century, randomly appearing across time and space, disconnected from full integration within any specific social environment: "the common image of the homosexual has been a figure divorced from any temporal-social context. The concept of homosexuality must be historicized" (Katz 1992, 6). Jonathan Katz and other historians, as noted earlier, emphasize the need to reposition gay and lesbian experience in the mainstream historical narrative. Their work has uncovered an extensive and, most importantly, a continuous record of lesbian and gay history. What such research accomplishes is the foregrounding of people and events that provides the context necessary for full integration into society's consciousness. Like Nyla Wade these historians have reinterpreted the material and reclaimed what was previously dismissed. Completing the record enables those who have been displaced to find reference points that help solidify a sense of identity, a sense of place.

In the murder investigations of *The Beverly Malibu* and *Liberty Square*, Katherine Forrest also interweaves Kate Delafield's discovery of this expanded sense of lesbian history and of her need to connect with it. This movement is handled differently in the two novels: in *The Beverly Malibu* Delafield's involvement with the history of the McCarthy anticommunist witch hunts provides the motivation for the murder of Owen Sinclair and Dudley Kincaid. Underpinning the obvious political situation that she must unravel, is Kate's introduction to the intricate structure of gay and lesbian actors, producers, technicians, and directors that supported Hollywood.[7] Throughout the investigation Kate learns of the number and influences of homosexuals in the movie industry. For Kate, this is the one positive outcome of the investigation, the recognition and pleasure in seeing the public display of that influence. An early scene in Paula Grant's apartment emphasizes the idea that the position of the observer impacts the facts and how to interpret them. After viewing the posters of famous lesbian centered films—*Queen Christina*, *Personal Best*, *The Hunger*—Kate "glanced at Taylor [her partner] to see if he had discovered the connection between most of these posters." Ed Taylor has not; he reads them from a surface viewpoint. However, Paula Grant, who "missed nothing of [Kate's] survey of the posters," acknowledged the link Kate's own reading has discovered between them (19).

Throughout *The Beverly Malibu*, and earlier works, Forrest has Kate take on the responsibility of becoming the bridge that connects her own and others' isolation from the wider lesbian history and community. Maggie Schaffer, the owner of the Nightwood Bar, has virtually ordered Kate to replace the outdated texts that she had "quickly, eagerly read" (60). Kate bankrolls Maggie's purchase of books and magazines, but they're added to the bar's library only when Kate has finished reading them. Although this brief flashback may seem like an interruption of the primary plot, it encapsulates the emphasis on knowing the past to understand the present. When factual gaps are closed, when the historical record is complete, positive action can result. Kate's reading, of history and of the crime scene, enables her to bring together the threads needed to solve the murders. Kate's historical investigations, in fact, duplicate Forrest's own research for *The Beverly Malibu*. At the end of the book Forrest lists those biographies and histories that helped provide the factual backgrounds for characters. Kate's reading, though, remains a private undertaking. She is not willing, yet, to expand her discoveries beyond the limited circle of the Nightwood Bar. The hurdle she must clear requires Kate to risk linking the private understanding with public revelation. Kate makes this connection during a review of the major suspects:

> *Cyril Crane.* Also had an ideological motive. Sinclair had informed on two gay acquaintances of his. ...
> She tapped her pen on Crane's name. Crane himself had an FBI file closed in 1975.... The non-political Cyril Crane had an FBI dossier because he had been known to them as a homosexual [209].

Her rising anger at the existence of this and other files, and her disgust at a government that would undertake such surveillance, marks a turning point in Kate's gradual movement from isolation to engagement. A line has been crossed from which Kate cannot retreat: she has discovered that the private and personal cannot always be protected from public scrutiny and interpretation. The file, after all, gives a slanted story of Crane, one that fulfills the FBI/government preconceptions. What Kate also comes to realize is that the majority will continue to impose its version of events and its justifications for such an imposition.

The Beverly Malibu is the first book in the Delafield series that specifically requires Kate to immerse herself in a particular historical period. She must become intimate with the events and participants to understand the motivations behind the murders. She must also through her study of the material learn to reconcile her own sense of how the various suspects are related to the outcome. It is not accidental that with each new interview of one of the Beverly Malibu tenants, Kate discovers more details about the McCarthy period. Nor is it surprising that this investigation demands that Kate frequently step out of any active participation to review, compare, read deeper into the background to bring about a successful conclusion. In many ways this investigation echoes the historian's process of weighing detail and interpretations against one another, of shifting versions of events to come to a more accurate record.

In *Liberty Square*, however, Kate's professional distance must be breached; it is only through her specific and intimate participation in the past that the murderer can be discovered. In important ways the investigation is not predominantly about who killed Allan Gerlack, the victim of the present day crime, but how Kate and the others can comprehend their shared experiences in Vietnam. This is the only book in the series in which Kate has no official jurisdiction over the crime scene; her outsider position to the progress of the investigation gives Kate the necessary intellectual and emotional distance from the immediacy of the murder. She and Aimee (her lover) are visiting Washington, DC, initially for Kate to attend FBI seminars, but Aimee has also forced Kate to attend a reunion of her Vietnam comrades. In this way, Kate is freed from any formal investigative responsibility and can pursue the "nonlegal" avenues of finding a resolution.

Kate, having reluctantly agreed to attend a reunion of Vietnam veterans with whom she served, is caught up both as suspect and investigator in the murder of one of the group. She is tentative about the outcome this meeting will have on the careful balance she has maintained in her life: "this weekend was reviving a number of unwelcome verities. About memory, mainly. Memory was lawless and illogical. Arbitrary. Capable of bending back on itself like a ribbon" (36). Kate resents the intrusion Aimee has accomplished; she describes it as being "careless with her past" (37). The exposure of her private self to public comment is not something Kate desires, particularly regarding Vietnam. However, at the novel's opening Kate's fears remain strictly individual; it is her own history that she is uncomfortable revealing, although Aimee looks forward to the promised revelations. Yet, the murder demands not only that Kate open the doors of memory, but that she integrate *her* past with that of others. Even though all the characters shared the same time of service, they have varying perspectives on it; each has a piece to the puzzle that the long night of reminiscences reveals. It will be through the sharing of stories and memories by the other reunion participants that the murderer and motive will be identified; it will also, more importantly, allow all of these characters the opportunity to begin reconciling their Vietnam experience with their present.

The cathartic sharing of the past itself does not solve the question of who killed Allan; what it does provide, through going beneath the basic facts of these characters' tours of duty, is insight into the emotional relationships and consequences this experience has created. Each of the participants moves from present to past with heart-wrenching clarity in order to exorcise the ghosts of real or perceived failures. All of them, including Kate, must return to the same event — the disappearance of Cap — to discover their roles in that event. Cap's absence is the real mystery to be resolved, and everyone keeps retelling the story to learn the truth. To achieve this, Kate must find and integrate several layers of connections among this group of veterans, since each has played a small part in the event; over the course of the evening the others will take up the major narrative or describe other happenings that occurred simultaneously with the story of Cap. As in *The Beverly Malibu*, Kate becomes the linchpin, reconciling the divergent versions of this core moment of shared history, balancing her roles of detective, interviewing suspects and witness, with participant in the experience, trying to get the story told correctly. She must filter events and outcomes from motivation; the public record must be laid out to reveal its inability to tell the whole truth; facts must be separated from speculations.[8]

Because Kate cannot act as the totally objective observer, Aimee Grant becomes Forrest's agent for this separation. Born after the Vietnam War, her questions and reactions frequently set the stage for Kate and the others to explain and comment. Besides learning the terms or the daily routines, Aimee discovers how this period in American history has been revisioned. For example, references are made to China Beach, and Aimee automatically thinks of the television show. During the interchange that follows she comes to realize the sanitizing that was required for television:

> "*China Beach*," Bernie said. "That show at least got some of it right."
> "It didn't get the real China Beach right. We went there together, Kate, remember?" Rachel said.
> "I do," Kate said, and Aimee looked up at her. "I couldn't watch the series. I found two hypo syringes sticking up in the sand, remember?"
> "Sure. Not to mention bloody bandages and assorted garbage washing ashore from *Repose* and *Sanctuary*...."
> "Those were hospital ships in the South China Sea," Doc said to Aimee [171].

Aimee's questions also force Kate to reevaluate her experiences twenty-five years ago and to reexamine her own understanding of them. During much of the evening, Kate develops a dual perspective on her past; at times intensely caught up in the memory, at others able to stand back from the young woman she was and reconcile her past actions with present awareness. One part of this process of integration is understanding the impact Kate's sexual identity has had on her past wartime experience and her present day life.

One of the issues raised for Kate by the reunion is what impact the public revelation of her sexual orientation will have on the others. As the novel develops, the response to homosexuality twenty-five years ago and the present moves to the center of the criminal investigation. As noted above, the key event is to discover what happened to Cap. As the night wears on, the memories begin to circle around the two major events that may have triggered his disappearance: his reporting of two of the reunion participants' shooting of a Vietnamese farmer's water buffalo and the increasing rumors about his sexual orientation. Kate comes to realize that, of the two, Cap's homosexuality proves to be *the* source of the mystery. Even after twenty-five years Cap's fear of exposure and its consequences reverberate into the present when the talk turns to the present-day situation of gays in the military. Kate's own lesbian identity put her at risk and forced her to become "a quick study, learning to skate carefully and discretely within this cesspool, with the advantage over other women marines of having an officer's rank to afford some protection" (133–134). The price paid for this, however, has been Kate's constant awareness of her isolation from any open expression of her identity.

During the novel Kate comes to understand the impact her experience with the institutionalized homophobia of the military has had on herself and others. In fact, the last discussions all deal in some way with homosexuality, whether it is gays in the military, one character comparing the nation's reaction to returning veterans to the treatment of gays and lesbians, to humorous comments on one another's sexuality; underneath the talk, however, strong emotions and reactions are brought to the surface that will set up the novel's climax. The reason the murderer offers for killing Cap during their tour in Vietnam is the water buffalo incident, but his nonchalant admission that "knowing Cap's queer and all, we … have a little fun with him" reveals to Kate the enormity of being gay and the vulnerability, especially during Vietnam (220). Cap's homosexuality privileges the physical assault by his killer; it is another reason to punish him. Cap's sexuality is also the impetus for the present day murder, as the victim, also a gay man, knew Cap was being transferred and was waiting for him. Kate, coming out at this reunion, would have reopened the past and revealed the original crime. The revelation during the evening that the others knew Cap was gay sets up for Kate's discovery that they all suspected her of being a lesbian. Surprising her, too, is their acceptance of this part of her. Kate discovers, perhaps, the most essential consequence of this evening of revelations: that these people have carried an image of her that encompasses her whole identity. Being a lesbian meant and means nothing to these men and women who have shared Vietnam with Kate. It is this recognition and acceptance that brings Kate to the point when she realizes "the essential lesson of this weekend lay in the difference between who she had been before she came here, and who she was now. She had restored the part of herself that she had tried to cut off. Unsparingly taken in her year in Vietnam and integrated it with her self" (234).

Throughout *Liberty Square* Kate and the others constantly look for connections—between time and place, between past and present, between memory and reality. As a woman in a man's world, as a lesbian in a straight environment, Kate Delafield faces the challenge of finding her place not only in the world, but also in the majority community's vision of that world. The movement in *Liberty Square* has been backward in time to redefine Kate's and Cap's experience as homosexual people. Her efforts to realign history's image of the gay presence in the military with the reality she knows allows the reconciliation that takes place at the Vietnam Memorial which closes the novel.

Mary Wings's *She Came by the Book* uses the subject of gay history more explicitly in the narrative; the murder occurs at the banquet celebrating the opening of the Howard Blooming Gay and Lesbian Memorial Archive and involves the content of the journals of Blooming, a Harvey Milk-like character, who had been assassinated during the early days of the gay liberation movement. Several characters, who have had previous personal and public relationships with Blooming, are concerned about what the journals may reveal. The pursuit and preservation of gay and lesbian history parallels the criminal investigation as Emma Victor, Wings's private detective, investigates who murdered the Archive's executive director. Since the motive for the crime is situated in what is written in the journals, the investigation requires Emma to relive the past in order to find the murderer. Digging through the past, however, reveals the tensions among the many gay and lesbian voices that are attempting to control the version of the history that will be preserved and published. Like their straight counterparts, the directors of the Blooming Archive are determined to control and define what is and is not appropriate for inclusion, leaving Emma to comment, that "our Archive looked like any other mausoleum. A cold and dead repository, available for anyone who wanted to hold up a distant mirror, raising facts and feelings from the artifacts of time gone by" (111). It is, in fact, the Archive's refusal to accept the manuscripts of a lesbian writer of popular fiction that sets up the murder.

Emma, who was a participant in the early movement as Blooming's press secretary, takes an ambivalent stand on the meaning and value of preserving the past. Visiting the Archive, in a chapter fittingly called "Preservation," Emma is fascinated to discover evidence of a gay and lesbian historical presence, but she is also wary of the jingoism and chauvinism that drives the ostentatious displays and fuels the turf wars over acquisitions. At the same time, Emma expresses a real sense of loss for what cannot be saved: "I was surrounded by ribbons fading, images fading, the weak ink of early nineteenth-century dyke America, fading, even as we worked to save them" (112). As the novel continues, personal history and community history become tangled and confused, leading to the manipulation of the community for selfish ends on the part of the murderer. Uncovering the past has revealed the identity of the criminal but at the cost of relationships; knowing what happened in the past does not always offer a way to avoid its pitfalls.

Forrest, McConnell, and Wings portray the intense battles over what is included in the historical record and who controls access to it. Nyla Wade, Kate Delafield, and Emma Victor experience the difficulty of claiming their legitimate place within that record. In the fictional world of the detective genre their efforts generally meet with success: Nyla's crusade to save the Ketcham mansion rallies the entire West Coast gay community. Kate's rewards are more private but just as far-reaching; she is able to integrate her private life with the public world she must inhabit as a police officer, enabling her to move in that world with greater comfort and assurance of her lesbian identity. Even Emma achieves some accommodation with the way the past impinges on the present; although Frances, her lover, leaves at the end of the novel, Emma takes stock of what she still has and knows, and plans for the future. These outcomes offer the lesbian reader the potential image of a reconciled relationship with the heterosexual majority; the lost history is proven to be valuable to the entire community. The mansion will provide the draw for tourists to the new Burnton resort center; the military hierarchy does not collapse if the presence of homosexuals is acknowledged; the words and images of the past can be salvaged. Outside of fiction, however, such accomplishments are not always achieved so quickly.

Yet this reality does not undercut the value these texts have for the lesbian reader. The very act of reading as a lesbian, especially reading specifically lesbian texts, encourages a conscious engagement with the explicit and implicit narrative. I read not only for the obvious pleasure of finding out who did it, but I also keep returning to these stories to discover more about who I am and who I am in the world. Terry Castle asserts such a view in the introduction to *The Apparitional Lesbian* (1993):

> We need to recognize how fully, if invisibly, the lesbian has always been integrated into the very fabric of cultural life. This is a paradox of course: just how thoroughly, despite all the hostility ranged against her, she has managed to insert herself into the larger world of human affairs. ... The very feeling of being obliterated by one's society may prompt a wish to assert oneself all the more aggressively — to enter more fully, as it were, into the larger scheme of things [17].

What Delafield, Wade, and Victor accomplish is to bring the invisible background to light. They have not only reread the past, but compelled the present majority to acknowledge their new version of previously determined events.

Much of the theory concerning how lesbians read texts concentrates on how "they actively disassemble the dominant heterosexual plot" (Inness, 1997, 83). Given a text, particularly a straight text, the lesbian reader consciously reinterprets the story and its overt meaning to her own purposes. She takes the explicit narrative, thematic, and character conventions of the work and reassigns them a lesbian centered emphasis, one that satisfies her need to see her experience reflected there. Such a reader engages in what Bonnie Zimmerman (1993) calls "perverse reading," that is consistently and actively reading as a lesbian (139). Reading perversely does not destroy the integrity of the text; rather it encourages responding to a work from a new perspective, "imagining possibilities otherwise ignored and suppressed" (144). This is not a new strategy, especially for women readers; Zimmerman's perverse reading echoes the strategy Judith Fetterley calls the resisting reader, the woman who refuses to accept the portrayals of women found in fiction written by men. Both critics call for an active engagement between the text and its reader that is both enriching and subversive; reading this way opens a work to wider interpretations and brings a marginalized presence into the center of the narrative. Applying these interpretive strategies to overt lesbian texts does not alter the intense connection between reader and work noted above. The fact that a text is written by a lesbian for a lesbian audience may increase the desire to discover oneself within the pages. By presenting diverse images of lesbians and stories that detail the variety of lesbian experience, lesbian authored texts assert the reality and continuity of my community. Narratives like Forrest's, McConnell's, and Wings's show that the mainstream mediated version of lesbian participation in history can be rewritten; as Gillian Whitlock

(1994) attests, such texts "intervene as agents of change, displacing and replacing negative representations of lesbian women with positive ones appropriated from the dominant culture and transformed in the process" (97).

Other lesbian detective writers use a strategy more common to mainstream historical detective fiction; they assume the presence of a recognized set of lesbian-centered references. These may or may not be familiar to the reader, but the author does not use the story itself to challenge the particular historical background incorporated into the narrative. The world that the main characters of these mysteries inhabit is complete and requires no explanations. Because of this total and self-contained presentation, the lesbian reader need not be a perverse or resisting reader; the presumption of normalcy in the descriptions of the main characters' thoughts, behavior, and experience allows the lesbian reader to relax the vigilance usually required when dealing with a text written by a straight author. Unfortunately, the number of historical detective novels written by lesbians is small; I have found three—by Deborah Powell, Lisa Davis, and ReBecca Beguin—who create fully realized historical periods in which lesbians appear as fully involved participants in those worlds.

Houston Town and *Bayou City Secrets*, by Deborah Powell, utilize a specific historical framework, late 1930s Texas, in very traditional ways. Powell has clearly researched the period in order to provide the necessary contextual accuracy, from the glass-topped gasoline pumps to the layout of streets and décor of buildings. Both novels also incorporate references to actual figures in Texas history, such as Ima Hogg, an important person in Houston's political and cultural life of the time, as well as well-known national figures in entertainment, politics, and other areas. Both novels also incorporate the character types familiar to readers of hard-boiled detective novels—gangsters, corrupt politicians, mysterious women, and tough reporters. What then, it may be asked, distinguishes Powell's work from any other mainstream historical mystery. The obvious, but incomplete, answer is the sexual identity of Hollis Carpenter, Powell's lesbian reporter and amateur detective.

More important is Powell's narrative insistence on the complete integration of Hollis into that historical period. Unlike Nyla Wade or Kate Delafield, Hollis does not need to find a way to connect to her surroundings; unlike Emma Victor, Hollis does not express any ambivalence about her relation to events. She is not isolated from any community, whether it's the newsroom or her relationships, because she is a lesbian. Hollis enters *Bayou City Secrets* (the first novel in the series) confident of her sexuality and conscious of how others are aware of it. Confronted by another come on from a coworker, Hollis expertly cuts him off and knows that "[h]e would spend the rest of the morning stumbling around the newsroom telling everyone within earshot what a 'goddamned queer' I was. ... It didn't take too many experiences like that to make you fall down on your knees and thank god you preferred women to men" (6–7). This sense of presence is the hallmark of Hollis Carpenter in both novels; there is no uncertainty, anguish, or fear connected to her sexuality. Neither does Hollis worry what the straight world thinks of her. In fact, her profession has required Hollis to build extensive relationships with people who know that she is a lesbian.

This confidence should not be read as Hollis being blind to the hostility directed toward her as a lesbian. The threats of blackmail, the contempt and disgust directed toward her underscore the danger always present. However, Hollis does not retreat from confronting these reactions. At the climatic confrontation at the end of *Bayou City Secrets* Hollis, in an attempt to goad the murderer into confessing, taunts him: "Are you going to kill her [Lily, his wife] and blame that one on me — the jealous lesbian..." (203). These encounters take place in public and private places, but in each instance Hollis does not retreat from asserting her right to be taken seriously; the "three inch tall bulldyke" that sits on her shoulder goads Hollis to react quickly and forcefully (6). Throughout both novels Hollis's main concerns are getting the story and solving the murders, not on how to reconcile her lesbianism with the larger world.

Hollis, and Powell, assume a familiarity with the signals that identify Hollis as a lesbian to the reader. Descriptions of appearance and clothing, occupations, cultural events, and personalities appear in both works; in *Bayou City Secrets*, for example, Hollis wakes up, looks in the mirror, and reacts, "Oh my God! I look just like Gertrude Stein!" (14). The reference to Stein operates on several levels — historical accuracy for the period, indicator of Hollis's breadth of knowledge, and signifier of lesbian context. The lesbian reader ties the reference to Stein to her own knowledge of Stein's place in a specifically lesbian history. When Hollis identifies herself as Alice Toklas later in the novel, the reader is given another link that widens her associations of lesbians and lesbian history. Not only is the lesbian reader able to link these references, but she becomes aware of the joke Hollis is playing. The Toklas allusion is made during Hollis's attempts to enter a building to meet someone who can help her; the man standing in her way has no idea who Alice Toklas is. But Hollis and the reader do, and this shared sense of pulling one over on the straight world strengthens the reader's sense of connection to the text.

Powell's deliberate utilization, with no explanation, of recognized lesbian historical figures marks a distinct difference from the other works examined here. Unlike those other texts, there is no character who requires that the references to the past be explained: Forrest includes Aimee in Kate's reunion to have a reason for the long explanations of the Vietnam experience of the others; even Emma Victor, who has participated in the very history being saved at the Blooming Archive, finds that she must have certain images explained to her. In this sense *Bayou City Secrets* and *Houston Town* present hermetically sealed worlds that establish the sense that these places and characters are credible. References in *Houston Town*, for example, to the portrait Lily is having painted by Romaine are there to indicate the jealousy Hollis feels about their new relationship. It is the reader who must recognize the full name of the artist — Romaine Brooks — and her position in the circle of lesbian artists, writers, and society figures living in Paris during the 1920s and 1930s. Would the reader's appreciation of this scene be diminished if the reader, even a lesbian reader, had no idea what this reference meant? Since its purpose is to reveal Hollis's fear of Lily breaking off their relationship, knowing the full background of the artist is not essential for understanding the story at this point. But as with the Toklas reference noted above, the reader who does know the complete story has an additional sense of satisfaction, because in a different, perverse sense, by not having to be explained, this history has become standard and needs no explanation.

The recognition of lesbian history and, more importantly, its inclusion in a genre text, reinforces the value of Zimmerman's perverse reading strategy. Powell's Hollis Carpenter books accomplish the foregrounding of a distinctly lesbian sensibility that offers no explanation or justification for existing. Genre fiction, especially, gives the reader the opportunity to practice such reading. Since a genre like the mystery adheres strictly to its conventional requirements, the adaptations made by a writer become spotlighted:

> The pleasures and transgressions involved in the experience of popular fiction are a constant reminder that a better, more fulfilled life is a possibility. Popular fiction engages in modernity's need to colonise (sic) the future, to project new worlds for ourselves. It engages with the modern sense of the ambivalent, indeterminate nature of the present, a sense that the past has not finished who we are and that the future is still open [McCracken 1998, 14].

More importantly, such reconfigurations of the detective story's conventions, so long as the author does not violate them, allow the incorporation of characters, relationships, and outcomes less likely to be found in other types of fiction. Throughout *The Reader and the Detective Story* George

Dove examines the nature of this relationship and the interdependence that exists between audience and text. So long as the basic expectations of the crime and the pursuit of its solution are met, the mystery writer can manipulate setting, motives, the process of the investigation, and its resolution.

Hollis's world, then, simply is; her sexuality simply is. She inhabits her world fully and easily, achieving all of her desires—the solution to the crime, the scoop for her paper, and "finally begin my vacation. With Lily" (*Houston Town*, 20). The view of the world has been shifted because Hollis is a lesbian who moves through a clearly described setting that assumes the inevitability of her history, and this new perspective revises the implications a reader may take from the text. After all, it is the power of "popular fictions [to] saturate the rhythms of everyday life ... and define our sense of ourselves, shaping our desires, fantasies, imagined past and projected futures," and by reconstructing the frames of reference, Powell has created an environment that encourages the lesbian reader to imagine herself fully integrated in time and place (Bromley 1988, vii).

This same immersion of the reader into the world of a 1929 air derby or the1949 gay club life of New York City is found in Beguin's *Hers was the Sky* and Davis's *Under the Mink*. Both books contain the same richly detailed descriptions that concretize time and place and provide the appropriate backgrounds for the characters. In Beguin's mystery, the emphasis of the story rests on the determination of the women "to demonstrate," as Hazel Preston says, "that we women are ready to be career pilots" (3). However, a second narrative appears as the derby plot develops; the reader becomes privy to the ways that lesbians in this period expressed their sexuality and sexual lives. The relationship between Hazel and Jo, one that seems solid in the beginning of the novel, begins to unravel as Hazel finds herself attracted to other pilots in the derby due to Jo's increasing discomfort with being identified as a lesbian, an identity Hazel willing accepts, as the following exchange shows:

> Jo's head tilted back as she laughed incredulously. "Ha!—You are one for living notoriously after all. At my expense now, I see. I just didn't dream you'd take up with someone at the drop of a hat...."
>
> [Hazel replies] "Yes, I do like to be around people who accept me for what I am, no pretenses. I wanted it to be with you, damn it. You have done nothing to encourage me. Well, I can't live like that. I don't live notoriously: I simply live about as honestly as I can" [117].

Jo's ambivalence continues until the end of the novel when she tells Hazel that " I can't live like you and Maxie. I don't know whether the looks I get, the whispers I hear are because of ... of that or just because I'm a pilot" (177).

As with Powell, Beguin does not break the narrative movement to explain what "that" is, although there have been clear indications of the attraction of one woman for another and the consummations of such attraction throughout the story. There is no secondary character who becomes the recipient of another's explanation of the context (like Aimee) nor is there any other method of slipping in information that would help frame Jo's attitude and behavior (like Nyla being able to read the unpublished history of the Ketcham house). The date of the derby, Jo's reference to high school crushes, and other almost incidental references provide the means for a reader to understand Jo's reluctance to be identified as "that." Two views of women were competing at this period in history: one was of the woman who had broken with the restrictive beliefs and expectations about her abilities and desires; the other responds to the reactionary impulses that saw the liberated woman as a threat to decency and society. The lesbian, who during the 1920s had enjoyed a level of acceptance and admiration not seen again until the era of lesbian chic in the late 1980s and early 1990s, was by the 1930s being labeled a sexual invert, a deviant who could not fit into the mainstream.[9] Hazel's acceptance of Jo's departure and her finding the chance of a new relationship is not sufficient to erase the undercurrents of unease and threat directed at women who reject male society's vision of their abilities. R. Taggart, who is revealed as the cause of the accident that kills one of the female pilots, articulates this position: "You girls ought to know better than to play a man's game. You should've thought about that before you started the race. We play rough to win" (182).

Not surprisingly, the motive for Taggart is not homophobia so much as it is greed; however, in Davis's *Under the Mink*, what today is called gay panic is the reason for the death of Skip Fletcher-Payne. In 1949 New York, gays and lesbians exist in a shadow world of mob protected clubs, fear of police harassment and brutality, constant derision from heterosexuals, and limited options for creating a successful life. By this time lesbians and gays have disappeared from the notice of mainstream society. Their existence has been compromised and contained by the legal, medical, religious, and other social institutions. Yet, as Blackie Cole illustrates, if you are willing to accept the restrictions placed on your behavior, you can create some semblance of an ordinary life. Once known as Blanche Cohen, Blackie has reinvented herself as a cabaret-style singer at the Candy Box Club; here dressed in a tuxedo and crooning like Frank Sinatra, Blackie enjoys a large following of gay and straight admirers. Although her involvement in the murder and investigation is accidental, Blackie becomes intent on finding out who killed Skip and why. During the course of the novel the reader follows Blackie and her friends as they maneuver between the cops and crooks, acceptance and dismissal. As the investigation continues Blackie will be arrested in a raid on the club, face the anger of Stevie, the Club's manager, and escape being beaten by thugs. Even when the killer is found, Blackie must face the consequences of becoming involved with the power brokers who manipulate the legal systems that control the lives of the gay and lesbian characters. Skip's father, John Jay Fletcher Payne, is a newspaper publisher who is willing to sell his endorsement for mayor to the highest bidder; the police hierarchy is full of officers who give lip service to ending corruption yet make their weekly runs for payoffs from gangsters like Stevie. Like much hard-boiled detective fiction, the resolution of the initial crime does not reflect the earnest commitment to justice of a detective; rather the end comes when the majority of players are trapped in a widening spiral of corruption among the various people involved. Most are trying to save themselves and shift suspicion to others rather than work for justice.

While the investigation progresses, Blackie takes the reader into the reality of lesbians and gay men of the time. What is particularly stressed is the seemingly strict delineation of homosexual representation: although gender postioning may be fluid — women dress and behave as men and men assume the dress and attitudes of women — gender behavior is rigid. Blackie, for example, is stereotypically butch, with the all of the outward cues of masculinity — dress, look, and behavior. Frequently Blackie is mistaken for a young man, which is a response she prefers. Interestingly though, at the novel's conclusion, Blackie is dressed in a skirt and blouse — what she refers to as "travel[ing] in drag" — as she boards a train with her girl friend Renee (262). In order to escape being abducted by thugs Blackie uses her easily mistaken identity to get away. As she is being forced into a car, a police officer, assuming she is a young man, interferes and Blackie reacts: "No matter how much she didn't trust cops, she feared a spin with Stevie's button men more. She dropped her voice into its lowest register. 'I got nuthin' to do with them dirty stinkin' faggots'" (255). The officer, following the surface cues that say Blackie is, indeed, a young man, turns his attention to the gangsters and Blackie manages to escape.

This tension between a character's surface presentation and intrinsic identity becomes an important point of connection between the text and the reader. The reader is given a glimpse into the tenuous world of pregay liberation and comes to appreciate the desire for claiming a safe space revealed by these characters. Throughout the novel, none of the gay or lesbian characters indicate any sense of internalized homophobia; they are seen as a group that shares in the positive and negative responses of others and have developed a loose support system among themselves. It is the straight characters who reveal discomfort with their own sexuality (most of them end up visiting Lucille Martin's bordello). Not surprisingly, the only family described in the novel — the Fletcher-Paynes — exhibits a range of dysfunctions, including the mother's alcoholism, the daughter and son's promiscuity, and the father's abuse. Skip's desire to become a member of the Candy Box chorus line underscores not only his sexual orientation, but his need for a supportive community as well. As with Powell and Beguin, Davis's novel, while fulfilling its genre requirements, presents an accurate picture of this historical place and time. Davis does not indicate the degree of research she did for her novel, but the settings and cultural markers described in the novel reflect the actual experience of gays and lesbians of the period. The reality behind Davis's fiction is provided by George Chauncey's *Gay New York*, which presents the history of the development of the city's gay community and culture in the first half of the twentieth-century.

In a 1989 interview Katherine Forrest asserted, "I don't have any confusion in my mind about who my audience is. I'm a lesbian writer and I write for a lesbian audience..." (qtd. in Marchino 1995, 65). Finding a history for this audience has required the deliberate reimagining of the dominant majority's version of the past. It has demanded the identification of lesbian and gay men as participants in and makers of those events. As the authors examined here show, the key issue is who controls the telling of the story and what story is to be told. In all of these texts the narrative perspective belongs to the lesbian, whether she tells her story personally or not. She directs not only the investigative process, but also guides the reader through the revision of events to uncover the hidden specter of the lesbian past. Through these characters' efforts the reader is encouraged to recognize that lesbians have been present in the world from the beginning and that their contributions cannot be written out of the record.

Conclusion: Gathering the Evidence

> This process of seeing oneself in print in a mass-market format provides a kind of identification which carries the mark of a subcultural identity and the authority of a mass-cultural reality. Lesbians describe this event variously as making them feel joyful or "quite cold and frightened." The image is there, widespread and readily available material for the process of lesbian identification. The process by which we react to that image is highly variable, but nevertheless, an identification.— Meredith Miller, 2001, par. 53

> In my thirty years on this planet, I have probably read hundreds of mysteries.— Jaye Maiman, *I Left My Heart* 25

I began my investigation of lesbian detective fiction with a basic question — what is the value in these texts for lesbian readers? Marilyn Farwell (1996) provides one answer:

> As a single, "severely literal" heroic figure, the lesbian character in popular lesbian fiction offers a sense of power and possibility to hungry lesbian readers who have encountered little either inside or outside of school which portrays them with anything but disdain. As could be expected, these stories are satisfying because writers assign the active narrative role to a self-conscious lesbian who makes her own decisions and decides her own fate. It is a role that most lesbians see as their chosen or unchosen role in life, and they want it given heroic status [137].

Heroism isn't just facing danger, rescuing the girl, or catching the crook; for the lesbian, heroism also includes braving social antagonism for declaring her sexuality, daring to build a community with other lesbians, deliberately seeking to be a participant in the public institutions that direct one's life, and building a complete and satisfying romantic relationship with another woman. Most of us, lesbian, gay, or straight, look to our culture for models; we hope to find ourselves represented in the wider world.

We also hope that those images show us in the most positive light, that we see acceptance, support, and possibility. Those of us on the margins know, however, that we must look long and hard for those portrayals. Even in the twenty-first century, popular forms still show us through negative stereotypes: young black men are gangsters or rappers; Mexicans are all illegals; gay men are pedophiles or fashion experts; lesbians just need a good man to set them straight. But cracks in these surfaces are beginning to show and, perhaps not surprisingly, popular culture itself is often the catalyst for reframing these dominant images.

I have referenced Philip Fisher's concept of the transformative power of popular literature several times throughout my examination of lesbian detective fiction. Fisher's contention that such texts perform a valuable function by making the unthinkable person, place, or action part of ordinary experience is shown to be true with the increasing visibility of gay and lesbian characters on mainstream television, with Hispanic or African American actors in luxury car advertisements, with disabled people eating at fast food restaurants. When the reader or viewer no longer comments on such "rainbow" casting, Fisher's transformative process has worked. This is not to suggest, however, that such inclusion is sufficient; there is still much that has to be done for the full integration of all minorities into the mainstream. But, with Fisher, I would suggest that popular forms, especially genre fiction, can effectively help in moving that process forward.

In genre fiction, whether it is romance, detective, or science fiction, utilization of clearly articulated narrative and structural conventions gives the reader a sense of familiarity and security; the reader knows what to expect when a book opens with a dead body or a young woman in an isolated mansion, and as critics of popular literature assert, "Formulas enable the audience to explore in fantasy the boundary between the permitted and the forbidden and to experience in a carefully controlled way the possibility of stepping across this boundary" (Cawelti 1976, 35). Popular fiction is able to balance the conservative literary expectations of the reader with the radical ideological explorations of the author, and instead of the book being thrown aside, the reader accepts the adaptation because it fits in with one's requirements for satisfaction. The critics of feminist detective fiction remind us that what could have had the potential to turn away readers—the introduction of the female investigator and crimes dealing with women's issues—instead achieved a widening of its readership: "[t]his is due in part to the crossover potential of genre fiction, which appeals both to readers who identify with the often marginalized identity of the detective and to those who identify with the conventions of the genre itself" (Walton and Jones 1999, 40). What was once unthinkable is now commonplace. This movement of popular forms incorporating previously omitted groups has now brought lesbian lives into focus. While the majority of lesbian detective novels are still published by small presses, a number of those written by major lesbian authors have found major publishing houses or their imprints willingly publishing and marketing them.[1] The first indicator of the growing acceptance of innovations within a popular genre is the increased availability of the work; obviously, the more access to a work, the more readers. Entering the mainstream also brings the attention of the reviewers; for example, Redmann's paperback edition of *The Intersection of Law and Desire* (1997) contains blurbs not only from gay newspapers and magazines (*Lambda Book Report* and *Seattle Gay News*) but major mainstream ones as well (*Kirkus Review* and *Library Journal*). Sandra Scoppettone's *Everything You Have Is Mine* (1992) was reviewed by the *New York Times Book Review*—the epitome of mainstream critical attention. The next marker of acceptability for the marginal text is its inclusion by academic critics in their surveys and examinations of a particular genre or literary time period. My own bibliography lists the works of many of the dominant figures in the fields of popular culture and literature and detective fiction who have brought such writers as Forrest, Wilson, Wings, and McConnell into their analyses. While not all of the writers mentioned in my preceding chapters have enjoyed the same level of attention, part of my intent has been to widen the circle to show the expanding production of this fiction. That so many writers are choosing the detective genre, regardless of the publisher or reviews, may be seen as another indicator of the renegotiation of texts once seen as undesirable. What such an increase also suggests is that lesbian readers find something compelling in these stories to keep them entertained.

As I have shown throughout this book, what attracts the lesbian reader centers first on the basic fact that she sees herself reflected in the characters; for those who have never had this experience, the result is often stunning, to realize that you are not the only woman who feels an attraction for another woman, that you have discovered models on which you can fashion a sense of who you are. Ann Bannon, in an interview with Katherine Forrest (2002), summarizes the exhilaration felt by the author who creates these images; what she describes easily fits the response of the lesbian reader opening the pages of a lesbian authored and centered text: "We did achieve something. We built a bridge to isolated, frightened women and told them they were not alone. And we told the tales that moved our own hearts. We were exploring a corner of the human spirit that few others were writing about, or ever had" (9). Once this moment of recognition has been assimilated, the reader is given the opportunity to match her experiences with those portrayed by the characters. The lesbian reader is able to compare her position within society to that of the characters; like the detective she investigates the situations that confront the development of a successful engagement with that larger society. As the lesbian characters in the work devise strategies to guarantee their survival, the reader is free to evaluate the possibility of success and understand the consequences of failure. The lesbian reader follows the detective's progress, sees her overcome professional and personal obstructions, and applauds her triumphs.

Besides finding a sense of belonging through the reading of such texts, the lesbian reader is given an understanding and appreciation of the ways being lesbian has changed and what has contributed to those shifts. She uncovers, through those novels that position the narrative within a specific historical period, how sexual difference was played out in that environment, and she gains an appreciation for the methods her predecessors devised to maintain their place in that world. A lesbian reader today may pick up a detective novel from the early 1980s and learn about the substantive issues gay men and lesbians faced; she may also find out about the controversies discussed within the homosexual communities; for example, the shifting portrayals of the AIDS crisis or the debates over lesbian sexual practice.[2] She can also enjoy the descriptions of the various ways lesbian culture was lived; for example, the transformation from the flannel shirt, work boots, and short hair to shaved legs, makeup, and decorator furniture. The lesbian reader watches the characters move from almost subsistence living conditions to attain middle-, even upper-class status, and she listens to them discuss marriage, having children, and balancing work and home. The reader discovers that she has a wide range of social, sexual, and cultural positions from which to construct her life; she appreciates that she is not locked into being butch or femme. Carol Ashton, for example, the tough police inspector, looks like a fashion model. The reader realizes that gender is fluid so she can fashion herself as feminine, masculine, or something in between. Katherine Forrest's most recent novel, *Hancock Park* (2004), has the secondary plot of Kate Delafield becoming involved in finding her missing niece; at its conclusion the reader and Kate discover that the niece is transgendered. Simply stated, these works "develop a complex and contradictory set of expectations about lesbian identity, a representation of lesbianism which is finely tuned in historical and social detail" (Whitlock 1994, 113).

Perhaps the greatest value to be found in lesbian detective fiction is its assertion of the ordinariness of lesbian experience; like anyone, the detective desires to create a range of relationships that answer all of her needs. She craves intimacy with a loving partner as well as a circle of friends, straight and gay, with whom she can interact. She wants to have a career that challenges her skills and rewards her talents. And, as the detective searches for the answers to the crime and to her own mystery, the reader is encouraged by the success in both of the investigator's endeavors. This list may appear to sugar-coat the dangers and limitations faced by marginal groups; however, the lesbian reader is also shown the deep-seated hatred many people hold toward her and the outcomes of that response. Even if lesbians are not actively discriminated against in these texts, characters are shown pushed to the margins or their efforts disregarded by those is control. But, the conventions of genre fiction provide a temporary containment, even punishment, of the hostility that provokes such behavior and disrupts the everyday, commonplace events of life. Detective fiction, particularly, asserts that through the committed efforts of the investigator the routines of life can be restored, and because of the strong identification made between the reader and the detective, "it becomes possible for readers to move, on occasion, from the world(s) of mystery fiction to the real world, expecting to apply what they have learned from the former to the demands of the latter" (Kelly 1998, 194).

This portrait of the lesbian as just like everybody else parallels the real radical impact of the fiction; while showing that lesbian experience can be placed within frames of reference understandable to mainstream, heterosexual society, at the same time, these texts can be seen as encouraging their readers to revolution. When I pick up a detective novel, written by a lesbian author, detailing the ability of lesbian characters to engage with people and institutions unwilling to acknowledge their existence and succeeding, I become part of a community of readers experiencing the same recognition and approval for those efforts:

> The breaks we have made as lesbians come from acting, from daring to create something new, and from being willing to risk making mistakes. Further, what we create, including change in our reactions and perceptions, is not valuable because of its permanence but because it contributes to a lesbian ground of be-ing, because it sparks and stimulates and helps create a context in which lesbians can continue to engage, to create, to make choices [Hoagland, 1988, 301].

I will close the book and return to my daily life, but I will carry with me possibility.

Chapter Notes

Introduction

1. Lauren Wright Douglas's Caitlin Reece series was published by Naiad Press, which has undergone financial troubles and organizational difficulties in recent years. Naiad Press is no longer publishing, although some of the authors from Naiad have been picked up by Bella Books. Douglas's novels have not been picked up by Bella or so far as can be determined any other publisher. Redman's early Micky Knight novels were originally published by New Victoria, a small independent press. Later works were published by W.W. Norton, indicating the increasing popularity of some lesbian authors and their marketability.

2. The dependence of the mystery genre on maintaining its rigid structure is central. The format such structures take and the relationship of the reader to the mystery novel varies depending on the particular critic's viewpoint. For example, John Cawelti in his now standard analysis, *Adventure, Mystery, and Romance: Formula Stories as Art and Popular Culture* (Chicago: University of Chicago Press, 1976), highlights the connection between literary convention and an essential human need for recognition and engagement with the familiar. George Dove, in *The Reader and the Detective Story* (Bowling Green, OH: Bowling Green State University Popular Press, 1997) emphasizes the concept of the detective novel as a game that involves the reader as an "interested spectator" (19) who comes to the text knowing what the rules of play are and engages with the text in a pleasurable reading experience. The reader looks to see how the author works within the rules while offering enough experimentation to keep the reader's interest. R. Gordon Kelly's analysis of the detective story in *Mystery Fiction and Modern Life* (Jackson: University Press of Mississippi, 1998) incorporates the importance of trust between author and reader. Within the novel itself trust involves the ability of the detective to interrogate the circumstances of the crime with a certain reliance on the crediblility of testimony and action. The reader of the novel trusts that the author is working honestly with the established conventions.

3. See Maureen Reddy's *Traces, Codes, and Clues: Reading Race in Crime Fiction* (New Brunswick, NJ: Rutgers University Press, 2003).

4. This comment was made by Wilson during a question-and-answer period held after a panel discussion on the mystery novel held in Philadelphia during Equity Pride Week in 2001.

Chapter 1

1. A representative sample of such critical approaches includes John G. Cawelti, *Adventure, Mystery, and Romance: Formula Stories as Art and Popular Culture* (Chicago: University of Chicago Press, 1976); Greg Forter, *Murdering Masculinities: Fantasies of Gender and Violence in the American Crime Novel* (New York: New York University Press, 2000); Christine Jackson, *Myth and Ritual in Women's Detective Fiction* (Jefferson, NC: McFarland, 2002); R. Gordon Kelly, *Mystery Fiction and Modern Life* (Jackson: University Press of Mississippi, 1998); Stephen Knight, *Crime Fiction, 1800–2000; Detection, Death, Diversity* (Basingstoke, Hampshire, UK:

Palgrave Macmillan, 2004); and Erin A. Smith, *Hard-Boiled: Working-Class Readers and Pulp Magazines* (Philadelphia: Temple University Press, 2000).

2. Because the word *lesbian* carries with it a multiplicity of meanings and responses, any study of lesbian texts requires some definition of the term itself. Theories of lesbian identity range from Adrienne Rich's concept of the "lesbian continuum," which suggests that woman-to-woman attraction covers the widest possible varieties of relationships, from sexual to emotional to ideal. This concept can be found in Rich's *Of Woman Born* (New York: Bantam, 1977) and among the essays collected in *On Lies, Secrets, and Silence: Selected Prose, 1966–1978*. (New York: W. W. Norton) More recent queer theory deals with the concept of the fluidity of sexual orientation/identification, particularly the notion of the performance of gender, a social construct which one manipulates to respond to or match specific situations (cf. Kate Bornstein's *Gender Outlaw: On Men, Women, and the Rest of Us* (New York: Routledge, 1996) and Marjorie Garber's *Vested Interests: Cross-Dressing & Cultural Anxiety*) (New York: Routledge, 1992). The social and psychological history of lesbians also contributes to the debate regarding the term's meaning as well as stability. My own understanding and use of the word *lesbian* rests, first, on my own identification as a woman whose emotional, physical, and relational experience is woman-focused and centered. This description falls into what can be considered a middle-of-the-road position. While I accept that there is some flexibility in how the word is applied and expressed, I believe there is a fundamental construct that characterizes a lesbian based on how the lesbian positions herself in relation to and in contrast with the various environments within which she is situated. (My definition pulls together a number of theoretical strands from such critics as Lillian Faderman (1981; 1991), Terry Castle (1993), Julie Abraham (1996), Judith Roof (1991), and others. My examination of the authors and the main characters in the novels uses the word *lesbian* according to this traditional, perhaps conservative, definition.

3. For an introduction to the history of sexuality and sexual identity see Joseph Bristow's *Sexuality* (London: Routledge, 1997).

4. The ways by which one lesbian recognized another varied according to time, place, class, and race. See Lillian Faderman"s *Odd Girls and Twilight Lovers: A History of Lesbian Life in Twentieth-Century America* (New York: Columbia University Press, 1991) and Elizabeth Lapovsky Kennedy and Madeline D. Davis, *Boots of Leather, Slippers of Gold: The History of a Lesbian Community* (New York: Penguin Books, 1994). The difficulty or ease of finding a community also fluctuated. Sometimes homosexuals were able to congregate freely with little interference from the law; at others, they were constant targets. George Chauncey's *Gay New York: Gender, Urban Culture, and the Making of the Gay Male World, 1890–1940* (New York: Basic Books, 1994), while focusing on the history of gay men, provides a full description of such shifts.

5. Given my focus on detective novels, I have limited this overview of lesbians in literature to fictional representations only.

6. Castle (1993) asserts that "[t]he spectral figure is a perfect vehicle for conveying what must be called — though without a doubt paradoxically — that 'recognition through negation' which has taken place with regard to female homosexuality in Western culture since the Enlightenment. Over the past three hundred years, I would like to suggest, the metaphor has functioned as the necessary psychological and rhetorical means for objectifying — and ultimately embracing — that which otherwise could not be acknowledged" (60). Inness, in *The Lesbian Menace* (1997) states, "Lesbians are always aware that the dominant heterosexual narrative of most fiction is a myth that fails to reveal the content of lesbian lives. Thus lesbian readers search for the lesbian subtext that speaks to them and their experiences" (83). For both critics, lesbian characters and narratives must be teased out of mainstream literature.

7. Marilyn Farwell (1996), in describing the impact of the introduction of a female into the dominant position in a narrative, points out that such a change in the narrative subject's gender creates a shift within the text itself, as well as in the expectations of the reader, breaking through the traditional descriptions and representations of action and response: "Thus, when a woman occupies the space of the hero or lover she is differently aligned to power but not necessarily either devoid of it nor necessarily absorbed by the maleness of the binary structure" (59). Standard categories of narrative organization and development become

reconfigured, particularly when the alterations result from the introduction of a lesbian character by a lesbian writer.

8. The "blue wall" is a feature not only of many police procedurals, but reflects the reality of life in the precinct. In *Armed and Dangerous: Memoirs of a Chicago Policewoman* (New York: Tom Doherty, 2001) Gina Gallo continually references the importance of an officer's success being based on her ability and willingness to "cover her ass" and watch her partner's back.

9. It is interesting to note that more and more, particularly in books published since 2000, the chain of command embodies a more accepting attitude toward out lesbian officers. The tensions between superior and subordinate more often emphasize standard work-related issues—following procedure, maintaining acceptable arrest statistics, and the like. The main character's sexuality, instead of being seen as a detriment to the smooth operations of the institution, may actually be an asset because of the specialized insight or connections the officer brings to an investigation. See, for example, the Hate Crimes Unit in the Lieutenant Maglione series or the special pornography task force in Detective Sergeant Rebecca Frye Justice series. More often the detective's sexuality becomes a nonissue. What seems to be happening, especially for lesbian readers, is a repositioning of sexuality not only within the context of the narrative, but outside the boundaries of the text. As Cathy Cole (2004) asserts, "[c]rime fiction also makes use of its temporality, of its times, in ways that many other forms of fiction fail to do, and an understanding of the cultural and political context of its stories generally offers readers new insights into the world in which the text is set" (199). Being a lesbian cop is no longer the issue; being a good cop is.

10. The cliché of the detective, regardless of her status as amateur, professional, or police officer, as a loner reaches back to Poe's Auguste Dupin, and despite the adaptations in narrative and characterization, this quality of being separated from others, whatever the cause, remains constant.

11. Examples of the first scenario include Lauren Wright Douglas's Caitlin Reece, Mary Wings's Emma Victor, and E. Reece Johnson's Cordelia Morgan. In the second category can be found Lori Lake's Dez Reilly and Jaylynn Savage, Radclyffe's Rebecca Frye and Catherine Rawlings, and Kaye Davis's Maris Middleton and Lauren O'Conner.

Chapter 2

1. Juhasz's discussion deals specifically with lesbian romance novels and points out a basic gap in my research. I have found very little formal discussion of romance within the standard criticism of the detective genre, and when romantic or sexual relationships are treated, they generally fall into examinations of the femme fatale and the hard-boiled detective (Cawelti, Haut 1999, Knight 2004, Malmgren 2001, and Erin Smith 2000) or the negative effects sexual encounters or romance have for the female detective (Patricia Johnson, Pope, Reddy in *Sisters in Crime*). These views are based on heterosexual relationships; most of the critics do not deal with lesbian or gay texts in their work. Feminist critics of the genre do treat lesbian texts, but I have found a certain repetition in the selection of texts examined; the critics will mention other writers and works but tend to concentrate on Barbara Wilson's Pam Nilsen novels, Mary Wings's early Emma Victor books, and Katherine Forrest's first Kate Delafield procedurals. The subject matter of their analyses, the way the romantic plot intrudes on the detective plot or the reinforcement or reinterpretation of heterosexual relational dynamics, dominate their analyses. More often the emphasis of the discussion shifts away from sex to sexuality and the ways in which these texts and characters address the broader concerns of gender identity and behavior. Romantic attraction and sexual behavior get pushed aside when the critical attention changes.

I have found it necessary, therefore, for my discussion of the roles sex and romance play in lesbian detective fiction to look at the critical work done on lesbian pulp fiction, as well as general studies of the romance novel itself. I will also be highlighting the romance plot over the criminal investigation in my references to the novels.

2. For a fuller discussion of the negative critical response to the romance see Pamela Regis, *A Natural History of the Romance Novel* (Philadelphia: University of Pennsylvania Press, 2003).

3. I am taking for granted that the primary reader of a romance is a woman.

4. Radway identifies the Smithton readers as the regular customers of a bookstore salesperson named Dorothy Evans, whose recommendations for romance novels were highly regarded. Over a nine-month period, using interviews and questionnaires, Radway explored these women's romance reading preferences and habits.

5. Radway identifies a thirteen-step narrative sequence (see chapter 4 "The Ideal Romance"). Regis reduces the number to what she calls the "eight essential elements" (see chapter 4 "The Definition Expanded") in the romance's narrative movement (30). Each critic, obviously, interprets the heroine's progress through these stages differently. Radway emphasizes the heroine's loss of identity and the role of the hero in reestablishing it; Regis positions the heroine as the principal actor in her movement toward achieving the desired outcome of an engagement/wedding.

6. See Janet Todd, *Women's Friendship in Literature* (New York: Columbia University Press, 1980) and Nina Baym's *Women's Fiction: A Guide to Novels by and about Women in America, 1820–1870* (Ithaca, NY: Cornell University Press, 1978).

7. See Judy Hilkey's *Character Is Capital: Success Manuals and Manhood in Gilded Age America* (Chapel Hill: University of North Carolina Press, 1997). For a more complete discussion of the historical processes at work at the end of the nineteenth century see Faderman's *Surpassing the Love of Men* (1981) and *Odd Girls and Twilight Lovers* (1991). For overviews of the psychological influences see Lynda Hart's *Fatal Women* (1994) and chapter four, "Freud Reads Lesbians," in Judith Roof's *A Lure of Knowledge* (1991).

8. It is interesting to note that the detective who is a member of a police force, whether male or female, does not operate within the same set of behaviors. Unlike the private detective, the police officer's procedures for investigating a crime are prescribed by the institution; the officer must adhere to these guidelines or face censure, even dismissal for any infraction. While it is true that many fictional officers believe in and do bend the rules to bring in the perpetrator, it is also important to note that those rules are not broken. The officer who crosses the line by engaging in illegal activity becomes a rogue cop, an exile, and is no longer part of the community.

9. For a fuller description of the transformation of the romantic hero see Radway, chapter 4, "The Ideal Romance."

10. See Reddy (1988), Plain (2001), C. Cole (2004), and Munt (1994).

11. The scholarly work on lesbian pulp novels remains available predominately through individual articles that can be found in both academic and popular journals. To my knowledge no full-length study of this material is currently available. While the references I have consulted do not provide a total view of these works, they do offer some of the dominant historical background and theoretical discussions taken towards the pulps.

12. All of the critics of the pulps emphasize their value for the readers. Yvonne Keller summarizes this impact this way: "Thus, pro-lesbian pulps constitute — along with literary fiction, nascent homophile organizations, and the public space of gay bars — the beginnings of a readily available representation of lesbian community and resistance that was soon to erupt to a new level with the 1969 Stonewall riots and their aftermath" (20).

13. A random selection of such books includes Cath Phillips's *River's Edge* (1997), Kim Baldwin's *Hunter's Pursuit* (2005), Gerri Hill's *Hunter's Way* (2005), C. N. Winters' *Irrefutable Evidence* (2003), and Talaran's *Vendetta* (2001).

Chapter 3

1. Cathy Cole (2004) presents a detailed discussion of this essential contradiction that is the foundation of all mystery stories. She wonders why crime writers "give voice to the murderous ravings of lunatics?" (86). Throughout the chapter in which she examines this question, Cole looks at the kind of violence and the extent to which it is described; she concludes by stressing the mythic/symbolic values embodied in the sometimes ritualistic character of the crimes and their perpetrators, highlighting the point that detective fiction replays a fundamental human tension between good and evil. She ends her discussion, quoting from Sandrine Berges' unpublished doctoral dissertation, that "[crime novels] force us to confront and reflect on the presence of evil that we face on an everyday basis. And by presenting it in the context of a criminal

investigation, the crime novel makes the ordinary evil extraordinary, forces us to divorce it from conventional perceptions, and to react to it in new, unprejudiced ways ... that what is being depicted is part of our world, and that it is a part that we could do well not to ignore" (120).

2. Throughout her memoir, Gina Gallo points out the role sex plays within the Chicago Police Department. Expectations that men and women will, and do, use sex as a means to promotion, a method to control others, and a way to maintain status are expressed at every level of the institution: " Sex as a stress reducer is as common for some cops as sex to relieve boredom, sex to dispel anger, sex because it's there. Sex as a tool to facilitate release. Sex for any imaginable reason..." (244). Chapter 21, "COP-ulation," particularly, highlights the ways in which sex permeates the institution.

3. Donna Wade's 1996 article on lesbian officers from *The Lesbian News* relates the experience of several out lesbians and describes how they still confront discrimination, although such acts generally take less overt forms.

4. The parallels between Lewis's fictional representation of a woman's experience and Gallo's memoir are striking, despite the five years that separates them. The range of attitudes and behaviors Gallo and the fictional Fitzpatrick face and how they confront them are also eerily consistent.

5. Society's smooth functioning relies on the trust of the individual that the various systems will operate smoothly and honestly. Kelly (1998) references the work of Anthony Giddens (1990) on the importance for the expert/professional to negotiate this relationship by developing the appropriate expertise in a particular situation: "Learning, perfecting, and maintaining the requisite demeanor is thus a critical part of the socialization of those people who staff access points, particularly in circumstances involving risk and danger. Perfecting the requisite professional demeanor means managing one's emotions and subordinating spontaneous emotionality to rational control" (5). The police force and the individual officer illustrate clearly the importance of the transaction of trust. The risk and danger referenced in the quotation apply both to the officer and to the civilian, and both put their faith in the unarticulated agreement that each party will fulfill its part by following departmental procedures, in the case of the officer, and by obeying the enforcement of the law by the citizen.

Chapter 4

1. The silent, passive, docile woman has been a standard literary figure throughout history, from *The Odyssey*'s Penelope through Shakespeare's Desdemona, from Alcott's Beth March to Fitzgerald's Daisy Buchanan. Such fictional characters embody a set of particular social and cultural concepts that delineate what being female is. Of course, what constitutes appropriate feminine behavior changes over time, but certain characteristics remain constant: reticence in speech and action; limitations of options in the public realm; denial of expressing sexuality; and acquiescence to others' definitions of one's self. Numerous critical discussions of this particular history are available: see, for example, Frances B. Cogan, *All-American Girl: The Ideal of Real Womanhood in Mid-Nineteenth-Century America* (Athens: University of Georgia Press, 1989); Joanne Dobson, *Dickinson and the Strategies of Reticence: The Woman Writer in Nineteenth-Century America* (Bloomington: Indiana University Press, 1989); Karen Halttunen, *Confidence Men and Painted Women: A Study of Middle-Class Culture in America, 1830–1870* (New Haven, CT: Yale University Press, 1982); Diane Price Herndl, *Invalid Women: Figuring Feminine Illness in American Fiction and Culture, 1840–1940* (Chapel Hill: University of North Carolina Press, 1993); Mary Kelley, *Private Woman, Public Stage: Literary Domesticity in Nineteenth-Century America* (New York: Oxford University Press, 1984); Barbara Welter, *Dimity Convictions: The American Woman in the Nineteenth Century* (Athens: Ohio University Press, 1976).

2. Kate Borenstein, transgender activist, identifies such behavior as "gender attribution, whereby we look at somebody and say, 'that's a man,' or 'that's a woman.' And this is important because the way we perceive another's gender affects the way we relate to that person" (*Gender Outlaw: On Men, Women and the Rest of Us* (New York: Routledge, 1994, 24). In her study of cross-dressing Marjorie Garber (1992) emphasizes the relationship between the superficial social codes that a society uses to delineate and assign suitable constructs of gender

and the actual performance of gender (see particularly chapter 1, "Dress Codes, or the Theatricality of Difference").

3. This rather broad summary is based on standard critical studies of detective fiction, particularly those highlighting the hard-boiled narrative, including Cawelti (1976; 2004), Forter (2000), and Knight (2004): Woody Haut, *Neon Noir: Contemporary American Crime Fiction* (London: Serpent's Tail, 1999); Carl D. Malmgren, *Anatomy of Murder: Mystery, Detective and Crime Fiction* (Bowling Green, OH: Bowling Green state University Popular Press, 2001); Erin A. Smith, *Hard-Boiled: Working-Class Readers and Pulp Magazines* (Philadelphia: Temple University Press, 2000).

4. Cathy Cole's (2004) analysis of crime fiction highlights the ways in which female detectives influence the construction of the crime novel and the implications of incorporating specifically feminist ideology into the storyline. Cole asserts that the female detective must "be familiar with male ways and, while challenging them, move within male spaces *to decode male ways of doing things*" (139; emphasis added).

5. Other critics emphasize this ritualistic, mythic aspect of the uses of violence within the detective genre. Violence and its perpetrators represent the dark, unknowable aspects of life. They traffic in death, forcing the rest of society, as portrayed in the text, to confront the reality of the body's annihilation. Many times the detective will experience some symbolic death, or real near-death experience, and her return offers hope of redemption for the individual and for the community. See Cole's chapter "The Moral Zone of Crime Fiction"; Christine A. Jackson's *Myth and Ritual in Women's Detective Fiction* (Jefferson, NC: McFarland, 2002)

6. See Greg Forter's *Murdering Masculinities: Fantasies of Gender and Violence in the American Crime Novel* (2000) for a discussion of the relationship between masculinity, violence, and identity.

7. The focus of Mizejewski's analysis is film and television representations of female detectives; however, her examination of how this figures' sexuality is defined in the show and, interestingly, by the audience indicates an ambiguity in the range of responses, from corporate executives who call for reworking of characters to make them appear less masculine or butch to lesbian fan clubs for these same women. Mizejewski frames her position in chapter 1 and expands it more fully in chapter 3.

8. For a fuller discussion of the motives of female readers, see Cathy Cole's *Private Dicks and Feisty Chicks* (2004), particularly chapter 1, "The Box Under the Bed (On Reading and Writing Crime."

9. Lynda Hart's study, *Fatal Women: Lesbian Sexuality and the Mark of Aggression* (1994), examines the mechanisms by which violence in women becomes a marker of the lesbian. Freud's and other psychologists' ideas about the nature of desire between men and women included the perceived inability of women to develop fully integrated personalities, and women's innate moral weakness that makes them more prone to criminality. Using these ideas Hart argues that in order for female hostility, particularly as embodied in the woman criminal, to be rationalized and contained it is projected onto the body of the lesbian: "Criminal anthropology, sexology, and psychoanalysis shared in the complex historical construction of the female offender. Each in its own way linked criminality with deviant sexualities. These discourses overlapped and sometimes contradicted each other. If it is in their imbrications that we can read a hypostatization of the 'lesbian' as criminal, it is in their internal disturbances that we can see a series of phobic displacements of criminality only lesbianism" (28).

10. Farwell gives a close analysis of the relationship between the lesbian as subject and the broader idea of woman as subject: "Each construction of the lesbian subject, I argue, oscillates between sameness and difference, utopian essentialism and deconstructive nonessentialism, and woman and not-woman" (68). See her fuller development of her position in chapter 3 "The Lesbian Subject: A War of Images."

11. Sherrie Inness, in *The Lesbian Menace* (1997), and Judith Roof, in *A Lure of Knowledge: Lesbian Sexuality and Theory* (New York: Columbia University Press, 1991) examine the uses of the term *butch* as it is applied within and outside of a homosexual context. Both provide detailed analyses of the multiplicity of meanings of butch, whether it reflects a style of dress or behavior, a sexual identity, or a political/ideological construct for the lesbian. They also show how the term and its meanings have shifted over time, and both critics stress that who is butch and what butch signifies

must remain fluid for lesbians. For Inness, "we need to make sure that we do not create definitions that function to delineate who is a 'proper' lesbian and who is not. Articulating the elements that make up various queer identities ... is vitally important in order to understand how gender is produced and performed among lesbians and gay men" (203). For Roof, "[l]esbian sexuality exists more at the interstices of multiple differences rather than necessarily constituting a core identity strong enough to completely fix an individual. Such an essential identity tends to come from outside — from a phallocentric culture, for whom the category lesbian is sufficient" (251).

12. Although I agree with Walton and Jones's assertion that "[t]alking back to masculine authority traditionally has been viewed as inappropriate behavior for women," I disagree with their contention that "it is a mode of resistance more plausible and ethical — and potentially subversive — than, say, physical violence" (131). The quick response that challenges a criminal's reputation or ability can momentarily distract his intentions, and does provide a concrete representation of the female detective's intelligence and toughness. However, the criminal's most common response to such wisecracks or comments is to begin or continue a physical assault on the detective. Should she be able to avert the attack, when the characters next meet, the residual effect is an increase in the felon's anger and possibly more intense violence when she is not able to evade the situation.

Chapter 5

1. These opening paragraphs are meant to present, to my best ability, a broadly framed discussion of this complex subject. Analyses of morality involve a number of scholarly disciplines, from philosophy to psychology to sociology, not to mention the numerous differences in viewpoint and interpretation offered by critics and theorists. Even finding a language that tries to present a value-free discussion is difficult. I will, for example, be using the terms *moral* and *ethical* (and their variations) synonymously, although in formal philosophical discussions they are sometimes seen as distinct. As noted above, McGinn asserts that our basic knowledge of what is moral or good behavior ultimately rests on a shared sense of, basically untranslatable, understanding. He also states, "the human ethical sensibility works best when dealing with particular persons in specific contexts; abstract generalities are not the natural *modus operandi* of the moral sense. Partly because philosophy is so wedded to generalities, such moral *concreta* tend to be ignored — they are felt to be too saturated in detail; but this shows a naïve and oversimplified view of the relation between the particular and the general" [3]. Suggesting, in other words, that attempts to establish all-encompassing descriptions of moral behavior (and by implication, immoral behavior) do not provide a sense of completeness because they ignore the variety of specific moral representation.

2. See Colin McGinn's (1997) discussion of this point in his chapter, "The Evil Character."

3. In *Murder Most Foul: The Killer and the American Gothic Imagination* (Cambridge, MA: Harvard University Press, 1998) Karen Halttunen examines the content and meaning of the variety of nonfictional descriptions of crime, especially murder. Her basic premise is that "through salvation history was losing cultural power in the late eighteenth century, the search for meaning in the face of violent transgression did not disappear with that older framework. The new secular accounts of murder endeavored to replace the sacred narrative with a new mode of coming to terms with the crime" (3). What were once published as vehicles for showing the power of God's redemptive grace or as warnings of the just punishment for breaking the law, became stories of inexplicable horror that were no longer comprehensible. Instead of reminding the reader that everyone was capable of such acts and to behave according to shared moral precepts, these tales began to separate the criminal from society and labeled the act deviant, views, which Halttunnen believes, have become intrinsically embedded in modern day attitudes toward crime and its perpetrators.

4. I find it intriguing that the primary literary text Walker uses to establish her discussion of moral repair is Toni Morrison's novel *Jazz*, which uses a murder as the starting point for Morrison's exploration of love, jealousy, and the consequences of their collision.

5. See Cawelti's *Mystery, Violence, and Popular Culture* (2004) and *Adventure, Mystery, and Romance* (1976). This view of the

hard-boiled detective has also been discussed by Greg Forter (2000) and Woody Haut (1999), among others.

6. Much critical commentary focuses on the language of the hard-boiled detective; it is typically described as terse, concrete, colloquial, and clear. Such linguistic mannerisms "give a feeling of straightforwardness and authenticity ... [and] the impression of objectivity — [the detectives'] reticence implies a refusal to engage with and thus become implicated in the corrupt world that surrounds them." (Walton and Jones 1999, 123). I would also suggest that such hesitation to speak may reflect a lack of experience with the language of relationships and intimacy as well as a fear of revealing a more sympathetic component of his personality. Further discussion of the hard-boiled detective's language also appears in Erin Smith's *Hard-Boiled: Working-Class Readers and Pulp Magazines* (2000).

7. See Katherine Klein's discussion of the well-known feminist detectives V. I. Warshawski, Kinsey Milhone, and Sharon McCone in *The Woman Detective: Gender and Genre*, 2nd ed. (Urbana. University of Illinois Press, 1995).

8. Sandra Tomc in her essay "Questing Women: The Feminist Mystery after Feminism," suggests that in the final confrontation between the detective and the criminal she assumes the status of the victim, since, as a woman, she is also subject to the same forces that have brutalized the original victim (50). Tomc's examples, it must be noted are all heterosexual women, usually members of a police force and, therefore, more likely to be trapped in this conflict of allegiance. Tomc does indicate that the female private detective has the ability, although constrained, to "put a dent in the machinery responsible for [her own victimization's] perpetration. And in a sense her defeat of the criminal each time is what allows her to entertain options, like living and working alone, since it illustrates to her, and to us, the possibility of her altering the conditions of her victimization" (52).

9. Rebecca Pope's essay, ""Friends is a Weak Word for It': Female Friendship and the Spectre of Lesbianism in Sara Paretsky," examines the intensity of the relationship between V. I. Warshawski and Lotty Hershel, noting how V. I. turns to Lotty for moral, emotional, and physical support that she feels no one else can give her. Their relationship, Pope suggests, is more than mother-daughter, but less than lovers.

10. See Winnie Tomm (1992), especially pages 101–104.

11. What follows is an overview of Hoagland's theoretical position. I am, of course, interpreting her ideas and applying them to my own analysis, where the fit may not be exact. Hoagland, after all, is examining the way lesbians must operate within the dominant society as well as within their own communities. She carefully describes the extent of patriarchy's efforts, what she calls the "society of the fathers," to deny the existence of lesbians (and other marginalized peoples) through its control of access to systems of power and its ability to force the marginalized to submit to its demands. Hoagland is also concerned with explaining the strategies that lesbians must develop to insure their survival, especially the importance of creating and maintaining lesbian identity and community: " When we interact as lesbians, out of that interaction comes the meaning of our lesbian lives. When we do not interact as lesbians, there can be no lesbian value" (9).

12. The implied threat of Delta Stevens losing her badge came to fruition in the subsequent novels in the series. She is no longer a member of the police force and has left the country in later novels in the series.

13. The idea that gender is not fixed, but rather a series of performances that individuals create has been discussed from a variety of theoretical positions. See Marjorie Garber's *Vested Interests* and Kate Borenstein's *Gender Outlaw*.

Chapter 6

1. The critical response to the way history is incorporated in a text depends to a great extent on how the text is perceived. Toni Morrison's *Beloved*, for example, receives extensive attention for the way the actual Margaret Garner's experience has been transformed to perform a variety of interpretive tasks. Overly simplified, the real Garner acts as a palimpsest for Sethe, allowing Morrison the opportunity to explore the intersection of past and present. Margaret Mitchell's *Gone with the Wind*, while considered a book worthy of critical study, is looked at more as a representative of a specific cultural moment and for the

accuracy of its depictions of time and place. Criticism of Mitchell's novel can most often be found in studies of popular fiction or culture as well as in examinations of historical changes in the roles and views of women. Barbara Hambly's mysteries, set in antebellum New Orleans, receive no critical attention at all, except for reviews.

2. For fuller discussion of the rationale and method of how history is shaped see Roger Bromley's *Lost Narratives: Popular Fictions, Politics and Recent History* (London: Routledge, 1988); James W. Loewen's *Lies My Teacher Told Me: Everything Your American History Textbook Got Wrong* (New York: Touchstone, 1995): David W. Blight's *Race and Reunion: The Civil War in American Memory* (Cambridge, MA: Belknap-Harvard University Press, 2001); and Michael Kammen's works. (1993, 1997)

3. Even a cursory summary of the efforts taken by scholars and critics to bring women's lives and experiences out of the background would extend well beyond the scope of my study of lesbian detective fiction. Their efforts have forced a reevaluation of the position of women throughout time and required a reexamination of the impact and influence women have had in society. Just in the field of literary study, the critical work of Annette Kolodny, Judith Fetterley, Nina Baym, Sandra Gilbert, Susan Gubar, bell hooks, Adrienne Rich, and many, many others has essentially altered the nature of text, the variety of interpretation, and the value of representation.

4. Perhaps it is not so surprising that lesbian romance novels more often use historical settings to develop the story. One of the best known, and earliest, is Isabel Miller's *Patience and Sarah*, originally published in 1969. Miller's novel effectively combines history as literary convention and subject matter in her reimagining of the lives of real persons (See Miller's "Afterword.") Miller's book echoes another historical couple — the Ladies of Llangollen, whose relationship may have inspired the numerous romances set in the Regency period of England. Other common historical periods for historical lesbian romances include, the American West, ancient Greece, the eighteenth century, especially stories of pirates, the Civil War, the early twentieth century, as well as World War II.

5. I have consciously chosen not to include mystery novels that build the narrative on family histories (Joan Drury's *Silent Words*). First, to do so would require much more time and space than I have in order to bring in the appropriate critical support and consider the points of connection and difference between personal and public history. Second, of the mysteries I have read that use the family history plot, none make any deliberate connection between the particular family and the wider world. While there may be historical references, they usually only provide accurate descriptive detail or settings.

6. For a full discussion of the cancelled Hiroshima exhibit see Edward T. Linenthal and Tom Engelhardt, eds. *History Wars: The Enola Gay and Other Battles for the American Past* (New York: Henry Holt, 1996). One of the numerous studies published during the lead-up to the 500th anniversary of Columbus's first voyage is John Noble Wilford, *The Mysterious History of Columbus: An Exploration of the Man, the Myth, the Legacy* (New York: Knopf, 1991).

7. Anyone interested in fuller discussions of the history of homosexuals in Hollywood can begin with Diana McLellan, *The Girls: Sappho Goes to Hollywood* (New York: LA Weekly Books, 2000); Axel Madsen, *The Sewing Circle* (New York: Birch Lane Press, 1995); David Ehrenstein, *Open Secret: Gay Hollywood, 1928–2000* (New York: Perennial, 2000); William J. Mann, *Behind the Screen: How Gays and Lesbians Shaped Hollywood, 1910–1969* (New York: Penguin, 2002); Vito Russo, *The Celluloid Closet: Homosexuality in the Movies*, rev. ed. (New York: Harper & Row, 1987).

8. As with *The Beverly Malibu*, Forrest provides a short list of books she used to research the background for *Liberty Square*. The following works update and expand those sources: Zsa Zsa Gershick, *Secret Service: Untold Stories of Lesbians in the Military* (Los Angeles: Alyson Books, 2005); Allen Berbue, *Coming Out Under Fire: The History of Gay Men and Women in World War Two* (Northampton, MA: Free Press, 1990); Winni Weber, *Lesbians in the Military Speak Out* (London: Madwoman Press, 1993).

9. For a more detailed discussion of this period of transition see Lillian Faderman's *Surpassing the Love of Men* (1991) and *Odd Girls and Twilight Lovers: A History of Lesbian Life in Twentieth-Century America* (New York: Columbia University Press, 1991). Lynda Hart's *Fatal Women* (1994) and

Lisa Duggan's *Sapphic Slashers* (2000) also describe the process by which the sexologists and psychologists of the time constructed a picture of lesbians and their relationships that placed them outside of society.

Conclusion

1. A small sample of this transfer of publishers includes, Ellen Hart's Jane Lawless series moving from Seal Press to Ballantine and St. Martin's; Katherine V. Forrest from Naiad to Berkley; J. M. Redmann from New Victoria to Avon. Other lesbian authors have been connected to mainstream publishers from their first books: Randye Lordon with St. Martin's; Sandra Scoppettone with Ballantine.

2. In a large number of novels set in the 1980s and early 1990s, AIDS frequently becomes the motive behind the initial murder, either as a punishment for being infected (Molly Hite's *Breach of Immunity*), fear and shame by the family (McNab's *Dead Certain*, 1992), or the "justification" for a hate crime (Forrest's *Murder by Tradition*, 1993). Very briefly and oversimplified, during the 1980s and early 1990s there were sometimes heated discussions in popular and academic formats of what forms of sexual expression were considered "correct" for lesbians. These conflicts were connected to the on-going debates over the impact of pornography on women. Some lesbians advocated the appropriation of the language and practice of sadomasochism as a way of rejecting the dominance of conservative and patriarchal notions of proper sexual behavior; others saw S/M as a mimicking of heterosexual roles that were just as detrimental. Barbara Wilson uses this issue as the narrative base for *The Dog Collar Murders* (1989), and Kate Allen has her main character, Alison Kane, become part of the S/M subculture.

Works Cited

Abraham, Julie. *Are Girls Necessary?: Lesbian Writing and Modern Histories*. New York: Routledge, 1996.
Allen, Kate. *Tell Me What You Like*. Norwich, VT: New Victoria, 1993.
Avenue, N. H. *For Pete's Sake*. New York: iUniverse, 2004.
_____. *Letter Perfect*. Lincoln, NE: Writers Club, 2001.
Baldwin, Kim. *Hunter's Pursuit*. Philadelphia, PA: Bold Stroke, 2005.
Baym, Nina. *Women's Fiction: A Guide to Novels by and about Women in America, 1820–1870*. Ithaca, NY: Cornell University Press, 1978.
Beal, M. F. *Angel Dance: A Classic Lesbian Thriller*. Freedom, CA: Crossing 1990. Orig. pub. 1977.
Beale, Elaine. *Murder in the Castro*. Norwich, VT: New Victoria, 1997.
Beguin, ReBecca. *Hers Was the Sky*. Norwich, VT: New Victoria, 1993.
Berges, Sandrine. "The Hardboiled Detective as Moralist: Ethics in 'Crime Fiction.'" From an unpublished doctoral dissertation, Department of International Relations/Philosophy, Bilkent University, Ankara, Turkey.
Bird, Delys, ed. *Killing Women: Rewriting Detective Fiction*. Sydney, Australia: Angus & Robertson, 1993.
Blight, David W. *Race and Reunion: The Civil War in American Memory*. Cambridge, MA: Belknap-Harvard University Press, 2001.
Bohan, Becky. *Sinister Paradise*. Northboro, MA: Madwoman, 1993.
Bornstein, Kate. *Gender Outlaw; On Men, Women and the Rest of Us*. New York: Routledge, 1994.
Bowers, Sharon. *Lucifer Rising*. Tacoma, WA: Justice House, 1999.
Bravmann, Scott. *Queer Fictions of the Past: History, Culture, and Difference*. Cambridge, UK: Cambridge University Press, 1997.
Bristow, Joseph. *Sexuality. The New Critical Idiom*. London: Routledge, 1997.
Bromley. Roger. *Lost Narratives: Popular Fictions, Politics and Recent History*. London: Routledge, 1988.
Browne, Ray B. "Introduction." In *Heroes and Humanities: Detective Fiction and Culture*. Ed. Ray B. Browne. Bowling Green, OH: Bowling Green State University Popular Press, 1986.
_____ and Lawrence A. Kreiser, Jr. eds. *The Detective as Historian: History and Art in Historical Crime Fiction*. Bowling Green, OH: Bowling Green State University Popular Press, 2000.
Burch, Beverly. *On Intimate Terms: The Psychology of Difference in Lesbian Relationships*. Urbana: University of Illinois Press, 1993.

Castle, Terry. *The Apparitional Lesbian: Female Homosexuality and Modern Culture.* New York: Columbia University Press, 1993.

Cawelti, John, *Adventure, Mystery, and Romance: Formula Stories as Art and Popular Culture.* Chicago: University of Chicago Press, 1976.

———. *Mystery, Violence, and Popular Culture.* Madison: University of Wisconsin Press, 2004.

Chandler, Raymond. "The Simple Art of Murder." In *The Longman Anthology of Detective Fiction.* Eds. Deane Mansfield-Kelley and Lois A. Marchino. New York: Pearson Education, 2005. Orig. Pub. 1944.

Chauncey, George. *Gay New York: Gender, Urban Culture, and the Making of the Gay Male World, 1890–1940.* New York: Basic Books, 1994.

Christianson, Scott. "Talkin' Trash and Kickin' Butt: Sue Grafton's Hard-boiled Feminism." In *Feminism in Women's Detective Fiction.* Ed. Glenwood Irons. Toronto: University of Toronto Press, 1995.

Clare, Baxter. *Bleeding Out.* Ithaca, NY: Firebrand Books, 2000.

———. *Last Call.* Tallahassee, FL: Bella Books, 2004.

Cobley, Paul. *Narrative. The New Critical Idiom.* London: Routledge, 2001.

Cogan, Frances, B. *All-American Girl: The Ideal of Real Womanhood in Mid-Nineteenth Century America.* Athens: University of Georgia Press, 1989.

Cole, Cathy. *Private Dicks and Feisty Chicks: An Interrogation of Crime Fiction.* Freemantle, Western Australia: Curtin University Books, 2004.

Cole, Eve Browning and Susan Coultrap-McQuin. "Toward a Feminist Conception of Moral Life." In *Explorations in Feminist Ethics: Theory and Practice.* Eds. Eve Browning Cole and Susan Coultrap-McQuin. Bloomington: Indiana University Press, 1992.

Corliss, R. S. *Conspiracy of Swords.* New Orleans, LA: Jane Doe, 2001.

Cowart, David. *History and the Contemporary Novel.* Carbondale: Southern Illinois University Press, 1989.

Crosby, Sara. "The Cruelest Season: Female Heroes Snapped into Sacrificial Heroines." In *Action Chicks: New Images of Tough Women in Popular Culture.* Ed. Sherrie Inness. New York: Palgrave/Macmillan, 2004.

Davidson, Diane. *Deadly Rendezvous.* Huntington, NY: Rising Tide, 1994.

Davis, Lisa. *Under the Mink.* Los Angeles, CA: Alyson, 2001.

Davis, Todd F., and Kenneth Womack. "Preface: Reading Literature and the Ethics of Criticism." In *Mapping the Ethical Turn: A Reader in Ethics, Culture, and Literary Theory.* Eds. Todd F. Davis and Kenneth Womack. Charlottesville: University Press of Virginia, 2001.

Dobson, Joanne. *Dickinson and the Strategies of Reticence: The Woman Writer In Nineteenth-Century America.* Bloomington: Indiana University Press, 1989.

Douglas, Lauren Wright. *The Always Anonymous Beast.* Tallahassee: Naiad, 1987.

Dove, George. *The Reader and the Detective Story.* Bowling Green, OH: Bowling Green State University Popular Press, 1997.

Dreher, Sarah. *Stoner McTavish.* Norwich, VT: New Victoria, 1985.

Duberman, Martin, Martha Vicinus, and George Chauncey, Jr. eds. *Hidden from History: Reclaiming the Gay and Lesbian Past.* New York: Meridan, 1990.

Duggan, Lisa. *Sapphic Slashers: Sex, Violence, and American Modernity.* Durham, NC: Duke University Press, 2000.

Faderman, Lillian. *Odd Girls and Twilight Lovers: A History of Lesbian Life in Twentieth-Century America.* New York: Columbia University Press, 1991.

———. *Surpassing the Love of Men: Romantic Friendship and Love Between Women from the Renaissance to the Present.* New York: William Morrow, 1981.

Farwell, Marilyn. *Heterosexual Plots and Lesbian Narratives*. New York: New York University Press, 1996.
Fisher, Philip. *Hard Facts: Setting and Form in the American Novel*. New York: Oxford University Press, 1987.
Forrest, Katherine V. "Acts of Individual Valor: Katherine V. Forrest Talks to Fifties Pulp Fiction Queen Ann Bannon." *Lambda Book Report* Feb. 2002: 6–9.
———. *Amateur City*. Tallahassee: Naiad, 1984.
———. *Apparition Alley*. New York: Berkley Prime Crime Book, 1997a.
———. *The Beverly Malibu*. Tallahassee: Naiad, 1989b.
———. *Hancock Park*. New York: Berkley Prime Crime Book, 2004.
———. *Liberty Square*. New York: Berkley Prime Crime Book, 1997b.
———. *Murder at the Nightwood Bar*. Tallahassee: Naiad, 1989a.
———. *Murder by Tradition*. Tallahassee: Naiad, 1993.
Forter, Greg. *Murdering Masculinities: Fantasies of Gender and Violence in the American Crime Novel*. New York: New York University Press, 2000.
Foster, Marion. *The Monarchs are Flying*. Ithaca, NY: Firebrand, 1987.
Fox, Ellen L. "Seeing through Women's Eyes: The Role of Vision in Women's Moral Theory." In *Explorations in Feminist Ethics: Theory and Practice*. Eds. Eve Browning Cole and Susan Coultrap-McQuin. Bloomington: Indiana University Press, 1992.
Friedman, Marilyn. "Feminism and Modern Friendships: Dislocating the Community." In *Explorations in Feminist Ethics: Theory and Practice*. Eds. Eve Browning Cole and Susan Coultrap-McQuin. Bloomington: Indiana University Press, 1992.
Frye, Marilyn. "A Response to *Lesbian Ethics*: Why Ethics?" In *Feminist Ethics*. Ed. Claudia Card. Lawrence: University of Kansas Press, 1991.
Gallo, Gina. *Armed and Dangerous: Memoirs of a Chicago Policewoman*. New York: Tom Doherty, 2001.
Garber, Marjorie. *Vested Interests: Cross-Dressing & Cultural Anxiety*. New York: Routledge, 1992.
Gilligan, Carol. *In a Different Voice: Psychological Theory and Women's Development*. Cambridge, MA: Harvard University Press, 1982.
Gilligan, Sharon. *Danger in High Places*. Huntington Station, NY: Rising Tide, 1993.
Goldsby, Gabrielle. *Wall of Silence*. Nederland, TX: Quest, 2003.
Gomel, Elana. *Bloodscripts: Writing the Violent Subject*. Columbus: Ohio State University Press, 2003.
Graskey, Roselle. *October Echoes*. Port Arthur, TX: Renaissance Alliance, 2002.
Halttunen, Karen. *Confidence Men and Painted Women: A Study of Middle-Class Culture in America. 1830–1870*. New Haven, CT: Yale University Press, 1982.
———. *Murder Most Foul: The Killer and the American Gothic Imagination*. Cambridge, MA: Harvard University Press, 1998.
Hamer, Diane. "'I Am a Woman': Ann Bannon and the Writing of Lesbian Identity in the 1950s." In *Lesbian and Gay Writing: An Anthology of Critical Essays*. Ed. Mark Lilly. Philadelphia: Temple University Press, 1990.
Harne, Lynne. "Beyond Sex and Romance?: Lesbian Relationships in Contemporary Fiction." In *Beyond Sex and Romance?: The Politics of Contemporary Lesbian Fiction*. Ed. Elaine Hutton. London: Women's Press, 1998.
Hart, Ellen. *Hallowed Murder*. Seattle: Seal Press, 1989.
Hart, Lynda. *Fatal Women: Lesbian Sexuality and the Mark of Aggression*. Princeton, NJ: Princeton University Press, 1994.
Haut, Woody. *Neon Noir: Contemporary American Crime Fiction*. London: Serpent's Tail, 1999.

Heidensohn, Frances. *Women in Control?: The Role of Women in Law Enforcement*. New York: Oxford University Press, 1992.
Herndl, Diane Price. *Invalid Women: Figuring Feminine Illness in American Fiction and Culture, 1840–1940*. Chapel Hill: The University of North Carolina Press, 1993.
Herrmann, Anne. "Imitations of Marriage: Crossdressed Couples in Contemporary Lesbian Fiction." *Feminist Studies* 18 (Fall 1992): 609–24.
Hilkey, Judy. *Character is Capital: Success Manuals and Manhood in Gilded Age America*. Chapel Hill: University of North Carolina Press, 1997.
Hill, Gerri. *Hunter's Way*. Tallahassee: Bella, 2005.
Hite, Molly. *Breach of Immunity*. New York: St. Martin's, 1992.
Hoagland, Sarah. *Lesbian Ethics: Toward New Value*. Palo Alto, CA: Institute of Lesbian Studies, 1988.
_____. "Lesbian Ethics and Female Agency." In *Explorations in Feminist Ethics: Theory and Practice*. Eds. Eve Browning Cole and Susan Coultrap-McQuin. Bloomington: Indiana University Press, 1992.
Hodgman, Helen. *Passing Remarks*. New York: Ballantine Books, 1996.
Inness, Sherrie. *Intimate Communities: Representation and Social Transformation in Women's College Fiction, 1895–1910*. Bowling Green, OH: Bowling Green State University Popular Press, 1995.
_____. *The Lesbian Menace: Ideology, Identity, and the Representation of Lesbian Life*. Amherst: University of Massachusetts Press, 1997.
_____. *Tough Girls: Women Warriors and Wonder Women in Popular Culture*. Philadelphia: University of Pennsylvania Press, 1999.
Iser, Wolfgang. *The Act of Reading: A Theory of Aesthetic Response*. Baltimore: Johns Hopkins University Press, 1978.
Jackson, Christine. *Myth and Ritual in Women's Detective Fiction*. Jefferson, NC: McFarland, 2002.
Jamneck, Lynne. *Down the Rabbit Hole*. Tallahasee: Bella, 2005.
Johnson, Patricia E. "Sex and Betrayal in the Detective Fiction of Sue Grafton and Sara Paretsky." *Journal of Popular Culture* 27 (Spring 1994): 97–106.
Juhasz, Suzanne. "Lesbian Romance Fiction and the Plotting of Desire: Narrative Theory, Lesbian Identity, and Reading Practice." *Tulsa Studies in Women's Literature* 17(1998): 65–82.
Kammen, Michael. *In the Past Lane: Historical Perspectives on American Culture*. New York: Oxford University Press, 1997.
_____. *Mystic Chords of Memory: The Transformation of Tradition in American Culture*. New York: Vintage, 1993.
Kappeler, Victor, Richard Sluder, and Geoffrey Alpert. *Forces of Deviance: Understanding the Dark Side of Policing*. Prospect Heights, IL: Waveland, 1994.
Katz, Jonathan. *Gay American History: Lesbians and Gay Men in the U.S.*, rev. ed. New York: Meridian, 1992.
Keller, Yvonne. "Pulp Politics: Strategies of Vision in Pro-Lesbian Pulp Novels, 1955–1965." In *The Queer Sixties*. Ed. Patricia Juliana Smith. London: Routledge, 1999.
Kelley, Mary. *Private Woman, Public Stage: Literary Domesticity in Nineteenth-Century America*. New York: Oxford University Press, 1984.
Kelly, R. Gordon. *Mystery Fiction and Modern Life*. Jackson: University Press of Mississippi, 1998.
Kennedy, Elizabeth Lapovsky, and Madeline D. Davis. *Boots of Leather, Slippers of Gold: The History of a Lesbian Community*. New York: Penguin, 1994.
King, Laurie. *A Grave Talent*. New York: Bantam, 1995.
_____. *With Child*. New York: Bantam, 1997.

Klaich, Dolores. *Heavy Gilt*. Tallahassee: Naiad, 1988.
Klein, Kathleen. *The Woman Detective: Gender and Genre*. 2nd ed. Urbana: University of Illinois Press, 1995.
Knight, Stephen. *Crime Fiction, 1800–2000: Detection, Death, Diversity*. Basingstoke, Hampshire, UK: Palgrave/Macmillan, 2004.
Lake, Lori. *Gun Shy*. Nederland, TX: Quest, 2001.
Lewis, Catherine. *Dry Fire*. New York: W. W. Norton, 1996.
Lieber, Julia. *There Came Two Angels*. Los Angeles: Alyson, 2004.
Loewen, James W. *Lies My Teacher Told Me: Everything Your American History Textbook Got Wrong*. New York: Touchstone, 1995.
Lordon, Randye. *Brotherly Love*. New York: St. Martin's, 1993.
Lundeen, Kathleen. "Who Has the Right to Feel? The Ethics of Literary Empathy." In *Mapping the Ethical Turn: A Reader in Ethics, Culture, and Literary Theory*. Eds. Todd F. Davis and Kenneth Womack. Charlottesville: University Press of Virginia, 2001.
Maiman, Jaye. *Crazy for Loving*. Tallahassee: Naiad, 1992.
———. *Every Time We Say Goodbye*. Tallahassee: Naiad, 1999.
———. *I Left My Heart*. Tallahassee: Naiad, 1991.
Malmgren, Carl D. *Anatomy of Murder: Mystery, Detective and Crime Fiction*. Bowling Green, OH: Bowling Green State University Popular Press, 2001.
Marchino, Lois. "Katherine V. Forrest: Writing Kate Delafield for Us." In *Women Times Three: Writers, Detectives, Readers*. Ed. Kathleen Gregory Klein. Bowling Green, OH: Bowling Green State University Popular Press, 1995.
Marcy, Jean. *Dead and Blonde*. Norwich, VT: New Victoria, 1998.
Martin, Susan Ehrlich. *Breaking and Entering: Policewomen on Patrol*. Berkeley, CA: University of California Press, 1980.
McAllister, Melanie. *The Lessons*. Minneapolis: Spinsters Ink, 1994.
McConnell, Vicki P. *The Burnton Widows*. Tallahassee: Naiad, 1984.
———. *Mrs. Porter's Letter*. Tallahassee, F: Naiad, 1982.
McCracken, Scott. *Pulp: Reading Popular Fiction*. Manchester, UK: Manchester University Press, 1998.
McGinn, Colin. *Ethics, Evil, and Fiction*. Oxford: Clarendon Press/Oxford University Press, 1997.
McNab, Claire. *Accidental Murder*. Ferndale, MI: Bella, 2002.
———. *Blood Link*. Tallahassee: Bella, 2003.
———. *Body Guard*. Tallahassee: Naiad, 1994.
———. *Chain Letter*. Tallahassee: Naiad, 1997.
———. *Cop Out*. Tallahassee: Naiad, 1991.
———. *Dead Certain*. Tallahassee: Naiad, 1992.
———. *Death Club*. Tallahassee: Naiad, 2001.
———. *Death Down Under*. Tallahassee: Naiad, 1990.
———. *Double Bluff*. Tallahassee: Naiad, 1995.
———. *Fall Guy*. Tallahassee: Bella, 2004.
———. *Fatal Reunion*. Tallahassee: Naiad, 1989.
———. *Inner Circle*. Tallahassee: Naiad, 1996.
———. *Lessons in Murder*. Tallahassee: Naiad, 1988.
———. *Past Due*. Tallahassee: Naiad, 1998.
———. *Set Up*. Tallahassee: Naiad, 1999.
———. *Under Suspicion*. Tallahassee: Naiad, 2000.
Mickelbury, Penny. *Darkness Descending*. Atlanta: Kings Crossing, 2004.
———. *Keeping Secrets*. Tallahassee, FL: Naiad, 1994.

_____. *Night Songs*. Tallahassee: Naiad, 1995.
Miller, Carlene. *Death Off Stage*. Burke, VA: Women's Work, 2001.
Miller, Isabel. *Patience and Sarah*. New York: Ballantine, 1973. Orig. pub. 1969.
Miller, Meredith. "Secret Agents and Public Victims: The Implied Lesbian Reader." *Journal of Popular Culture* 35.1 (Summer 2001): 22 pp. Apr. 2005 http://proquest.umi.com
Mizejewski, Linda. *Hardboiled & High Heeled: The Woman Detective in Popular Culture*. New York: Routledge, 2004.
Modleski, Tania. *Loving with a Vengeance: Mass-Produced Fantasies for Women*. New York: Methuen, 1982.
Morell, Mary. *Final Session*. San Francisco: Spinsters, 1991.
Muller, Marcia. *Edwin of the Iron Shoes*. New York: Mysterious, 1993.
_____. *Trophies and Dead Things*. New York: Mysterious, 1991.
Munt, Sally R. *Murder by the Book?: Feminism and the Crime Novel*. London: Routledge, 1994.
Nealon, Christopher. "Invert-History: The Ambivalence of Lesbian Pulp Fiction." *New Literary History* 31(2000): 745–64.
Palmer, Pauline. *Contemporary Lesbian Writing: Dreams, Desires, Difference*. Milton Keynes, UK: Open University Press, 1993.
Paradee, C. *Deep Cover*. Port Arthur, TX: Quest, 2004.
Phillips, Cath. *River's Edge*. Sydney, Australia: Black Wattle, 1997.
Plain, Gill. *Twentieth-Century Crime Fiction: Gender, Sexuality and the Body*. Chicago: Fitzroy Dearborn, 2001.
Pope, Rebecca. "'Friends Is a Weak Word for It': Female Friendship and the Spectre of Lesbianism in Sara Paretsky." In *Feminism in Women's Detective Fiction*. Ed. Glenwood Irons. Toronto Canada: University of Toronto Press, 1995.
Powell, Deborah. *Bayou City Secrets*. Tallahassee: Naiad, 1991.
_____. *Houston Town*. Tallahassee: Naiad, 1992.
Radclyffe. *In Pursuit of Justice*. Nederland, TX: Quest, 2003.
_____. *Justice in the Shadows*. Gainesville, FL: Star Crossed, 2003.
_____. *A Matter of Trust*. Port Arthur, TX: Renaissance Alliance, 2003.
_____. *Shield of Justice*. Port Arthur, TX: Renaissance Alliance, 2002.
Radway, Janice A. *Reading the Romance: Women, Patriarchy, and Popular Literature*. Chapel Hill: University of North Carolina Press, 1984.
Reddy, Maureen T. "The Feminist Counter-Tradition in Crime: Cross, Grafton, Paretsky, and Wilson." In *The Cunning Craft: Original Essays on Detective Fiction and Contemporary Literary Theory*. Eds. Ronald G. Walker and June M. Frazer. Macomb: Western Illinois University Press, 1990.
_____. *Sisters in Crime: Feminism and the Crime Novel*. New York: Continuum, 1988.
_____. *Traces, Codes, and Clues: Reading Race in Crime Fiction*. New Brunswick, NJ: Rutgers University Press, 2003.
Redmann, J. R. *Death by the Riverside*. Norwich, VT: New Victoria, 1990.
_____. *The Intersection of Law and Desire*. New York: Avon, 1997.
Regis, Pamela. *A Natural History of the Romance Novel*. Philadelphia: University of Pennsylvania Press, 2003.
Rich, Adrienne. *Of Woman Born: Motherhood as Experience and Institution*. New York: Bantam, 1977.
_____. *On Lies, Secrets, and Silence: Selected Prose, 1966–1978*. New York: W.W. Norton, 1979.
Richardson, Tracey. *Last Rites*. Tallahassee: Naiad, 1997.
_____. *Northern Blue*. Tallahassee: Naiad, 1996.

Robinson, Jenefer, and Stephanie Ross. "Women, Morality, and Fiction." In *Aesthetics in Feminist Perspective*. Eds. Hilde Hein and Carolyn Korsmeyer. Bloomington: Indiana University Press, 1993.
Roof, Judith. *A Lure of Knowledge: Lesbian Sexuality and Theory*. New York: Columbia University Press,1991.
Ross, Sharon. "Tough Enough": Female Friendship and Heroism in *Xena* and *Buffy*." In *Action Chicks: New Images of Tough Women in Popular Culture*. Ed. Sherrie Inness. New York: Palgrave/Macmillan, 2004.
Scoppettone, Sandra. *Everything You Have Is Mine*. New York : Ballantine, 1992.
Schweitzer, Margie S. *Courting Death*. Tacoma: Justice House, 2001.
Silva, Linda Kay. *Storm Shelter*. San Diego: Paradigm, 1993.
_____. *Taken by Storm*. San Diego: Paradigm, 1991.
_____. *Weathering the Storm*. San Diego: Paradigm, 1994.
Slotkin, Richard. "The Hard-Boiled Detective Story: From the Open Range to the Mean Streets." In *The Sleuth and the Scholar: Origins, Evolution, and Current Trends in Detective Fiction*. Eds. Barbara A. Rader and Howard G. Zettler. New York: Greenwood, 1988.
Smith, Erin A. *Hard-Boiled: Working-Class Readers and Pulp Magazines*. Philadelphia: Temple University Press, 2000.
Smith-Rosenberg, Carroll. "The Female World of Love and Ritual: Relations Between Women in Nineteenth-Century America." In *Disorderly Conduct: Visions of Gender in Victorian America*. New York: Oxford University Press, 1985.
Talaran. *Vendetta*. Nederland, TX: Quest, 2001.
Taylor, Jean. *The Last of Her Lies*. Seattle: Seal, 1996.
_____. *We Know Where You Live*. Seattle: Seal, 1995.
Todd, Janet. *Women's Friendship in Literature*. New York: Columbia University Press, 1980.
Tomc, Sandra. "Questing Women: The Feminist Mystery after Feminism." In *Feminism in Women's Detective Fiction*. Ed. Glenwood Irons. Toronto, Canada: University of Toronto Press, 1995.
Tomm, Winnie. "Ethics and Self-knowing: The Satisfaction of Desire." In *Explorations in Feminist Ethics: Theory and Practice*. Eds. Eve Browning Cole and Susan Coultrap-McQuin. Bloomington: Indiana University Press, 1992.
Wade, Donna. "Crossing the Thin Blue Line." *The Lesbian News* May 1996: 32+.
Walker, Margaret Urban. "Moral Repair and Its Limits." In *Mapping the Ethical Turn: A Reader in Ethics, Culture, and Literary Theory*. Eds. Todd F. Davis and Kenneth Womack. Charlottesville: University Press of Virginia, 2001.
Walters, Suzanna Danuta. "As Her Hand Crept Slowly up Her Thigh: Ann Bannon and The Politics of Pulp." *Social Text* 23(Autumn–Winter, 1989): 83–101.
Walton, Priscilla L., and Manina Jones. *Detective Agency: Women Rewriting the Hard-Boiled Tradition*. Berkeley: University of California Press, 1999.
Wartenberg, Thomas E. *Unlikely Couples: Movie Romance as Social Criticism*. Boulder, CO: Westview, 1999.
Weir, Angela, and Elizabeth Wilson. "The Greyhound Bus Station in the Evolution Of Lesbian Popular Culture." In *New Lesbian Criticism: Literary and Cultural Readings*. Ed. Sally Munt. New York: Columbia University Press, 1992.
Welch, Pat. *Fallen from Grace*. Tallahassee: Naiad, 1998.
Welter, Barbara. *Dimity Convictions: The American Woman in the Nineteenth-Century*. Athens: Ohio University Press, 1976.
Whitlock, Gillian. "'Cop It Sweet': Lesbian Crime Fiction." In *The Good, the Bad and the Gorgeous: Popular Culture's Romance with Lesbianism*. Eds. Diane Hamer and Belinda Budge. London: Pandora, 1994.

Wilson, Ann. "The Female Dick and the Crisis of Heterosexuality." In *Feminism in Women's Detective Fiction*. Ed. Glenwood Irons. Toronto, Canada: University of Toronto Press, 1995.

Wilson, Anna. "Death and the Mainstream: Lesbian Detective Fiction and the Killing of The Coming-Out Story." *Feminist Studies* 22(Summer 1996): 251–78.

Wilson, Barbara. *The Dog Collar Murders*. Tacoma: Seal, 1989.

_____. *Murder in the Collective*. Seattle: Seal, 1984.

_____. "The Outside Edge: Lesbian Mysteries." In *Daring to Dissent: Lesbian Culture from Margin to Mainstream*. Ed. Liz Gibbs. London: Cassell, 1994.

Windrath, Helen, ed. *They Wrote the Book: Thirteen Women Mystery Writers Tell All*. Duluth, MN: Spinsters Ink, 2000.

Wings, Mary. "Rebecca Redux: Tears on a Lesbian Pillow." In *Daring to Dissent: Lesbian Culture from Margin to Mainstream*. Ed. Liz Gibbs. London: Cassell, 1994.

_____. *She Came by the Book*. London: Women's Press, 1995.

_____. *She Came in Drag*. New York: Berkley, 1999.

Winters, C. N. *Irrefutable Evidence*. Nederland, TX: Quest, 2003.

Zimmerman, Bonnie. "Perverse Reading: The Lesbian Appropriation of Literature." In *Sexual Practice/Textual Theory: Lesbian Cultural Criticism*. Eds. Susan J. Wolfe and Julia Penelope. Cambridge, MA: Blackwell, 1993.

_____. *The Safe Sea of Women: Lesbian Fiction, 1969–1989*. Boston: Beacon, 1990.

Index

Abraham, Julie 45, 178
abuse 14, 126, 128, 133, 134; of children 2, 11, 47–48, 110, 142; of women 47–48, 77, 110
agency 44, 127, 128, 130, 131, 132, 134, 137
aggression 13, 93, 94, 96, 98–99, 103, 105, 109, 111
Alpert, Geoffrey 70, 71
amateur detective 14, 19, 25, 27, 29
appearance 101–105, 107, 111, 134, 165, 169
assimilation 11, 13
authority 7, 13, 24, 70, 71, 75, 78, 79, 82, 87, 89, 100, 104, 131, 136, 137, 142, 155; see also power
autonomy 127, 128, 134

Beguin, ReBecca: *Hers Was the Sky* 150, 167–168
behavior 30, 95, 103, 120, 122, 123, 135, 155
body 100, 101–102, 103, 107, 111, 134, 182
Bornstein, Kate 178, 181, 184
Braverman, Scott 167, 248
Bristow, Joseph 21, 178
Bromley, Richard 155, 176, 184
Browne, Ray 125, 146
butch 22, 53, 169, 174, 182

Castle, Terry 8, 9, 23, 45, 109, 154, 163, 178
Cawelti, John: *Adventure, Mystery, and Romance* 4, 24, 38, 47, 68, 107, 172, 177, 179, 181, 183; *Mystery, Violence, and Popular Culture* 96, 99, 111, 124, 130
Chandler, Raymond 124
Chauncey, George 170, 178
Chauncey, George, Jr. 148
choice 11, 29, 44, 50, 54, 112, 115, 123, 127, 129, 130, 131, 132
Christianson, Scott 115
Cobley, Paul 145
Cole, Cathy 48, 97, 111, 119, 123, 128, 131, 178, 180, 182
Cole, Eve 125
Coltrap-McQuin, Susan 125

coming out 11, 12, 14, 20, 25, 27, 29, 30, 31–32, 34, 37, 41, 55, 57, 63–64, 74, 83, 87
community 12, 14, 21, 27, 28, 34, 35, 38, 41, 51, 54, 67, 69, 70, 81, 88, 104, 107, 115–116, 120, 123, 132, 150, 151, 153, 171
control 63, 66, 87, 114, 115, 116, 123, 126, 127, 129, 130, 134, 161, 170
conventions genre 3, 4, 6, 8, 17, 23, 25, 29, 58, 60, 68, 97, 98, 117, 122, 131, 145, 149, 163, 172, 175; mystery 12, 17, 37, 51, 58–59, 68, 75–76, 94–95, 111, 122, 124, 128, 131, 151, 166; romance 42, 44, 46, 50, 53, 57–59
Cowart, David 145, 149
Crosby, Sara 95

Davis, Lisa: *Under the Mink* 167, 168–170
Davis, Madeline D. 22, 178
Davis, Todd 121
desire 20, 21, 25, 42, 44, 49–50, 53, 55, 56, 57, 65, 103, 105, 130, 182; see also passion
deviance 68, 70, 93, 101, 105, 109, 117, 118, 142, 168
difference 7, 8, 11, 67, 90, 174
diversity 4, 84
Douglas, Lauren Wright: *The Always Anonymous Beast* 28, 113–114, 118
Dove, George 5, 6, 18, 29, 38, 59, 60, 76, 151, 167
Duberman, Martin 148

ethics 120, 121, 123, 125, 127, 131; see also morality
expectations 6, 8, 10, 14, 18, 22, 23, 25, 38, 42, 44, 61, 90, 91, 92, 104, 117, 125, 135, 168, 172, 178

Faderman, Lilian 45, 154; *Surpassing the Love of Men* 178, 180
familiarization 1, 3, 5, 11, 18, 24, 38, 60, 62, 172
family 12, 14, 35, 93, 101
Farwell, Marilyn 11, 23, 104, 171, 178, 182, 185
femininity 93, 96, 100, 101, 102, 112, 142, 181

femme fatale 37, 47, 50, 96, 179
Fisher, Philip 1, 3, 4, 5, 24, 38, 146, 172
Forrest, Katherine V. 162, 170, 173; *Amateur City* 82, 84; *Apparition Alley* 32, 88; *The Beverly Malibu* 19–20, 150, 156–158, 159; *Hancock Park*; 174; *Liberty Square* 144, 150, 152, 156, 158–161; *Murder at the Nightwood Bar* 35, 133; *Murder by Tradition* 84, 87–88, 109, 133
Forter, Greg 47, 177, 181, 182, 183
Fox, Ellen 128
friendship 31, 45, 46, 52, 97, 134, 169, 175

Gallo, Gina 57, 71, 72, 73, 178, 180
Garber, Marjorie 179, 181, 184
gender 5, 12, 14, 22, 42, 47, 89, 92, 93, 95, 98, 103, 105, 106, 112, 116, 117, 142, 148, 169, 178, 181
genre 9, 17, 18, 23, 34, 37, 44, 60, 75, 96, 108, 126, 131; *see also* conventions genre
genre fiction 2, 17, 24, 25, 38, 68, 137, 149, 166, 172; *see also* popular fiction
Gilligan, Carol 125–127
Gomel, Elena 92, 100, 107, 111, 151
goodness 119–120; *see also* value

hard-boiled detective 2, 4, 5, 19, 37, 46, 48, 61, 104, 105, 115, 116, 124, 137, 169, 179, 183
Hart, Lynda 104, 154, 180, 182, 183, 185
Haut, Woody 179, 181
Heidensohn, Francis 70
historical fiction 14, 144, 145, 146, 149, 154, 164
history 6, 14, 35, 174, 184
Hoagland, Sarah 131–135, 137, 140, 143, 175, 184
homophobia 13, 20, 28, 34, 73, 77, 78, 81, 82, 84, 88, 89, 90, 96, 106, 109, 133, 160, 168, 169

identity 6, 13, 19, 21–22, 36, 55, 71, 100, 139, 148, 169; construction of 21, 22, 25–27, 34, 38, 57, 63, 101, 103, 104, 105, 159; public 19, 22, 35, 37, 74, 75, 88, 161; sexual 19, 20, 21, 35, 38, 57, 73, 83, 100–101, 106, 160, 182
Innes, Sherrie: *Intimate Communities* 45; *Lesbian Menace* 9, 10, 20, 24, 163, 178, 182; *Tough Girls* 94–95, 98, 101, 102, 112
intimacy 13, 22, 27, 35, 38, 45–46, 51, 56, 143, 154, 174
Iser, Wolfgang 3
isolation 36, 41, 149

Jackson, Christine 177, 182
Johnson, Patricia 50–51, 179
Jones, Manina 25, 44, 56, 96, 98, 102, 105, 126, 131, 172, 183
Juhasz, Suzanne 41, 53, 54, 56, 179
justice 7, 8, 120, 123, 124, 128, 131, 136, 137, 169

Kammen, Michael 144, 145, 148, 155, 158, 185
Kappeler, Victor 70, 71
Katz, Jonathan 156
Keller, Yvonne 180
Kelly, R. Gordon 69, 91, 127, 175, 177, 181
Kennery, Elizabeth Lapovsky 22, 178
Knight, Stephen 177, 179, 181
Kreiser, Lawrence A., Jr. 146

language 48, 49–55, 56, 98, 100, 115, 151, 183
lesbian pulp fiction 53, 174, 179, 180
Lewis, Catherine: *Dry Fire* 76–78

Maiman, Jaye 59
Malmgren, Carl 179, 181
Marchino, Lois 40, 170
marginalization 5, 7, 10, 60, 90, 93, 101, 124, 127, 129, 147, 148, 149, 156, 163
Martin, Susan 71, 73, 76, 91
masculinity 22, 93, 95, 97, 100, 103, 106, 119, 138, 142, 169
McAllister, Melanie: *The Lesson* 89–90
McConnell, Vicki: *The Burnton Widows* 35, 150, 151–153; *Mrs. Porter's Letter* 14, 26–27, 150, 151, 153–154
McCracken, Scott 2, 3, 6, 7, 8, 40, 43, 122, 131, 166
McGinn, Colin 120, 121, 183
McNab, Claire: *Accidental Murder* 11; *Blood Link* 61; *Body Guard* 61; *Chain Letter* 111; *Cop Out* 64; *Dead Certain* 36, 63, 64, 109, 133; *Death Down Under* 17, 64; *Double Bluff* 61, 64; *Fall Guy* 65; *Fatal Reunion* 61, 62; *Inner Circle* 61; *Lessons in Murder* 36, 62; *Past Due* 64; *Set Up* 61; *Under Suspicion* 65
memory 153, 154, 155, 158, 160, 161
Micklebury, Penny: *Darkness Descending* 110; *Keeping Secrets* 84–86
Miller, Meredith 171, 174
Mizejewski, Linda 101, 102, 182
morality 18, 19, 35, 48, 69, 99, 120, 121, 122, 123, 125, 127, 129, 133, 135, 138, 142, 183
Morrell, Mary: *Final Session* 80–81
Munt, Sally 74, 79, 82, 91, 180

narrative/narrator 3, 6, 9, 10, 11, 33, 96, 98, 104, 105, 121, 164, 174; lesbian 10, 11, 27, 52, 55, 61, 78, 104, 112, 170
negotiation 106, 112, 115, 123
normalizing 11, 14, 56, 134, 164; *see also* familiarization

Palmer, Pauline 52, 90
passing 66, 73, 74
passion 38, 41, 42, 56, 60; *see also* desire
performance 88, 94, 104, 115, 142, 177, 184
Plain, Gill 57, 86, 88, 180
police 10, 25, 69; institutions 3, 7, 13, 20, 24, 32; lesbians 13, 29, 30, 31, 70, 74, 84, 91, 106; procedurals 13, 19, 35, 96

Pope, Rebecca 51–52, 179, 184
popular fiction 2, 3, 8, 10, 14, 38, 60, 94, 110, 122, 161, 166, 172, 184
Powell, Deborah: *Bayou City Secrets* 150, 164–166; *Houston Town* 150, 164, 166, 167
power 11, 24, 30, 70, 71, 78, 82, 85, 91, 100, 105, 113, 126, 128, 132

Radclyffe 103, 142; *In Pursuit of Justice* 140–141; *Justice in the Shadows* 140, 142–143; *A Matter of Trust* 141; *Shield of Justice* 138–140
Radway, Janice 43, 51, 57, 62, 179, 180
reader 1, 3, 5, 7, 10, 17, 68, 75–76, 98, 99, 102, 103, 111, 121, 123, 131, 138, 178; lesbian 8, 10, 11, 12, 18, 27, 29, 31, 34, 37, 38, 53, 64, 75, 105, 108, 112, 114, 150, 153, 165, 167, 169, 171, 173, 175
Reddy, Maureen 48, 51, 75, 82, 83, 84, 100, 128, 179, 180
Redmann, J.D.: *Death by the Riverside* 116
Regis, Pamela 42, 44, 57, 179
relationships 7, 14, 31, 37, 42, 46, 49–50, 51, 69, 95, 107, 119, 125, 127; lesbian 9, 10, 12, 25–27, 35, 37, 45–46, 131, 136
representation 8, 9, 15, 23, 35, 53, 68, 94, 104, 147, 169, 171
Rich, Adrienne 177
Richardson, Tracey 67; *Northern Blue* 72–75
romance 10, 19, 25, 37, 41, 42, 43, 49, 50, 53, 54, 56, 61, 65, 78, 83, 126, 153, 171; language 49, 52, 55–56; lesbian 41, 52, 53–54, 58, 179, 185
Roof, Judith 178, 179, 181, 184
Ross, Sharon 98

sex 13, 27, 40, 41, 56, 57, 72, 73, 179, 180
sexuality 5, 11, 12, 13, 19, 29, 30, 31, 33, 41, 53, 74, 77, 78, 80, 82, 85, 87, 101, 103, 105, 133, 135, 167, 171, 179
Silva, Linda Kay 31; *Storm Shelter* 136; *Taken by Storm* 79–80, 136; *Weathering the Storm* 136
Sluder, Richard 70, 71
Smith, Erin 177, 179, 181, 184

Smith-Rosenberg, Carroll 17, 22, 45
society 11, 14, 19, 67, 70, 78, 107, 126, 127; *see also* expectations

Tomc, Sandra 184
Tomm, Winnie 127, 129, 184
toughness 94, 99, 103, 104, 105, 111, 116
transformation 3, 4, 5, 24, 38, 41, 46, 56, 74, 122, 172
transgression 13, 67, 69, 74, 90, 91, 122, 132
trust 69, 83, 91, 97, 123, 126, 181

value 1, 2, 23, 35, 38, 67, 70, 76, 94, 107, 174; literary 1, 2, 6, 8, 34, 42, 100–102, 121, 132, 135, 152, 155
Vicinus, Martha 148
victims 35, 48, 126, 129, 133, 134, 150, 152, 184
Vietnam 14, 144, 150, 158, 159, 160, 161, 166
violence 4, 13, 27, 47, 48, 56, 61, 71, 92, 6, 99, 100, 103, 104, 108, 111, 115, 124, 129, 134, 136, 138, 180, 182

Wade, Donna 76, 81, 181
Walker, Margaret 123, 183
Walters, Suzanna 53
Walton, Priscilla 25, 44, 56, 96, 98, 102, 105, 126, 131, 172, 183
Wartenburg, Thomas 54
Weir, Angela 53
Whitlock, Gillian 34, 37, 163, 174
Wilson, Ann 106
Wilson, Barbara: *Murder in the Collective* 27–28
Wilson, Elizabeth 53
Wings, Mary: *She Came by the Book* 150, 161–162
Womack, Kenneth 121
women detectives 4, 30, 48, 49, 51, 52, 97, 100, 106, 126, 127, 130; roles 5, 42, 46, 71, 72, 96, 124, 129, 149; violence 4, 11, 48, 92–93, 98

Zimmerman, Bonnie: "Perverse Reading" 10, 163, 166; *Safe Sea of Women* 20

www.ingramcontent.com/pod-product-compliance
Lightning Source LLC
Chambersburg PA
CBHW032100300426
44116CB00007B/825